William Henry Davenport Adams

Mountains and Mountain-Climbing

Records of Adventure and Enterprise among the Famous Mountains of the World

William Henry Davenport Adams

Mountains and Mountain-Climbing
Records of Adventure and Enterprise among the Famous Mountains of the World

ISBN/EAN: 9783744750905

Printed in Europe, USA, Canada, Australia, Japan

Cover: Foto ©Andreas Hilbeck / pixelio.de

More available books at **www.hansebooks.com**

MOUNTAINS AND MOUNTAIN-CLIMBING.

RECORDS OF ADVENTURE AND ENTERPRISE
AMONG THE FAMOUS MOUNTAINS
OF THE WORLD.

BY THE AUTHOR OF

"*THE MEDITERRANEAN ILLUSTRATED*," "*THE ARCTIC
WORLD ILLUSTRATED*,"
&c. &c.

WITH THIRTY-THREE ENGRAVINGS

London:
T. NELSON AND SONS, PATERNOSTER ROW.
EDINBURGH; AND NEW YORK.

1883.

PREFACE.

MOUNTAINEERING has always had an attraction for the adventurous; and, indeed, in human nature seems implanted a thirst after novelty and a feeling of curious inquiry which impels men to attempt the ascent of "high places." No one, perhaps, ever reached the summit of a hill without a sense of gratification, nor without a desire to attain the summit of the next! It is the one thing which does not pall upon us. And this not only because we are conscious of having surmounted a difficulty, but because the changing prospect, the novel view, always interests and exhilarates the mind. When Milton spoke of hastening to "fresh woods and pastures new," he was certainly in error. We grow tired of wood and pasture; we refuse to believe that they are either fresh or new. But who could say so much in dispraise of the Mountains, with their varieties of configuration and elevation, their incessant changes of scenery, their marvellous diversities of form and colour?

Without entering, therefore, into any discussion of the *morale* of Mountain-Climbing, we may be content to affirm that it has strong attractions for the robust and bold; that it has been of good service to Science; and that it tends to cherish in the youth and manhood of a nation a chivalrous fearlessness and a heroic love of adventure. And hence we are inclined to hope that the following pages, descriptive as they are of the ascents of some of the world's most remarkable mountains, will find an eager and a grateful public. They are intended not only for readers who *have* climbed mountains, but for those who wish they *could* climb them, or who are wisely of opinion that when they cannot climb *in propriâ personâ*, the next best thing is to read about more fortunate enthusiasts. And then they are also intended for all who can sympathize with deeds of daring, or who find a rare enjoyment in studying descriptions of Nature's wilder, grander, and sublimer landscapes. For our little volume is dedicated not only to the Mountain-Climbers, but to the Mountains in all their high pure beauty and elevated magnificence. May what we have written find favour with those who read!

CONTENTS.

I.	VESUVIUS,	13
II.	IN THE HARZ,	58
III.	THE PYRENEES,	94
IV.	NORWAY: THE NORTH CAPE,	148
V.	THE PEAK OF TENERIFFE,	159
VI.	THE PETER-BOTTE (ISLAND OF MAURITIUS),	172
VII.	MOUNT ATHOS,	179
VIII.	MOUNT ETNA,	203
IX.	MONT BLANC,	225
X.	IN THE INDIAN ARCHIPELAGO,	263
XI.	CHIMBORAZO,	270
XII.	IN HAWAII,	297
XIII.	MOUNT ARARAT,	326
XIV.	MOUNT SINAI,	345
XV.	THE HIMALAYA,	362
XVI.	HEKLA,	398

List of Illustrations.

THE SPECTRE OF THE BROCKEN,	*Frontispiece*
VESUVIUS, AND BAY OF NAPLES,	17
ERUPTION OF VESUVIUS IN 1858,	27
ERUPTION OF THE GREAT CRATER OF VESUVIUS,	35
RUINS OF TORRE DEL GRECO,	45
A MINE IN THE HARZ—DESCENDING THE SHAFT,	63
SCENE IN THE ROSSTRAPPE,	79
THE PRINCIPAL SUMMITS OF THE PYRENEES,	97
VALLEY OF GAVARNIE,	105
CIRQUE DE GAVARNIE,	111
RAMOND'S ASCENT OF MONT PERDU,	143
THE NORTH CAPE,	151
PEAK OF TENERIFFE,	163
THE PETER-BOTTE, MAURITIUS,	175
MOUNT ETNA, FROM TAORMINA,	205
THE CASTAGNO DI CENTO CAVALLI,	209
MOUNT ETNA,	217
MONT BLANC, FROM MONT BUET,	229
GREAT CREVASSE AT THE FOOT OF MONT BLANC,	237
PIERRE DE L'ECHELLE,	247
VOLCANO OF BANDA—INDIAN ARCHIPELAGO,	265
PANORAMIC VIEW OF THE ANDES,	281
CRATER OF KILAUEA, ISLAND OF HAWAII,	303
A WAVE OF FIRE, CRATER OF KILAUEA,	307

LIST OF ILLUSTRATIONS.

CASCADE OF LAVA, HAWAII,

MOUNT ARARAT,

MONASTERY OF ST. CATHERINE, MOUNT SINAI,

THE RAS SAFSAFEH AND PLAIN OF ER-RAHAH,

PASS IN THE HIMALAYA,

GLACIER OF KOTHSADA.

MOUNT EVEREST,

KUNCHAIN-JUNGA,

MOUNT HEKLA,

MOUNTAINS AND MOUNTAIN-CLIMBING.

I.

Vesuvius.

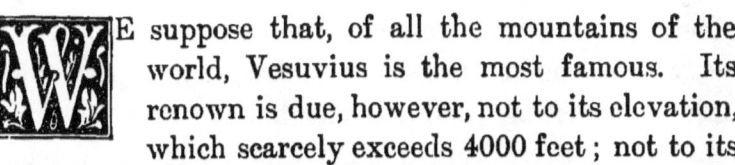E suppose that, of all the mountains of the world, Vesuvius is the most famous. Its renown is due, however, not to its elevation, which scarcely exceeds 4000 feet; not to its picturesqueness, though this is considerable; but to a variety of circumstances seldom found in combination. And, first, it is easily accessible, so that all its features have been carefully studied and are thoroughly known. Second, it is situated close to a great city, and on the shore of a bay which is unrivalled for its gentle beauty. Third, it has had the fortune to be sung by the old classic poets of Italy, and to have gathered around it the shadows of a thousand fantastic legends. Again: it is a volcano of exceedingly destructive character, which has repeatedly wrought the most terrible ruin; and this ruin has always been minutely described by competent observers, so that the name of Vesuvius has acquired a fatal and disastrous import. Further: in one of its awful outbreaks it overwhelmed two ancient

towns of more than ordinary importance; and the recent exhumation of those towns, and the consequent recovery of a series of remarkable memorials of that antique society which previously was but dimly seen in the pages of poets and historians, has reflected, as it were, a new and singular interest on the mountain so fatally associated with their annals. We cannot think of Herculaneum and Pompeii without thinking of Vesuvius, which was at once their destroyer and preserver; suddenly arresting their current history and checking their flow of prosperous life, in order, as it would seem, that later generations might be able to contemplate that history and survey that life in all their original freshness! Thus it is, we think, that Vesuvius has acquired a world-wide fame, to which no mere considerations of height or grandeur could have entitled it.

The ascent of Vesuvius has been so frequently accomplished and so often described, that it has passed into the category of "things familiar and indifferent." Time was when the undertaking was regarded as one of heroic proportions; and a flourish of trumpets announced its successful accomplishment. But in these days, when men speak of climbing Mont Blanc as a holiday excursion, to ascend Vesuvius is simply the ordinary pastime of the ordinary tourist. Still it cannot properly be omitted from a volume which has "Mountains and Mountain-climbing" for its *raison d'être;* and, indeed, it is always attended by features of interest which fully engage the attention of the reader. We suppose we have read some fifty or sixty accounts of the ascent of the great Italian volcano, and yet with unabated curiosity we turn to each new narrative. Which of these fifty or sixty we should place before the intelligent student of our graphic pages has caused us some anxious thought. But we have finally decided on selecting the lively tale told by a French writer of eminence, M. Marc Monnier; on the ground that it is, in all probability, the least familiar. We believe, indeed, that it has never before been rendered into English; so that to its intrinsic merits of accuracy and vivacity it will add the adventitious one of comparative novelty.

Vesuvius, as the reader knows, rises with a gradual slope from the shore of the Bay of Naples, the ancient Parthenopean Gulf, at a short distance from the sunny city renowned for its memories of Masaniello, Murat, and Garibaldi. Numerous small towns and villages stud its vine-clad flanks, and are too often buried beneath the lava and ashes it pours from its depths during the throes of its frequent eruptions. From one of these, named Resina, the ascent of the mountain is generally undertaken; and it is from this point we now propose to start, under the competent guidance of M. Marc Monnier.

In most cases you leave Naples about noon, and a carriage conveys you to Resina, which lies at the foot of the mountain. Immediately, a crowd of obliging plebeians surround and seize upon you. One offers you an ass, a mule, or a horse; another, a choice of torches; a third, a supply of provisions; a fourth is loaded with ropes; others carry poles; others bring up more beasts of burden; and a score or more proclaim their merits as faithful guides. As you descend from your vehicle, a host of lads relieve you of your cloak and provisions, and start ahead. Make haste and follow them! You may shout as you will, and objurgate as you will; clap your hands, stamp your feet, brandish your stick; a Neapolitan crowd takes no notice of the exhibition. Twenty men or more accompany you in your advance with their instruments and their animals. Others pick you up on the road, and join themselves to the caravan; they offer for sale Vesuvian pebbles, or coins embedded in pieces of lava, or litters for your repose and refreshment in case of need. These officious and troublesome parasites lie in wait at every corner. They expect you, they know you; they address you as "cavalier," or "caballero." They beset you from your arrival at Resina to the very summit of the cone. And as the road is free to all, you cannot get rid of them,*—except, indeed, by flinging among them a shower of small coin; and this is your wiser plan. Otherwise, after all the toil of the ascent, you will see nothing of Vesuvius; and the only result of six hours' toil will be your own eruption, —a tremendous outpouring of wrath and indignation, hard words and harder blows!

The experienced traveller, however, on reaching Resina does not quit his vehicle; calmly and composedly he selects from the crowd besieging it an official and duly licensed guide; and it is but fair to admit that some of these guides are honest and faithful fellows, who will spare your piastres, and save you from extortion. Your

* This was written in 1862. Thanks to the Italian Government, the nuisance now is not so great as it was formerly.

VESUVIUS, AND BAY OF NAPLES.

guide will undertake everything, and he knows the secret of dismissing the importunate beggars that waylay you. In fact, on his appearance by your side, the most shameless own themselves beaten; well do they know they will not receive a stiver. So suffer yourself to be led in peace, and climb like a true athlete, troubling yourself about nothing but your boots. A hundred to one but they will be reduced to tinder. But if that is all, you will have no cause for regret.

Vesuvius, as seen from Naples, is a two-headed mountain: the peak to the left is the Somma, that to the right is the volcano itself; they are separated by a deep valley. At the mouth of the valley, on a plateau forming quite a natural belvedere, are situated the Hermitage and the Observatory. The first stage of our ascent takes us to the former.

Of old it was reached by a well-made and noble road, the chef-d'œuvre of King Ferdinand. Roads as well-made and beautiful issue from Naples in all directions, and secure the justly-deserved admiration of travellers. They extend in a truly majestic manner for several leagues. Then they assume an air of neglect, and preserve an accumulation of mud or dirt until they reach the mountains, where they diminish into rugged and abominable tracks, which soon become impracticable, and finally disappear altogether. Many villages can be reached only on foot; hamlets there are to which you must climb by ladders. However, to the Hermitage you can progress comfortably with a couple of horses to your carriage; it is situated about two leagues from Naples.

At one time the road, in its earlier course, wound through orchards blushing with fruit, and vineyards flowing with excellent wine; when drunk quite pure, but execrable stuff when adulterated under the sacrilegious designation of *Lacryma Christi*. Higher up, it clambered rocks of lava, and skirted black and rugged ravines. The traveller descended from his carriage at the Hermitage, with all his energies unimpaired, to begin the ascent.

Unfortunately, the lava-flood of 1858 broke up the main road at two places; and before repairing it the new kingdom of Italy had other work to do. In M. Marc Monnier's time, therefore, you were compelled to mount on horseback at Resina, and to climb as quickly and directly as possible, by a very ill-defined route, to the humble house where, according to a hemistich of Victor Hugo's,—

"Prays a priest on bended knees."

The real, living hermit, however, does not pray—at least, in public; but concocts omelettes *à l'huile*, which he sells at an abominably high rate. He sells also *Lacryma Christi*, manufactured at Naples. Moreover, he has a collection of very curious volumes, being the registers, or "albums," in which visitors write their names and any remark that suggests itself to them. Some precious signatures occur here, among a host that are trivial and unimportant. We recognize, for instance, those of Lamartine; Alexandre Dumas (1837); Maria Malibran (1833); Monti (April 18, 1812); Lord Byron; Goethe (September 7, 1792); and Alfieri, with this phrase, which to Italians seems sublime,—" Qui Vittorio Alfieri, nel 1782."

When you have turned over the album and remunerated the hermit,—admiring, with Chateaubriand, " the spectacle of Christian hospitality enshrined in a little cell, at the foot of a volcano, and in the midst of a tempest,"—you may seat yourself in the shade of the leafy boughs, and survey at your leisure the smiling, graceful coast, from Misenum to Sorrento, bending and breaking and winding into a thousand sinuosities, as if to embrace more lovingly the warm waters of that glorious sea. The sight is splendid; especially in the evening, when the sun halts for a moment over the island-rocks of Ischia, like a wheel of fire, before it makes haste to sink behind the peaks which it touches with glorious flame. But the picture which lingers longest in the memory is a "moonlight effect;" such as was seen from the Hermitage, on the occasion of the last eruption. Then half the mountain slept in shadow, while the rest was luminous, as was the kindling sea; the heights of Sorrento were tinted with bronze on their sides, and silver on their brow; Capri shone in a shimmering "milky way" of light; afar off, in the mist, lay Misenum, and Ischia, the distant Mediterranean, and, beyond, a world of dreams; nearer, the city, with the lighthouse on its mole, and the pale reflections of its lighted quays — a row of glow-worms under a border of houses; all unfolded before us at our feet; and behind us, the mountain on fire, with its indescribable glories of leaping flames and strange electric coruscations.

But we must resume our march, we have so much to see. Above the Hermitage no other mode of locomotion is available than an ass, or our feet. We pass in front of the Observatory, from which the astronomer Gasparin has discovered so many planets or planetoids; his successor, Luigi Pannieri investigates with more interest the phenomena of earthquakes. It is well-stocked with curious instruments, which do not prevent these commotions, but accurately define them; such is their sensibility that they are affected by the slightest movement of the soil. Thanks to the seismograph of Vesuvius, and the wise men who kept their eyes fixed upon it, we learned that Torre del Greco (in 1862) was crushed by a landslip. And yet men can lament the vanity of human Science!

After leaving the Observatory, we plunge into the valley which separates the two summits, and skirt the cone of the volcano until we find a point where its ascent seems practicable. It is then that we first grow sensible of fatigue. There are no longer either roads, bridle-paths, foot-paths, or tracks; nothing but a mass of cinders and scoriæ. These scoriæ, to use a happy image, exactly resemble iron sponges. "There are also heaps of stones, earth, iron, sulphur, alum, glass, bitumen, nitre, baked earth, copper, petrified or cast in a kind of *foamy* pattern, in the shape of marcassites or iron dross. And these the rains have washed for a considerable period, so that one is able to distinguish the earlier and the later overflows. There is nothing more frightful to see, or fatiguing to traverse, than these masses of *iron sponges*, which are not less hard than rugged. You cannot figure to yourself aught more disgusting than these hideous ejections; you drag yourself across them with inconceivable weariness. The lumps of dross are incessantly rolling beneath your feet; so that, thanks to the detestably rapid movement of the soil, you descend a couple of fathoms each time you think you are receding only a step." Such is the faithful description given by the President de Brosses.

It is needless to say, then, that you will not be sorry to have made the ascent with a companion. All my life I shall recollect one of my friends, a Swiss, with the limbs of a mountaineer, who smiled with pity on catching sight of the cone of Vesuvius. "What!" cried he, "is that all?" And he sprang towards the cone. At the end of a hundred paces he halted, blowing and gasping; then he resumed his course. I marched slowly, very slowly, behind him. The scoriæ rattled under his feet like the stones of a falling house. He accomplished another hundred steps, and fell flat upon the ground, grazing his hands and knees. He rose without uttering a word, ran forward splendidly; a second fall; this time he tore his clothes from top to bottom. Then only did he condescend to yield. At first he took the arm of one guide; next, the rope of another; and at length he consented to be propelled from behind, like a *bourgeois* of Paris or a citizen of London.

But, after all, this is nothing. We cannot ascend always upon the scoriæ. We must sometimes scale the gentle slope, the yielding side of the cinders; and this is a thousand times worse. These cinders are of very fine sand, reddish, and so friable that they may be dusted, without inconvenience, instead of gold powder, over the ink of a freshly-written page. When you see this smooth slope before you, you feel reassured; you take to it with a light heart. Alas! before long you are regretting the scoriæ. It is true that the stones are no longer crumbling and slipping beneath your feet, but oh! the dust is hard and compact into which at every step you sink knee-deep! You extricate one of your limbs from this solid pool, and perform some astonishing manœuvres in order to carry it forward. Lost labour! The other leg is set fast, and you have no *point d'appui*. You think to help yourself with your hands. Utopian! They sink immediately into the moving soil, and drag your arms into it up to your shoulders. Get out of your "fix," if you can.

At length we reach the summit. Keen blows the air, and we are thankful to wrap ourselves in our cloaks. And now we advance to the edge of the crater;......it is a smoky gulf, the shape of which changes daily. I have never seen there, for my part, except on the occasion of an eruption, more than one sees in a cauldron: a great white humid cloud. But others, more fortunate, and favoured by a wind from the north which swept down the edges of the gulf, have succeeded in catching sight of the soil, which appeared to be composed of sulphur and iron ore,—the inner walls, of solid rugged rock, burnt even to calcination, like limestone; white, but stained with the yellow stains in a thousand places of pure sulphur and saltpetre; in other places tending to vitrification, in some ferruginous, everywhere cloven and fissured by long crevasses, from which issue volumes of malodorous smoke. Not a few adventurous travellers have descended, by means of ropes, to the bottom of the crater; among others, the French poet Chateaubriand. There may be seen huge blocks of granite curved into the shape of acanthus-leaves, rose-work, girandoles, and a swan beautifully moulded in white lava.

For my part, when there is no eruption I turn my back on the crater, and cast my glance over the plain.

The view is similar in character to that from the Hermitage, but extended, developed even to infinity. But I will not describe it, I have still so much to describe; I will only say that from this elevation we discover three gulfs, three islands, I know not how many promontories, on which the eye rests, with the blue sea beyond, stretching to the far horizon, where it mingles with the sky; an immense plain, a great city, five small towns at least, to say nothing of villages, innumerable mountains, bare or wooded, green or gray, white even in January;—all the wonders of the world!

But during an eruption the traveller forgets this calm and radiant picture. Then his gaze is attracted to the crater, as it vomits flames, ashes, masses of rock, and even a kind of red and burning snow; which, falling back in flakes of fire on the slopes of the cone, accumulates there, to roll down headlong in formidable avalanches, and cover the lands, and swallow up houses, and bury cities, and defy the strength and skill of man to arrest its progress.

The spectacle is dangerous when contemplated from the great crater. But, of late, eruptions have rarely taken place from thence. Since 1850, some mouths have been opened at the foot of the cone, in the ravine which separates the two mountains; and from these the lava hoarsely flows, like the rivers which issue from glaciers. The traveller, therefore, may approach without peril the incandescent streams. In 1855 and in 1858 it rolled slowly in the ravine, like a Thames which had caught fire. The accidents of the soil changed it here and there into a lurid cascade, falling like metal in a state of fusion, and leaping up again in foam, in glowing dust. Elsewhere the surface was perfectly smooth, resembling a bed of embers traversed by red-hot coals. All this you saw in safety on the brink of the ravine; spectators were numerous, and none were afraid. People flocked thither as to a pyrotechnic display, and those who had read a little called it "a beautiful horror!"

But the spectacle was very commonplace. To feel a sensation of real fear, you should not overlook the lava. You should see it coming towards you, as I saw it in 1855, at the base of Vesuvius, between Massa and San Sebastiano. Then it is no longer a flaming Seine, with waves of coal instead of water, but a rampart of ice resistlessly pressing forward. This wall was at least a mile in breadth and twenty feet in height. It advanced slowly, fatally, surely, blocking up the hollows, setting fire to trees, and winding at first in among the houses it encountered on its course, to surround them afterwards, and overwhelm them. We were forced to retire before it, like a captain before his company; and

ERUPTION OF VESUVIUS IN 1863.

I saw what seemed to be billows of stones, rolling up to within three feet of the summit of this wall, which still advanced, with an irresistible power and an implacable persistency. At every descent the progress of the lava seemed to be arrested; but afterwards came another wave, accumulating at my feet a fresh heap of stones, then another heap; and, sinking always before it, this lava filled up the ravines and invaded the plain, and menaced all the villages situated at the foot of the volcano. It was, in truth, an awful sight. Curiosity-seekers did not resort to this side of the mountain; but terrified villagers and stricken labourers rent the air with their cries. Some of them, in their frenzy, threw themselves in front of the rolling lava, that it might bury them in its depths; but, owing to its insupportable heat, before reaching them the river of fire raised them again to their feet, flung them afar, and completed their ruin by denying them the boon of death.

But at a higher level, on the occasion of eruption, I saw something more beautiful than the fiery inundation. As thus:—

We are above San Sebastiano, on the western flank of Vesuvius. A guide offers to conduct us one or two miles farther, and a hundred feet higher: we have seen the river and the torrent; he promises to show us the cataract. Two torches are lighted, and we set out. We—that is, two young women and myself—climb at first an almost perpendicular path through the brushwood. We cling to the stems to steady our steps, and put them aside in order to effect a passage. At the top of the path a ravine opens; but for the glare of our torches we should have fallen into it. And now we speed across the fields, without any regard for the beans of the cultivator. We skirt the lava-river along a way which is narrow enough for one, as Nadaud says, and not broad enough for two, to the brink of the gulf. A false step, and we should be precipitated into the fire. We traverse defiles and pathways, hollow, twisted, rocky, rugged, through the darkness of night, for about an hour. We are three in number, at the mercy of a couple of scouts who have already fleeced us, and are preceded by numerous vagabonds hideously picturesque. Nevertheless, our two young girls march bravely, unhesitatingly, with an almost feverish ardour. And yet they are not Englishwomen; they do not traverse the streets of Naples on foot; they scream at the sight of a spider; they look under their beds before retiring to rest. But the intoxication of the fire carries them out of themselves.

At length we reach the border of a kind of moat or trench. I ask the younger guide what it is called. "The *fosse de Farellone*," he replies. The other takes him up sharply, and laughs at him as a blockhead. "It is the *fosse de Pharaon*," he says; and turning towards me, he adds,—"Pharaoh, your excellency, the Roman emperor!"

We are now upon a plateau. At our feet, on the left, runs the river of lava, red as a glowing furnace. It boils, it seethes! On the other bank, a great black mass conceals an oven whence the smoke issues in whirlwinds. Before us, beyond the fosse, is the cataract. And how shall we describe it? Have you seen an avalanche descend from the summits of the Alps? Have you seen the Rhine throwing itself headlong at Lauffen into a foaming gulf? Well: combine in one picture both these images; add to it the clattering downfall of ruined houses; mingle together the cascade, the avalanche, the crash, and embrace them all in a mighty conflagration. The declivities of Vesuvius shine luridly in the night, from top to bottom, like a sheet of lightning. Masses of kindling rock bound, and crack, and splinter. In front of us the accumulated waves, vomited by the unseen crater, rear themselves every moment, and from a height of one hundred feet fall back into the fosse, carrying everything with them, sweeping everything before them. A bush is whirled off by the torrent; its fire pales in the floods of lava. There, above, enormous chestnut-trees are burning, and their fiery skeletons stand out with ghastly distinctness against the dull white gleams. The terror of the night is chequered with every possible shade or tint of fire. Garnets redden in the fosse; rubies sparkle in the torrent; glowing coals roll down the mountain-side; draperies of purple flutter from every peak; constant lightnings enkindle the shadows; rills of blood trickle at our feet. A hillock which projects on high, gradually invaded by the fiery surge, rears for a moment its base towards the sky, and falls headlong, crushed...... We all start back in mingled awe and admiration. This time it is no longer an overflowing torrent, but a mountain on fire which rolls and sweeps before us.

Another reminiscence, and I come to the eruption of 1862. In 1855 and 1858 we enjoyed some superb views, but no spectacle so frightful as that of the preceding catastrophe. The fire did not leap from the great cone like a glowing column, mounting six thousand feet in the air, and ejecting stones, rockets, ashes, fragments of rock with the roar of a tempest or a bombardment. This sight I saw only in 1850.

I found myself then at the Hermitage with a company of Germans, among whom was a Pole who had partaken freely of the hermit's *Lacryma Christi*. He announced his intention of drinking a bottle in the jaws of the volcano, and begged us to accompany him *en route*. We entered into the valley; and not content with having seen the new gulf that had opened between the two summits, we wished to reach the edge of the great crater which flamed and thundered above us. In vain our guide opposed us; we only laughed at him. It was not courage, however, which inspired us, but, as I have said, the intoxication of fire. A gendarme barred the way with his bayonet; but how could he bar a road a mile in width? Nor did his musket alarm us; he could not reasonably kill us in order to save our lives! "But there is danger," said the guide. "Own that you want a piastre more, and you shall have it, coward!" And we all set forth.

We had advanced but a few paces when we fell in with an Englishman, who was being carried down on a litter. He had attempted the ascent, but a stone had broken his arm. "What did I tell you?" resumed our guide. We acknowledged he was right, but the acknowledgment did not satisfy him. He demanded his piastre.

To conciliate all parties, we seated ourselves in the middle of the cone, on a mound of ashes between the two craters. We could lift our eyes towards the one, or lower them towards the other, at pleasure. Two steps from us, a rill of lava descended into the gulf; and this gulf, opened up the day before, was a veritable sea, losing itself on the horizon in clouds of smoke—a liquid sea which whirled and roared, breaking against the piled-up reefs its billows of flame, hurtling its floods, which leaped up, shattered in the air, and fell back in foam of fire on the lofty rocks they illuminated with weird splendour. And meanwhile, above our heads, the great crater vomited iron, sulphur, flakes of lava, red-hot bullets, and bombs weighing three hundredweights. I have already described a moving conflagration, a rolling mountain; now figure to yourself a bursting, leaping volcano, undermined by subterranean besiegers; figure to yourself a combat of Titans,—the burning of Sodom, or rather Sodom thundering against heaven. All Vesuvius quivered; an earthquake shook the crust of cinders on which we were seated; we heard beneath our feet the hammer of the Cyclops, and around us a confusion of noises, like the roar of breakers—the roll of surf on a rocky shore—the reverberation of long-continued thunder.

Meantime the Pole, in spite of guides and gen-darmes, had scaled the cone with his bottle of *Lacryma Christi*. He had outstripped all our party, and climbed precipices which would have struck terror to the heart of a muleteer of Schwytz. He reached the summit of the volcano; then he turned round to rally the prudent individuals who had followed him with so much caution. He brandished his bottle—and fell as if stricken by a thunderbolt! A bomb had smashed his leg. The word "bomb" which I here make use of is not a figure of speech, but the word always employed at Naples; and the bomb is an enormous stone, heavy and hard as granite. A flake of lava one day fell upon my hat, and did nothing more than burn the rim; but a bomb—crushes you!

The Pole was lying on the ashes of the crater, and a hail of burning stones was rained around him. One of his friends, who had seen him fall, hastened to rejoin him. He gained his side, and, through the roaring fire, carried him behind a rock of lava; then he lay down upon him to shelter him, and endeavoured to bandage the wound. The rest of the party had fled for safety to the Hermitage, and to Resina in search of assistance. But the Hermitage was one league distant, and Resina two leagues. The two friends remained alone on the summit of the volcano, in the darkness of night, under the fire, under the bombs. All the clothes they had about them did not suffice to save the unfortunate Pole, who bled to death. His friend, however, did not leave him; he was fain to contend for this lifeless body with the crater which had killed it. Alone and exhausted, he could not carry that bleeding burden into the valley, over rugged declivities and blackened steeps; so for several hours he remained stretched upon the corpse.

I invent nothing. The incident occurred exactly as I have related it, at just one hundred feet above my head.

ERUPTION OF THE GREAT CRATER OF VESUVIUS

It was related to me on the following day by all the guides, and by a German who had been one of the party.

Throughout that lonely night, around the heroic man who thus constituted himself the living shelter of a dead body, Vesuvius poured forth bombs and stones enough for the bombardment of a town. Patient and motionless he remained, uttering no sound, for the thunder would have stifled his voice, and risking a thousand deaths to save a corpse, with an obstinacy of devotion which assuredly was not the intoxication of fire. When we meet with such acts of nobleness, we certainly do not come to the conclusion that man is a god, but we are somewhat consoled at being only men.

Such accidents are fortunately rare, and usually befall the imprudent. In the eruption of 1862 there was but one victim,—a poor guide, who approached too near the mouths of fire. In 1858 an Englishman fell into the "Fosse of Pharaoh;" but this, perhaps, was a suicide. It is easy to keep account of the limited number of mishaps that overtake the cautious. Eruptions seldom occur without warning; generally they are heralded by symptoms which give time to the inhabitants of Vesuvius and its vicinity to take the necessary precautions. The wells dry up, and the soil trembles in the neighbourhood of the mountain. True it is that these prognostications are not infallible, and that the crater sometimes opens fire without first giving a warning shot; but it confines its bombardment to the cone. As for the lava-river, it has a long way to flow before it reaches the houses and cultivated grounds; it marches, moreover, at so slow a rate, that no one can be surprised by it. Thus the eruptions themselves are more ruinous than murderous; and the peasant who sleeps at the foot of the mountain would be very fortunate if he had as little cause to fear for his vines as he has for his skin.

Unfortunately, the magnificent spectacles which I have so weakly described are often accompanied by earthquakes. The shocks convulse the slopes of Vesuvius even to the sea, and not unfrequently destroy at a single blow the most flourishing towns,—compelling their inhabitants to a precipitate flight. Let us hasten to survey one of these terrible disasters.

We will descend, therefore, from the cone which we climbed with so much difficulty. The ascent occupies an hour or more; the descent is accomplished in ten minutes. One has nothing to do but to let oneself slide down the sandy slope, holding one's body well forward, so that the weight of the head may not make one tumble head over heels. At each step you glide fully twenty feet, if you will, over ashes which glide along with you, and without supporting you drag you downward. Thus you float, as it were, upon a Niagara of dust, rarely standing erect, nearly always seated or else lying on your back, when you do not roll on one side like clowns at a fair! I do not advise you to have any delicate articles about you, or any feeble muscles, for you will surely come in contact with a painful number of stones hidden in the sand where you cascade so bravely.

At length, and, I hope, without accident, we reach

the foot of the cone. Immediately we pull off and empty our boots, into which quite a mineralogical collection has insinuated itself. Then we remount our horses,—good old beasts which would cut a sorry figure in Rotten Row or the Bois de Boulogne, but march hardily over the scoriæ, and wind their way without stumbling among the rocks, and along paths which you could not travel on your two feet. At the end of an hour you are at Resina; and from Resina to Torre del Greco is but a gallop.

Some months ago * it was the cleanest, neatest, and most populous town in Naples. It manufactured articles of coral, with which it supplied the world. About twenty thousand souls lived there peacefully at the foot of the terrible neighbour which already had several times destroyed their town. Without going back much more than a century,—on the 21st of April 1737, "a current of lava," says the President de Brosses, who recorded the event two years afterwards, "dashed against Torre del Greco, broke down the wall of the Carmelite convent, entered the sacristy and the refectory, where it made but a light repast on all it found, thence crossed the highroad, and finally halted on the margin of the sea at six o'clock in the evening."

Half a century later,—in 1794,—occurred a terrible eruption. The lava-river, fifteen hundred feet broad and fourteen feet high, flowed onward for a course of three and a half miles, and advanced six hundred feet into the sea. The English ambassador, Sir William Hamilton, embarked in a boat, on the third day of the

* This was written in 1862.

eruption, to see this glowing wall. For a radius of three hundred feet, the lava made the water boil and smoke; and it rose to an extraordinary height, especially at a point where two currents met. To a distance of two miles the fish perished; even the "fruits of the sea," as the Neapolitans call shell-fish! Sir William Hamilton was compelled to make for the shore in all haste, his boat leaking at every seam, owing to the pitch having melted in the boiling sea.

The ashes vomited by the crater in this unfortunate year were so dense, that a burden of thirty-one ounces was found on a single branch of a fig-tree, though the branch weighed only five. Eruptions of cinders frequently accompany the other volcanic outbursts, and sometimes are very terrible. It was an eruption of cinders that overwhelmed Pompeii. It may be added that the dust of Vesuvius was more than once carried by the wind as far as Rome; and even as far as Egypt, if Dion Cassius be not a terrible liar! At all events, the eruption of 1862 covered all the surrounding country, and incrusted Naples with a black and red powder, which, when wetted by the rain, lay everywhere in a stratum of thickest mud.

We return to 1794. The lava of that year descended upon Resina, then diverged so quickly and abruptly towards Torre del Greco that the population had scarcely time to save themselves. Fifteen stragglers, old and feeble, perished. A monk saved the lives of seven aged nuns, who were loath to leave their convent. One of them, who counted ninety years, warmed her hands by the lava which flowed beneath her window, and thought it delightful. They had to be removed almost by force, imploring for dispensations from the Pope, and fearing Vesuvius less than purgatory. When requested to take with them their little valuables, they left their money, and carried away some sweetmeats.

Many curious things were noticed on the occasion of this catastrophe. A thief, as Sir William Hamilton informs us, got into a house surrounded by lava to steal a pig. When pursued by the owner, he endeavoured to hide himself behind the English ambassador, and wheeled round and round him for a long time, with the pig in his arms, while the despoiled proprietor similarly wheeled round on the other side. Never before or since was diplomatist in such a position!

The eruption being at an end, the Torresi—that is, the inhabitants of the Torre—rebuilt their town upon the lava in absolute contentment. The old engulfed houses became the cellars of the new; the upper windows were enlarged and made into doorways, and after a few months the disaster was forgotten. Thus, for seven-and-sixty years, the Torresi lived, without the least fear, on this platform of scoriæ.

But suddenly, on the 8th of December 1861, a violent shock of earthquake aroused them from their security. And directly afterwards, with frightful detonations, a mile above the town, four or five mouths abruptly opened, hurling stones and bombs, vomiting ashes and cinders, and darting here and there pale blue flashes of lightning. Figure to yourself the scene that followed. Immediately the population, in a terrible state of alarm and anxiety, abandoned the town, fleeing for safety towards Resina, and even as far as Naples. The highroad was crowded with scattered families, who shrieked and rolled upon the ground, with all those outbursts and convulsions of passionate emotion in which the Italians so readily indulge. Children sought their mothers; women tore their hair, calling loudly on their husbands or fathers; old men, forgotten by their kindred, wept and groaned in the rear; carriages, hastily loaded with valuables, rattled through the crowd at full gallop; the trains on the railway did not suffice to carry away the fugitives. For several days the tumult and confusion lasted. It is needless to prolong the description; enough if you picture to yourself the headlong flight for life of twenty thousand men, women, and children.

The first shock, however, did but shake the city; several others followed, and completed its destruction. It is true that some scientific authorities deny the disastrous effect of the shocks, and attribute the misfortune to a sudden subsidence of the soil—a kind of subterranean dislocation. The lavas on which the city stood were disjointed, yawning everywhere in great crevasses, and bringing down the houses in masses of ruin. Whatever the cause, I content myself with speaking to the effect. I have traversed these dismal streets, which formerly I had seen full of life, of labour, of gaiety. The broken pavements were everywhere split up by broad fissures. In the market-place a kind of well had been suddenly excavated, at the bottom of which were visible blocks of lava; and even, it is said,—though I myself did not see it,—the pavement of the ancient city. Nearly all the houses were rent and shattered, open here and there from top to bottom; balconies torn from the walls and suspended over the street; the floors sunk in the cellars, perhaps in the old mansions, which opened in wide chasms, the depth of which could not be fathomed. Elsewhere, the very façades had crumbled, so as to expose the inner walls with pictures still adorning them. I recognized a copy of Titian's "Venus." In many of the balconies I saw plants abandoned in their pots, which no one dared attempt to reach; they flowered among all the ruin, asking only for a little sunshine. Entry into some of the streets was forbidden, as fresh houses toppled daily, and would have killed the passers-by. In the midst of all this, the desolation, the silence, not a vestige of the life of yesterday, not a house inhabited, not a shop open, a cruel and fatal abandonment: some sight-seers—a few priests—paupers stealing sadly along—an old woman bemoaning the misfortune of her beautiful country—and a vendor of apples philosophically selling his fruit in the market-place. He was the only inhabitant whom I found at his post, and had not quitted the hovel where he slept. "Are you not afraid?" I asked of him. "Ah, well! I was born here, and can very well die here."

What most impressed me was the solitude and silence. The curious and the scientific have bestowed their admiration on other phenomena, of which abundant descriptions have been published; particularly on the appearance of *mofetti*, or gaseous emanations, along nearly the whole shore between Torre del Greco and Resina. One of these *mofetti* broke out in a small church of the latter village, and diffused an odour of so much potency that it drove the faithful from their knees. Nearer Torre, dogs, cats, pigs, even (it is said) a cow, were choked by the unwholesome exhalations. Long afterwards an almost unendurable stench pervaded the whole town; and travellers from Castellamare or Vietri, stopping but a minute or two at the pestiferous station, were inconvenienced so much as to hasten the departure of the train. Poor slain city! It was like the stench of its corpse.

Scientific men, moreover, turned their attention to the peculiarity of the stones vomited by the eruption. They conversed learnedly among themselves about iron and lead, sulphur and muriate; they took note of the various species of lime of which the Neapolitan artisans manufactured tobacco-boxes, brooches, ear-rings, or paper-weights; the idiocrase, manufactured into a thousand articles; sodalithe; maionite, poetically named "Vesuvian jacinth;" sarcolithe, which when wrought forms a blood-red ruby; bricolatate, humboldtilithe, and all the *lithes* possible, with the names of *savants* tagged on to them. With the materials which it ejected to ruin the labourers, Vesuvius, at all events, enriched the dictionary of the mineralogists.*

Others were astonished and afflicted by the deluge of

---

* The eruptions change the form of the crater and the cone, but have not modified their height since 1749. Measured then by Nollet, the volcano rose 3558 feet above the sea-level. Pole, in 1794, estimated it at 3636; Colonel Visconti, in 1816, at 3950 feet. Montecelli and Covelli, prior to the eruption of 1822, computed the elevation at 3888 feet; after the eruption, Humboldt found it to be only 3642 feet—and a little later, 3730 feet. (See Professor Phillips, *Vesuvius*.)

RUINS OF TORRE DEL GRECO

ashes; and, in truth, they issued in whirling clouds, not only from the new mouths, but also from the new crater. I have already noted that they were blown as far as Naples, but it was more particularly the plains and the sea which they covered with a dense black cloud. The railway-trains were compelled to slacken while traversing this palpable fog; a steam-packet, coming from Palermo, was forced to lay-to in the latitude of Capri, for her helmsman could no longer steer. It was feared that the vapours would do much harm; but scientific authorities have predicted that they would blight only the tender shoots and flowers. They assure us that after the eruption of 1794 the vineyards yielded such a crop of grapes that it could not be got rid of, and the vintage fetched but half its price through this superfluous abundance. This phenomenon, which has been more than once observed, reassured the poor vinedressers. Moreover, all the slopes of Vesuvius boast of a soil of wonderful fertility. The nearer you approach the cone, the more exquisite are the grapes and other fruits. At Somma, especially, though it has a northward aspect, the fig-trees preserve their vigour even to the month of November.

Others betook themselves to the examination of the little river of lava, which, after having descended straight upon the town, was arrested in its course at a point distant one hundred and seventy-five feet from the houses. The river broke off into two branches; one of which marched towards the villa of the Cardinal Riario Sforza, but did not touch it. Behold, a miracle! We shall hear of many others by-and-by. These rills in no way resembled the torrents of which I have spoken; they were not, like those of 1822, a mile broad and fifteen feet high. Nor did any of the details recall the conflagrations of 1858, 1855, or 1850,—still less those of 1834 and 1822. The upper crater (extinct, or at least for a long time tranquil) vomited an abundance of red-hot cinders, which at night resembled the glare and smoke of a fire; but there were none of those enormous plumes, those columns nine thousand feet in height, expanding at the summit like the branches of a pine—those marvellous spectacles which the gray-beards of Torre had seen in their youth, and to which Pliny calls attention in his account of the eruption that destroyed the two Campanian towns. And imagination therefore fails to conceive the horrors of some of those earlier eruptions; as, for instance, of that of 1631, when, according to the Abbé Braccini, three thousand persons, according to other authorities, ten thousand persons, perished. For a long period the volcano was silent; the crater filled up, trees flourished on the cone. At the bottom of the gulf, which measured five miles in circumference, and from which issued three springs of hot water, the cattle of the mountain peacefully pastured. Figure to yourself the extent of the disaster, when these pasturages were rent apart, upheaved, and hurled towards heaven by a subterranean conflagration.

And what shall be said of that historic eruption of A.D. 70, which simultaneously engulfed Stabiae, Pompeii, Herculaneum, and many villages whose names are forgotten—that eruption so tragically described in Pliny's famous epistle? Prior to this catastrophe, the terrible forces of the volcano were unknown, or at least were spoken of only as a venerable tradition or a nurse's tale. In the time of Augustus, the summit, much less elevated than it is at present, was clad with vineyards, and traversed by a cavern. To this recess penetrated eighty-four of the gladiators of Spartacus in their retreat before the overwhelming forces of the prætor Claudius, who blockaded them on the mountain. By means of the subterranean gallery, they passed under the Roman army; and issuing at its other extremity, put the prætor to flight by the suddenness of their attack, and saved their gallant leader.

Some years later broke out the eruption of Pliny. It was an awful cataclysm, which burned up trees and crops, overwhelmed cities, which still lie partly buried, and suffocated their inhabitants, whose bones and memorials are now rewarding the curiosity of explorers. As far as Misenum, it enveloped the Parthenopean gulf and the whole country in a sinister darkness. It was not merely an outburst of lava, an overflow of ashes, but whirling clouds rained down floods of fire and boiling water.

I ask the reader's pardon for repeating details which have been so often recorded; but it is impossible among the recent ruins of Torre del Greco not to think of the classic ruins of Herculaneum and Pompeii. Vesuvius, that terrible and implacable enemy of the Neapolitan land, has a thousand ways of slaying its people and destroying its towns. Torre del Greco is a striking example. Since 1731 it has been seven or eight times consumed by fire. In digging deeply under the soil, we find the remains of Roman villas; a little higher, several strata of ruins superimposed upon one another. The lavas which have made and covered them tremble incessantly at the shocks and eruptions of the volcano. Along the littoral, the shore has risen nearly four feet; and this is not the least curious phenomenon. At other places, as at Puzzuoli, the sea has receded fully as much. This upheaval of the soil began the disaster; men are now afraid of a subsidence, which will complete it. The inhabitants, therefore, are forbidden to rebuild their shattered houses.

Curious spectators contemplated also the ebullition of the sea, even at a distance of fifty feet from the shore. At two or three points, and in the same direction, the water spluttered on the surface as if swollen by a breath, or heated by a subterranean fire. Finally: they took note of the extraordinary copiousness of a spring which, with its tenfold volume, converted a small stream into a torrent. So far as I was concerned, all these "objects of interest" spoiled the spectacle: they attracted too many people. I preferred the market-place—fissured, depopulated, stretching seaward between two rows of houses in ruins, and that aged woman, who walked to and fro alone and in tears, repeatedly sobbing forth,—"My country! O my beautiful country!"

And yet I could not but smile, even in that desolate spot, at the remarks of my guide. He pointed out the church uninjured, and explained to me the causes of the eruption. The poor fellow spoke with much more assurance than the *savants* of the Observatory would have done. He possessed the faith of which science deprives us—to restore it to us again, thank God!

He told me that on the Sunday of the catastrophe, during prayers, some young persons entered the church with a tricolor scarf, and were fain to decorate the Madonna with it. The curé exclaimed against what he regarded as a profanation: "Hand me the scarf, if you will, but do not touch the holy Virgin."

"She is a wooden image," replied the sacrilegious crew.

"She is made of thunder, and will kill you."

The young men, however, would not listen to the priest; and, afraid of being killed, he gave way. Of course, I am simply repeating what my guide told me. Immediately the earthquake occurred, and the terrified crowd fled from the church with the curé, who murmured,—"I told you the truth, you see!"

I have since learned that the whole of this pretty little narrative was false. How it got abroad I know not, but the curé himself contradicted it; without shaking the faith, however, of the inhabitants of Torre del Greco.

"Were you present in the church?" I asked of one of them.

"Undoubtedly."

"Did you see the incident?"

"No; I saw nothing at all."

"How then do you know it took place?"

"Because I was told so."

"Who told you?"

"Nicole."

"Was Nicole in the church?"

"She was there with me, on my left hand."

"Then *she* saw it?"

"No more than I did; ask her."

"But if the story is true, some person or other must have witnessed the transaction."

"But if it were *un*true, Torre del Greco would still be standing!"

I make no comment; these facts speak for themselves. Superstition lifts its head everywhere in this country; and the eruptions of Vesuvius are associated with innumerable fables. Each catastrophe is followed by an increase of external devotion, unless despair seizes on the crowd. Then they seem to grow delirious, and abandon themselves to every excess. In 1707, for example, when the Neapolitans thought destruction inevitable, they indulged in the most terrible orgies. The Church had to send her missionaries among them, to revive their hopes and restore their confidence. This is the only similar case known to me in the history of Naples; but it is pregnant with lessons, and invites our patient consideration.

In ordinary outbreaks, I repeat, they address themselves to their saints; and the cessation of the eruption they invariably ascribe to some supernatural interposition. You know, perhaps, that hitherto the city of Naples has been saved from the vengeance of Vesuvius by Saint Januarius. One evening, the statue of the martyr stood, with head lowered and arms drooping, at the entrance to the town. Next morning it was found with head turned and arms outstretched towards Vesuvius,—as if to say to the lava, then flowing towards Naples, "Thus far, and no farther." And, wonderful to tell, the lava was arrested in its course.

Since this memorable event, the statue of the saint has always preserved the same attitude. During the eruption of 1779, the French ambassador, M. Clermont d'Amboise, fled from Portici, and hastened, full gallop, towards Naples. On the Madeleine Bridge his carriage was stopped by a dense, tumultuous crowd, who wished the diplomatist to kneel before St. Januarius. Unfortunately, M. Clermont d'Amboise understood not a word of the dialect in which their directions were shouted. His ignorance would have cost him dear, had he not skilfully extricated himself from his unpleasant position by flinging a handful of piastres at the foot of the statue: the mob plunged eagerly upon the booty, and demanded no other satisfaction.

Let not the reader suppose that this patronage of the illustrious martyr is only a popular superstition. The Government professed to believe in him in the time of the Bourbons. During these eruptions I have seen the relics of "San Gennaro" transported to Fort Saint-Elmo, which was illuminated for the occasion. The precaution, however, was neglected in December 1861; and this is one reason—among many others—why Torre del Greco suffered so severely.

Some people say, however, that San Gennaro protects only Naples; and, therefore, the inhabitants of the neighbouring villages show but little respect for him. They resort more willingly to San Antonio, the patron-saint of Fire. And yet, in 1850, San Antonio was powerless. The people of Ottajano, who were then particularly menaced, addressed themselves to Pio Nono; but the Holy Father replied that he did not work miracles, and could only offer his prayers. In this singular country, however, the people do not believe in prayers, only in miracles; and the people of Ottajano accordingly betook themselves to the mariners of Torre Annunziata. These coral-fishers boast of a Madonna, which they fished up from the bottom of the sea. Many of the boatmen of the neighbouring coasts had attempted to carry off this treasure, but not one had been successful. In the hands of the mariners of Castellamare or Naples the image weighed tons, even without its setting. But in those of the coral-fishers it was a feather—nay, light as air. They hauled up the Madonna, and placed it in their church.

The people of Ottajano came, then, to beg those of Torre Annunziata to lend them the venerated image. "Take it," said the latter. But this the former found themselves unable to do. They could have more easily uplifted the whole church for removal to their own territory. It was necessary that the coral-fishers themselves should repair to the scene of disaster with their precious Madonna. There they placed it in front of the lava, and — the incandescent river immediately ceased to flow!

I tell the story as it was told to me. Unfortunately, the men of Torre Annunziata never thought of carrying their Madonna to the assistance of their neighbours of Torre del Greco.

Young ladies who read these truthful pages, remember that the beautifully-wrought stones and the rich necklaces of rose-tinted or vermilion-coloured beads which adorn your charms, were manufactured in the unfortunate city. The inhabitants of the Neapolitan seaboard maintain a constant strife with Nature; but it does not seem to weaken their devotion to Art.

To the foregoing details, we desire to add some particulars embodied in a letter addressed to M. Elie de Beaumont by M. P. de Tchihatchef, immediately after the occurrence of the catastrophe:—

Yesterday, the 8th of December, at half-past one P.M., there was felt at Naples a very light shock of earthquake,—which I did not remark, being at the time in the Rue de Toledo. But about three o'clock, towards the Riviera de la Chiaja, I was surprised to see the horizon in the direction of Vesuvius enveloped in a dense smoke, which, I was told, proceeded from the very foot of the south-south-west slope of the mountain.

At nightfall, about seven o'clock, the heights of Torre del Greco appeared illuminated by four or five fiery columns, echelonned on a line, the direction of which seemed to be from north-north-east to south-south-west. These columns were united by less luminous wreaths, and formed in some degree one great curtain of flames.

This morning, the 9th, I hastened to Torre del Greco. At Naples the air was serene, the sea perfectly calm; but as I approached the village the sky became dull and sombre, owing to the smoke and the ashes which fell at Portici like very fine rain.

I found the inhabitants of Torre del Greco in a state of the most violent agitation, and preparing to emigrate in a body, with all the effects they were able to carry.

They told me that on the previous day they had experienced more than twenty-one shocks, which had succeeded one another at irregular intervals from eleven in the morning until three in the afternoon; and that about three o'clock loud subterranean detonations were followed by dense clouds of smoke and ashes, which rose at a short distance north of the village on the south-south-west slope of the mountain.

I penetrated into the village as quickly as possible, and could see that the walls of many of the houses were rent with great fissures.

I had scarcely got clear of the last enclosures of Torre del Greco when I found myself in the midst of an immense agglomeration of scoriæ, from the interstices of which escaped thousands of tiny jets of smoke.

The inhabitants of Torre del Greco assured me positively that not only was this immense heap the entire product of the preceding day's convulsions, but also two conical masses which I could see beyond (at about six hundred yards to the north-north-east of Torre del Greco, and about two thousand yards to the north-west of the convent of the Camaldules). These two cones, the summits of which gave forth thick columns of smoke, were inaccessible on account of the hail of stones and incandescent ashes which they ejected: these, seen from Naples in the midst of the obscurity, had been mistaken for columns of flame.

At a short distance to the south of these piles were found, echelonned on a line running in the main from east-north-east to west-south-west, three cavities hollowed out in the very soil, consisting of pre-existent volcanic sands; they were separated from one another by irregular walls or partitions. As to the cavities, they were shaped very regularly as funnels, the depth of which probably did not exceed twenty yards, and the circumference about forty. The bottom was level.

Columns of smoke, similar to those which issued from the summits of the two conical heaps, likewise proceeded from the bottom of these funnel-shaped cavities, probably through imperceptible fissures. The smoke escaped in sudden outbursts, and was preceded by a rumbling sound like the distant report of artillery.

After each detonation, the smoke sprang upward in gigantic sheaves, and unfolded into white or grayish masses of a globular form, presenting a truly sublime spectacle. An odour of sulphur made itself very distinctly appreciable.

For two hours I wandered about this fiery soil; and meanwhile I observed a curious oscillation in a broken-up mass of scoria, which twice rose and fell, without disturbing the loose fragments composing it: it seemed a transitory, local movement of expansion or upheaval.

On my way back to Naples, I found the shower of ashes gradually diminishing, and then disappearing. A dull white cloud obscured Vesuvius. At Naples the sky was of an intense azure, and the sun shone in all its splendour.

II.

In the Harz.

THE Harz—so called from the German *Hart, Harti,* "a wooded height"—forms an isolated mountain-mass, spreading into the four territories of Hanover, Brunswick, Prussia proper, and Anhalt-Bernburg. Geographically, it is divided into two parts: the Upper and the Lower Harz—*Oberharz* and *Unterharz*. It exhibits a rich variety of striking and romantic landscapes, and is associated with innumerable traditions, songs, and legends. Formerly the traveller found some difficulty in penetrating into its recesses; but now the railway has invaded it, and even the spectre-haunted Brocken has become vulgarized and commonplace. Fortunately it has been found impossible as yet to ruin its scenery, and the artist, in wandering through its sylvan regions and deep defiles, will find abundant material for his sketch-book.

We propose to accompany M. Carnot on a tour in this wild mountain-country, and shall join him at Klausthal, a town of 7000 to 8000 inhabitants, planted on the crest of a bare and rugged height, in the Oberharz. We arrive there in time to witness the incidents of a *Schützenfest;* which is, as everybody knows, the German national fête, and calls forth in the hearts of the people their most patriotic emotions.

It extends over a week. So far as the tourist is concerned, its chief feature would seem to be the misery he suffers from the brass instruments of itinerant musicians, who successively besiege every house in the town. A grand concert, moreover, is given for the benefit of the aristocracy of Klausthal, at a shilling per head. In the neighbourhood of the shooting-ground are planted all kinds of booths and stalls for the sale of pottery, cakes, bon-bons, refreshments, and a hundred articles; ambulatory theatres, with the attractions of gigantic women and African ostriches; and a German *Punch,* uttering his jokes in a curious dialect of Low Dutch.

The aristocratic concert is followed by a grand ball for the *bourgeois,* given in a large saloon erected for the occasion, decorated with wreaths of foliage and lighted by a limited number of candles. Near the orchestra a third of the space was allotted to the nimble movements of the dancers; the remainder was occupied by rows of long tables, at which were seated young men and women, and their parents, spending the tedious intervals between the dances in conversation and in pledging one another in cheap Rhenish wine. At a signal from the orchestra, everybody quitted his glass, proceeded in search of a partner, and took his place in the long line of couples,—every movement being performed with truly German phlegm, method, and deliberation. Then the waltz or galop began. Six or seven couples only started at the outset. But a signal being given, six others succeeded them; and the first six stationed themselves behind those who had not yet danced, or gravely promenaded round the saloon. On returning to his seat, everybody put on his hat, and resumed the pleasing task of refreshing his wearied frame. In the general soberness and decorous dulness of the scene, there was something surprising. Dancers and drinkers, all meant business; and all went through their work with edifying gravity. The fête was prolonged to so late an hour, that before quitting the dancing-hall we saw the sun rising above the Brocken.

The Harz is celebrated for its mines, and a visit to these is as indispensable on the part of the tourist as the ascent of the Brocken.

There are two ways of descending into the mines. Formerly, at regular intervals in a special compartment of the shaft, was arranged a succession of stages, platforms, or landing-places, communicating with one another by ladders; and the visitor ascended or descended by means of these. In many places this arrangement is still kept up. But the fatigue of climbing up or down vertical or almost vertical ladders, for a depth of 500, 600, or 700 yards, is very severe. The miners spent an hour or an hour and a half every morning and evening in the wearisome exercise, to the great trial of their strength and the loss of their time. So, in some of the mines, the ascent and descent are accomplished, as in our English mines, in the buckets, cradles, or suspended cages, used also for the removal of the ore or coal. These are lowered or raised by ropes passing over pulleys, and worked by hand or by steam power.

Peculiar to the Harz, also, is the ingenious apparatus known as the fahr-kunst, which enables you to effect a tolerably rapid ascent, with the minimum of fatigue and the maximum of security.

Picture to yourself, as suspended in a compartment of the shaft of the mine, two vertical beams supporting small platforms or foot-boards at regular intervals; suppose that these beams receive from above to below, and from below upward, a uniform movement, the extent of which shall be equal to the distance of the foot-boards; and suppose that these two beams move always in an opposite direction, the one rising as the other descends. At the moment when the two are arrested, and when consequently two foot-boards will be opposite one another, a man can easily pass from one to the other by clinging with his hands to the handles fixed for the purpose upon the beams. Now the reader will easily understand that if he changes in this way from side to side, each time the two foot-boards are brought together, —quitting the descending beam for that which is moving upward,—he will gradually rise from the bottom to the top of the shaft. In descending, all he has to do is to reverse the process.

In Belgium and in France, the apparatus established on this principle are much more novel and perfect than those in use in the Harz: instead of rough foot-boards, they are furnished with convenient platforms, on which two persons can easily stand at a time; but the honour of the discovery belongs to the engineers of the Harz.

Having accomplished our descent into a mine, our first inquiry will be as to its ventilation. How do the miners *breathe* in these underground recesses? How are they provided with a sufficient supply of pure atmospheric air? For we feel that the temperature is not disagreeable nor the odour oppressive. On the other hand, we are conscious that a cellar or subterranean excavation, if only a few feet below the surface, is by no means a healthy or agreeable residence. How, then, do the miners contrive to enjoy a tolerably healthy climate at a depth of two thousand feet in the bowels of the earth?

Well, the process of ventilation, though somewhat complicated in its details, is very simple as a whole.

Metallic mines, like those of the Harz, do not require a very active circulation of the air; all that is necessary is to carry off that which has already been respired by the workmen, which has fed their lamps, and been vitiated by the process of blasting. There is no occasion to fear, as in coal-mines, the irrespirable and explosive gas which is disengaged from the surface of the coal. Special machines, however, are sometimes made use of to renew the air in the inner parts of the mine. But frequently a natural ventilation is sufficient: the fresh air enters through the lowest openings, shafts, or galleries, grows warm in the mine, and accordingly rises and passes away through the higher shafts, just as the heated atmosphere of our rooms escapes through the chimneys. In all cases the direction of the air-current, and its proportion, is regulated by means of doors, which prevent it from seeking the shortest way, and compel it to feed those places most in need of it.

A MINE IN THE HARZ—DESCENDING THE SHAFT

The lights used by the Harz miners are lamps of classic form; which are supplied, before descending, with a lump of fat for distinguished visitors, or with oil for workmen. The same system of lightage is adopted for the solid galleries and those navigated in boats, in spite of the regret of all lovers of the picturesque, who naturally would prefer the weird effects produced by the shifting glare of torches.

And yet it is fortunate that such lamps, with their naked and powerful flame, can be safely employed. In coal-mines the presence of an explosive gas compels the miner, as everybody knows, to surround the flame with a metallic network, which prevents its combustion from spreading externally, and, at the same time, so masks the flame that darkness swallows up everything at a foot or two from the lamp.

The Harz miner is generally well-educated; at an early age having been sent to school, and having been properly instructed in everything that concerns his occupation. He speaks good German, often with elegance. On Sundays you meet him and his wife and his children repairing to the nearest church with their Bibles or psalm-books in their hands, for all are able to read. He is thoroughly religious, assembling his family every morning at prayers, before they betake themselves to the mines, each one to his post. He never fails, when he encounters you underground, to salute you with the word *Glückauf*,—an abbreviation of *Glückliche auffahrt*, "A good voyage," or rather, "A safe ascent,"—nor, at the close of a meal, with the kindly expression, *Gesegnete Mahlzeit* ("May the meal be blessed!"). He is strongly attached to his dogmas and religious rites; and some twelve years ago an attempt on the part of the late Hanoverian Government to introduce a new catechism, professedly to regenerate the true Lutheran doctrine, met with so vigorous an opposition that it was perforce abandoned.

From Klausthal it is customary to repair to Andreasberg, the *locale* of a very celebrated silver-mine. It has long been exhausted, and now retains only the tradition of its ancient glory; but it has still the honour of ranking at the head of the deepest mines in the world. As it cannot supply the wants of some silver-works situated in the neighbourhood, the proprietary, to keep alive their furnaces, are obliged to import, through Hamburg, the ore of the American mines; a remarkable circumstance in a country so difficult of access, and where there is not even the advantage of cheap fuel, the coke in use being procured from Westphalia!

The surrounding country is more picturesque than the neighbourhood of Klausthal: the undulations of the soil are more compact and better defined; the slopes are rapid, the valleys deep; the fresh verdure of the meadows and the deep green of the fir-woods intermingle in such a manner as to give a strong character to the landscape; —here is, indeed, the true mountain-land, the Harz of which one dreams over the rhymes of poets and the sketches of artists.

From Andreasberg a short journey carries us to Torfhaus, at the foot of the Brocken. The ascent of this famous mountain is neither a dangerous nor a difficult enterprise; it occupies little more than two hours, and the path is nowhere unpleasantly steep. It is curious that this mountainous mass of granite is covered on every side, and even on its most abrupt declivities, by a thick stratum of turf, in which the purple heather flourishes abundantly. Apparently there is nothing to arrest the flow of the water, and assist the formation of turf; yet it develops with great rapidity, and attains a depth which, in the more accessible parts, renders the collection of peat a profitable occupation.

Up to the very summit of the mountain, M. Carnot, on the occasion of his ascent, was protected by dense clouds against the glowing ardour of an autumnal sun. The peak is crowned by a very considerable inn,—the *Brockenhaus*. From this point, on a clear day, the tourist enjoys a panorama not less varied than extensive.

The celebrated legends of the Brocken, and the stories of the wild dances of witches and fairies, immortalized by the genius of Goethe, are familiar now to every reader. The tradition of the Walpurgis Night is still a living thing; only it is merry villagers who now, on the night of the 1st of May, take the place of the deposed sorcerers and sorceresses, and dance in company on the Brocken,—while, in the plain, the timorous peasants, apprehensive of all manner of evil plotting against them by the mountain-spirits, pass the night in devoutly making the circuit of their fields by the light of torches.

Some persons seek the origin of the terrible legends

of the Brocken in the reminiscences of the bloody sacrifices perpetrated there by the pagan Saxons, and continued long after the exterminating campaigns of Charlemagne, the great emperor of the West. The altars on which these sacrifices were offered up consisted of the large natural platforms which, supported in the air by huge pillars of granite, brought to light by the constant actions of the waters, present to this day, on the rugged slope of the Brocken, a weird and impressive aspect. It is easy to conceive that myth and fable would soon grow up about them.

We shall now take up a fuller description of the Harz and the Brocken, as supplied by the traveller Strobbant in 1862.

As Heine says, the Brocken is essentially German, for good as for ill, for the beautiful as for the hideous. The same is true of other parts of the Harz. The general aspect of the country is one of picturesque grandeur; and the mists which prevail there during a considerable portion of the year communicate to the landscapes an exceptional character and colouring. The peasant does not escape their influence; he seems marked on the forehead with a sombre hue, which gives to his physiognomy an air of fear and gloom. His gestures are abrupt; and if you wish to obtain from him the slightest information, you must speak to him in his own language, and speak accurately, for if he discovers that you are a stranger he will turn his back upon you, murmuring unintelligible words. It happened to us, during our excursion in this country, to be for a whole week seated at table with the same companions, and yet to find scarcely two of them disposed to reply to our questions on the manners and usages of the Harz; the others sedulously avoided conversation. Notably one opposite neighbour shrank even from looking at us, and shut himself up in silent phlegm. His countenance is photographed on our memory, because we had frequent occasion to meet him elsewhere: the traits of the visage sometimes differed, but the traditional gold spectacles never failed to be planted squarely on the nose of this mistrustful personage.

The visitor to the Harz must travel afoot, with his portmanteau on his back, if he would penetrate into the less frequented and the wildest localities; which, to the sketcher, are generally the most interesting.

Still, a guide is valuable on account of the services he renders during and after a long day's march. Generally, the guides are honest and sober; bread and beer are all they require. Food is not dear, and the pay they receive is very small. When crossing an immense plain, luxuriant with splendid crops, we perceived several young persons mounted on stilts, and making with a kind of rattle a deafening noise, intended to put to flight the few sparrows which came to peck at the ears bending over the furrowed way. These robust young guardians, who spent all the day in the fields, certainly received at each meal, in the shape of bread, more grain than the birds would have carried away in a week. The inaction of their vigorous arms bore testimony to the trifling value of manual labour.

The Harz is composed of enormous blocks of granite,

the base of which rises several hundred feet above the sea-level. Its area is thirty-six square miles. The mountains are generally isolated, and form huge conical peaks, separated by deep and narrow valleys, especially in the north of the Harz. A chain of mountains divides this country into two parts; several rivers rise in it. Of these the chief are the Bode, the Holzemme, the Wipper, the Tyra, the Ilse, and the Selke.

Our traveller reached Halberstadt at four o'clock on a bright and cloudless day. The town was completely deserted. With much interest he surveyed the antique houses that lined its streets, some of which were genuine masterpieces of wood carving. The caryatides and gargoyles assume forms so twisted, that it is necessary to follow closely the line of the principal subject to discover what the artist wished to represent. The Rathskeller House, which dates from the beginning of the fifteenth century, is a complete marvel. The three stories facing the street are each of a different design. The lower gallery is the most richly and artistically ornamented; and the artist has given to the figures and ornaments which form the angles the greatest importance, with a happy result as regards the general effect. The details above are broader, though lighter in form, so as not to overwhelm the lower part of the design.

Halberstadt is seen to most advantage on a market-day. There is a certain quaintness about the dress of the men, which harmonizes with the character of the scene. That of the women is semi-Oriental: they wear large blue mantles, striped with white or red, or capacious pelisses with three hoods, in which they wrap up and carry their children. The folds of these ample garments, and the calm, slow air of their movements, give to the women a monumental character. Through this strangely-attired and novel crowd pass carts and waggons drawn by oxen, which pace as deliberately as their masters.

The most important building in the market-place is the town-hall. Its architecture is a picturesque grouping together of different styles, the Gothic predominating. Amateurs notice with interest the happy arrangement of the lines; and a balcony at the corner of the market-place is a thing of beauty. The lower gallery is particularly distinguished by the fertility and originality of its decoration. Three grinning heads look out upon you from the stone, as if they had been suddenly endowed with life. Gaze upon them when the sunset touches them, and they seem to twist themselves into convulsive movements,—so that every moment you expect to hear a frightful laugh burst from the yawning mouths.

The cathedral is a noticeable structure. Of course, it has its legend; and, of course, in this legend Satan plays the principal part. In the centre of the market-place is preserved the enormous stone which he hurled at the cathedral with the intention of destroying it; though archæologists are found obtuse enough to declare that it is only a pagan altar.

It is a building of much beauty, which deserves to be included among the most remarkable and least-known monuments of Northern Germany. Like most erections of the kind, its architecture extends over a considerable period, marking the gradual development of the Gothic style, from early in the thirteenth to late in the fourteenth century. The lower part of the towers, the windows, the intercolumniation, and the doorway, all admirable in design and execution, date from 1180 to 1220; the principal windows and the buttress-pillars belong to 1300 to 1380. Very rich in details are the columns and arches; and in one of the niches is to be seen a fine head of Christ, with the twelve apostles grouped around it. On the upper portion of the capitals are skilfully wrought the four evangelists.

The interior of the cathedral is particularly worthy of attention. Its aspect is imposing, and its principal lines are majestic. The sombre tone which dominates everywhere lends prominency and effect to the details exposed to receive the light of day. The eye rests with delight on the screen which separates the choir from the nave. It bears the date of 1510. Its invention is rich, and forms a group of little spires of archivolts interlaced with foliage wrought as delicately as lace-work. Some curious tombs are found in the nave; one on the right hand surpasses anything the imagination can conceive in its varied arabesques of ornaments and figures. It resembles an engraving by Dieterlin transferred to stone. This masterpiece is inscribed with the name of "Bastian,......of Magdeburg," master-sculptor to the lords of Kannenburg. Bishop Scimka's monument is enclosed by an iron railing of superb workmanship; the recumbent effigy is very fine, but has been much injured by the names and dates foolishly carved upon the hands and figure. Some of these inscriptions are very ancient. Among other objects worthy of attention we may name the baptismal fonts, said to be of the twelfth century, the remains of a remarkable Gothic tabernacle, two very old and colossal candelabra, and the monument of the Margrave of Brandenburg, of 1558.

The first cathedral of Halberstadt was built by Charlemagne; and destroyed by Henry the Lion, Duke of Saxony and Bavaria, who laid siege to the town, carried it by assault, and set fire to its buildings. Several churches and four monasteries were reduced to ashes, and the priests and people who had fled thither for refuge perished in the flames.

The church of "Our Lady," on the other side of the market-place, is one of the best-preserved specimens of the Byzantine in Germany.

The town generally wears a calm and silent aspect. However, our traveller was witness of an incident which shows the emotional susceptibility of its inhabitants when once their political sympathies are aroused.

One night he was suddenly awakened by a great noise. Hastily rising, he threw open his window, and saw that a numerous throng had collected round a vehicle in front of the Hotel Prince Eugene. Two persons descended from it; and immediately a thousand arms were uplifted, and a formidable shout broke from every breast. A few minutes afterwards, he heard steps in the corridors of the house; then all was silent, and the crowd quietly dispersed. Next day, he learned that the acclamations were a welcome to the Duke of Saxe-Coburg-Gotha, who had arrived at Halberstadt to review the regiment of Prussian cuirassiers of which he was colonel.

Said the traveller to one of the attendants: " You are much attached, then, to the duke ? "

The attendant replied : " Yes, truly; we love the prince because his views are liberal."

Throughout the day the town was *en fête*, and in the evening several choral societies gave the prince one of those German serenades in which the dialogue with its political allusions is of more importance than the music. Old and tattered banners were unfurled above the crowd, and a hundred torches lighted up a scene which was certainly picturesque. Similar scenes were of frequent occurrence a few years ago, when almost every week brought to the Harz and its quaint little towns the news of a German victory, and of the further progress of German soldiers into the heart of France.

The reader will object, perhaps, that these particulars have little to do with mountains. But we are now sketching a mountainous region, and not any single height, and our object is to bring into relief its salient characteristics. The legends of the Harz, and the manners of its population, and even the prevailing sentiment of its architecture, are closely connected with, if they did not actually originate in, its peculiar and remarkable scenery. And we submit, therefore, that we are by no means overloading our pages with superfluous details in thus sketching the aspect of the country through which the persevering traveller ascends to the spectre-haunted Brocken.

From Halberstadt we proceed to Quedlinburg, where the old castle frowns from a precipice of sandstone. Thence we make our way to Blankenburg, crossing several pretty mountain-streams, which wind capriciously into the Bode.

Blankenburg is less picturesque than some other towns of the Harz, in spite of its *Teufelsmauer*, or Devil's Wall. The town is full of life, and the promenades are pleasant; but the castle which dominates it is heavy and gloomy. The traveller will prefer to visit the ruins of the Regenstein; a strong fortress, perched on the summit of a precipitous rock, and built by Henry the Fowler. It is now a shattered mass of stones, hardly distinguishable from the rock itself.

Some distance beyond rises the Hoppelberg, or Cradle Mountain; so called on account of its peculiar conformation. This is the culminating point of the Unterharz; the ascent is easy, and from the summit the view to the northward is extensive and romantic, and includes the Brocken.

By descending the mountain on this side the tourist reaches a curious accumulation of rocks, which the natives call volcanic mountains; they resemble colossal *dunes*. An isolated and fantastically-shaped mass terminates the chain. Towards nightfall, or in gloomy weather, this grand dentelated line, which recedes to the horizon, seems continued to infinity; and, saddened by the reflection of the gray, cloudy sky, invests the surrounding landscape with a peculiar air of melancholy and severity.

Next day, the traveller may visit the Hermit's Rocks, which lie in the same direction. These bare, denuded, and enormous blocks wear quite a monumental character. When seen in the glowing sunshine of a cloudless day, they seem to transport the spectator to the distant East, and he feels as if he stood before the huge palace-temples of Egypt, and their façades covered with hieroglyphical inscriptions.

M. Strosbant visited the Rosstrappe, he tells us, in very favourable weather. The sky was "deeply, darkly, beautifully blue;" the glossy foliage of the trees reflected its rays of subtle and sparkling light. All nature seemed to thrill with joy. It was one of those exceptional days when we forget the cares and sins of humanity, and dream for a while that earth is as happy and as pure as it is beautiful and grand.

A stork, perched on a chimney, contemplated with grave and anxious air the laughing groups that passed beneath and chatted in their gaiety of heart. Some sparrows, who had taken up their residence in her nest, and fluttered and chirped with active merriment, vainly endeavoured to divert the attentive and steadfast gaze, fixed on the scenes of happiness around her.

The road leading to the Rosstrappe is steep, but not difficult. When the traveller had gained the summit, the guide pointed out to him a horse-shoe shaped indentation, to which this locality owes the name of the Rosstrappe.

The princess Hildegard inhabited, with her father, a castle in the neighbourhood of the Bode; she was a maiden of great personal charms, and of much boldness of character. Mounted on her favourite steed, she loved to gallop afar over hill and dale. In one of her excursions she approached a cavern in which a giant resided, who had several times seen her splendid beauty, and now conceived the base idea of possessing himself of it. He rushed in pursuit of her. She fled; and her horse, spurred to full speed, crossed the valley at a single leap, and descended on an enormous crag projecting from the precipice. His hind legs finding no support, he rolled, with his living burden, deep down into the recesses of the Créfal, an excavation of the Bode. When the waters are low you may still see, it is said, the crown of the princess, who lives, and sits erect in the depths of the river. The story goes that, one day, a troop of woodcutters assembling at this spot, one of them endeavoured to draw the princess from the waters; he plunged several times to bring her to the surface, but each time an impetuous current forced him back; at last he seemed on the point of succeeding, when suddenly he disappeared beneath the waves, dragged down by an unseen hand. Some moments afterwards, the spectators were horror-stricken to see a jet of blood issuing from the waves. The princess, by sacrificing a victim, made known her will that men should no more trouble her resting-place. So the peasants fled affrighted; and to this day the country-people will make a long circuit to avoid the haunted and accursed spot. With the aid of a sympathetic imagination, the tourist may discover the imprint of a horse's hoof upon the rock.

In descending into the valley, he will find the rock somewhat precipitous; but by means of a rugged staircase of stones, piled upon one another, he accomplishes the descent, and proceeds along a narrow path to the Devil's Bridge. A little farther, and the rocky scenery assumes a wild and eery character, and only a strong nerve and a clear brain should face the dizzy heights.

Recrossing the Bode, he reaches a remarkable nook or corner, known as the Witches' Valley. It is closely shut in on every side, so that at first sight there seems no outlet for the river; and the surrounding crags present the most varied and fantastic outlines. They seem like so many colossal figures,—some recumbent, others erect; and each has its legendary associations. In fact, everything in this country is the subject of myth and tradition; and, therefore, it is not surprising that the peasantry, bred in so legendary an atmosphere, should be superstitious and timorous in all that relates to the *Hezen* or to the Father of Evil.

A staircase of about twelve hundred steps conducts the traveller to the Hezen-tanz platz—that is, the Platform of the Witches' Dance. Half way-down the mountain, he may rest upon one of the rocks which overhang the valley; a complete tranquillity reigns all around, and the sound of the flowing water does but enhance the impression of perfect harmony. Listen attentively, and you will think you detect the echo of an instrument blending with the murmur of the waves, and the general effect is that of an unearthly and dreamy music.

SCENE IN THE ROSSTRAPPE.

And now, most patient reader, behold us on the road to the Brocken.

The weather, hitherto so fair and favourable, has become gloomy; the heat is intolerable; and a few large drops of rain, like "the first of a thunder-shower," fall heavily on the dusty highway, to disappear immediately. Not a leaf stirs; the trees along the road are silent, yet seem disturbed; great belts of greenish-gray clouds rest upon the horizon. To the left, the Brocken shows itself above a framework of mountains, the upper portion of which is sharply outlined against the sky; a dull, leaden-coloured mist spreads over the valley, and obscures and confounds its various features. We hasten our steps, and, after a good walk, reach Ilsenberg just as the rain begins to fall abundantly. Several tourists have already taken up their quarters in the inn; and the threatening weather has induced them to defer their ascent of the Brocken until the morrow. They advise us to follow their example.

The rain, falling in torrents, renders us undecided; and seated beneath the shelter of the sloping roof, we spend a long time in watching the lapsing waters as they descend the surrounding mountains. The monotony of this contemplation makes us less capable than ever of forming a resolution. We return to the inn. But there the spectacle of the listless, weary, yawning, and lethargic tourist-company somewhat revives our energies. Away we speed, and find our way to the room where the guides are taking their ease; all rise, and willingly proffer their services for—the next day; all, except a little, squat, robust man in the corner. He looks at us with a careless air, then resumes his former posture, with his elbows on his knees, and his head supported between his two large hands. Turning towards him, we ask him if he will conduct us at once to the Brocken. He replies abruptly,—"Are you in earnest in making the proposal in such bad weather?" "Yes." "Will you take the paths, instead of the abominably ugly main road?" "Certainly." "But I shall not be able to redescend the mountain to-day." "I will hire you for several days." He rises slowly, buckles on his big gaiters, and prepares to strap my portmanteau to his lusty shoulders.

When they saw us reappear, accompanied by our man, the tourists burst out laughing, and the landlord joined them, not without cause; we pretended to see nothing, and bravely started on our enterprise.

At intervals the rain ceased; but the storm was incessant, and its roar was like the rattle of a hundred chariots. Occasionally a flash of lightning broke forth, and we took advantage of these gleams to reach the Ilsenstein.

The Ilsenstein is an immense rocky precipice, about 2500 feet in height, washed by the winding flood of the river Ilse, a stream very famous in song and fable. Heinrich Heine says of it:—It is impossible to describe the vivacity, the boldness, the grace, with which the Ilse descends on the fantastic groups of rocks she encounters in her career. Here the waters hiss wildly, or roll in spray and foam; there they leap in crystal arches over a labyrinth of crevasses; and, lower down, they dance across the mossy pebbles like frolicsome nymphs.

Yes; tradition is right. The Ilse is a princess who, with the laughter and freshness of youth, descends the mountain-sides. How her white robe of foam sparkles in the sunshine! How the silver ribbons of her bosom flutter in the breeze! How her diamonds glitter! The tall ash-trees stand erect beside her, like grave seniors who smile benignantly at the tricksomeness of a favourite child; the white birches balance themselves with the satisfaction of tender aunts who, nevertheless, are somewhat afraid of her daring escapades, the proud oak regarding them with the stern glance of a gloomy uncle, and counting their possible cost; the small birds of the air applaud her with joyous songs; and the flowers on the bank murmur tenderly,—"Oh, take us with you, take us with you, dear little sister!" But the wild young girl speeds on her way, and listens to none.

We rapidly descended into the valley towards a steep pathway, which would shorten the route, and conduct us in three hours to the summit of the Brocken (3700 feet). During the first hour of our march all went well; and so complete was my enjoyment that several times I asked the guide to stop and rest. However, his only reply was to quicken his steps; and before long his obstinacy explained itself. Just as we had arrived at a heap of scattered rocks, the storm, which had so long been threatening, broke forth in all its violence. A keen and violent wind lashed us in the face, the rain fell heavily and densely, the water rushed from the mountain in impetuous torrents, carrying along with it the trunks of uprooted trees; and with the clash of successive thunder-peals the Brocken seemed to tremble. Every now and then we were surrounded by whirlwinds of so much violence, that it was only by clinging together we could maintain our footing. On reaching the elevation at which all vegetation ceases, the gusts redoubled; the lightning-flashes apparently glided before us along the barren steep. Still, with firm and regular step, we continued our ascent. After a while, a spectacle of equal novelty and magnificence greeted our eyes: above our heads shone a splendid sun; beneath our feet rolled the terrible storm. The scene was grand and majestic; the clouds revolved one above another. From time to time a point of rock appeared; then disappeared immediately as in a furious sea. The coldness of the atmosphere, however, soon roused us from our contemplation; and we directed our steps in all haste towards the Brockenhaus, the roof of which we could see above a rising ground: we soon arrived there, wet to the bone. The innkeeper had seen us in the distance, and was waiting for us at the door; a good room and a blazing fire were prepared, and we soon forgot the inconveniences we had suffered on our way.

In the afternoon I explored the summit of the mountain, which is the highest in this part of Germany, and rises to an altitude of 3580 feet above the sea. Among the peasantry it bears the reputation of being haunted. According to a very old legend, the witches assembled on its peak yearly, on the Walpurgis nacht, or night of the 1st of May, under the presidency of their lord and master Satan. The rocks of the Brocken all bear names alluding to this nocturnal scene,—as the Devil's Pulpit, the Witches' Altar, the Witches' Dancing-Hall.

Goethe has cast the magic of his genius over the Brocken. One November morning, in 1777, at daybreak, and in spite of the snow which was falling in dense flakes, he mounted his horse, and ascended to the summit. He undertook the excursion, less to visit the famous mountain, than to fall in, as if accidentally, with a young man, suffering from hypochondria, who, after reading "The Sorrows of Werther," had addressed to him many bitter and foolish letters.*

Goethe was then twenty-eight years old. It was during this winter-journey, or on his return from it, that he wrote a beautiful though somewhat vague poem (*Die Harzreise im Winter*), from which we make the following extract:—

* Goethe's Harz journey was made in the November and December of 1777, with a twofold object: to visit the Ilmenau Mines, and to comfort an unhappy misanthrope who had sunk into *Wertherism*. He set out with the Duke of Saxe-Weimar, who had arranged a hunting-party to destroy a great boar then ravaging the country round Eisenach; but he soon quitted this jovial troop. Through hail, frost, and mud, lonely, yet companioned by great thoughts, he rode along the mountainous solitudes until he reached the Brocken. A bright sun shone on its eternal snows as he ascended, and looked down upon the cloud-covered Germany beneath him. "Here," says Mr. Lewes, "he felt the air of freedom swell his breast. The world, with its conventions, lay beneath him; the court, with its distractions, was afar; and the poet stood amid these snowy solitudes communing with that majestic spirit of Beauty which animates Nature." In due time he found his misanthrope, who was named Plessing, and lived at Wernerigode. He describes him as one who had read much, but had never studied nature; and he endeavoured to stimulate him to undertake this study, in order to divert his melancholy thoughts. "My young friend," he says, "appeared to get very restless and impatient at this, just as we do when we begin to be irritated at some foreign or entangled language, the meaning of which we cannot understand; on which I, without much hope of a successful result, but rather for the purpose of not remaining silent, went on speaking. To me especially, as a landscape painter, I said, did this appear evident, as my particular department of Art was in direct communication with Nature; however, since that time, I had observed with more assiduity and eagerness than previously — not only noted any remarkable natural landscapes and appearances, but felt myself more full of love for all things and all men. But in order that I might not lose myself in the

" Like to the vulture which, on the heavy clouds of morning reposing its light wing, descries its prey, may my song hover in the air!...

" In the sombre thicket the wild beast hides itself, and, with the yellow-hammers, the herons have long since plunged into their marshes.

" But whom see I here in the solitude? His track disappears in the forest; behind him the bushes agitate their branches, the mist rises, the solitude absorbs him.

" Oh, how shall we cure the wounds of him for whom balm has become a poison; who, in the floods of love, has satisfied his thirst with misanthropy! Despised of men, whom he despises in his turn, he secretly devours his genius in an insatiable egotism.

" If it be upon thy lyre, O father of Love, with sounds accessible to his ear, do thou appease his heart! Reveal to his clouded gaze the thousand springs which well out in the desert by the side of the soul athirst.

" Enfold the solitary in thy golden clouds, O Love; and while waiting until the rose blossoms anew, crown with winter-leaves the dripping locks of thy poet!

abstract, I related how even this compulsory winter-excursion, instead of being painful to me, had furnished me with lasting enjoyment. I described to him picturesquely and poetically, and still as truly and naturally as I was able, the course of my journey; I pictured the snow clouds which I saw that morning rolling above the mountains, with the most diversified appearances during the day-time; and then I presented to his imagination the curious turreted and walled fortifications of Nordhausen, as seen in the twilight; and further, in the night-time, the torrents rushing down the mountain-ravines, their waters illuminated transiently, and glistening in the flickering light of the guide's lantern; and, last of all, the miners' cavern....We parted in peace and quietness, his person leaving quite a peculiar impression behind....On going out," continues Goethe, "I found the sky quite cleared up, and twinkling with stars, the streets and squares covered with snow; and I stopped upon a narrow bridge, and stood quietly surveying the surrounding objects in the wintry night. At the same time I revolved the adventure in my mind, and felt myself quite resolved not to see the young man again; in pursuance of which I ordered my horse at daybreak, delivered an anonymous and apologetic slip of paper to the waiter,—to whom I was able, at the same time, to say many things in praise of the young person to whom he had introduced me, and which were quite true besides; and of which, no doubt, the dexterous fellow made good use for his own purposes. I now rode along the north-east slopes of the Harz in wild, stormy weather, with the snow-flakes drifting around me."—G. H. LEWES, *Life and Works of Goethe*, vol. 1., pp. 383–388.—The visitor to the Harz cannot fail to be interested by the fact that he treads in the footsteps of the greatest of German writers.

"By the gleam of thy torch, O Night, do thou guide him across the streams, in the impracticable paths and the desert plains; with the myriad-tinted morning, smile upon his soul; with the furious tempest, bear him aloft upon the heights; the torrents of winter dash headlong from the rock and respond to his strains: —it becomes for him the altar of the tenderest gratitude, that snow-clad crest of the dreaded peak which the credulous peasants have crowned with fantastic legends.

"Mountain with the unexplored flanks, thou risest, mysterious and unveiled, upon the astonished world; and thou contemplatest from thy clouds its kingdoms and their glory, when thou pourest out the floods which thy neighbouring sisters discharge from their fountains!"

One of the wildest and most eery of the scenes of "Faust" takes place in the Harz, above the mines, and on the summit of the Brocken. Faust is represented as traversing the region of the air with Satan:—

Mephistopheles. Hold fast to the skirt of my mantle. Here in the centre is a summit, from which one sees, astonished, the splendour of Mammon in the heart of the mountain.*

Faust. A twilight glimmer trembles sadly in the depth of the valleys! It glides into the farthest recesses of the abyss! Yonder rises a jet of smoke. Beyond, pestiferous exhalations wind their way. Here glitters a flame in the bosom of sombre vapours; there it leaps forth like a spring. Elsewhere it creeps in a thousand veins through the valley. There, in that narrow space close beside us, it suddenly gathers itself together. Near at hand the sparks are scattered abroad like a rain of golden sand. But, look! the rocky sides of the mountain are everywhere aflame.

Mephistopheles. Does not King Mammon splendidly light up his palace for this festival? Fortunate for you that you have seen these things; already I have a presentiment of turbulent guests.

Faust. How the storm rages in the air! With what violence it beats upon my shoulders!

* An allusion to the mines.

Mephistopheles. Hold fast to the ancient projections of the rocks, lest it dash thee into the bottom of these abysses. A mist obscures the night. Hark to the crashing noises in the woods! The owls fly away affrighted. Dost hear the splintering of the columns of the evergreen palaces, and the groans, the breaking of the branches, the deep murmur of the stems, the cries and complaints of the roots? In their confused and terrific fall, the trees hurtle one against another, and, through gulfs strewn with ruin, hiss and roar in the air. Hearest thou these voices on the height, both afar off and close at hand? Yes; all along the mountain rolls furiously the magic song.

Chorus of Witches.

>To the Brocken mount the witches;
>The stubble is yellow, green the barley;
>There the numerous host assembles;
>Urian seated on the summit!
>Thus we speed by hills and valleys...

A Voice. By what road didst thou arrive?

Another. By Ilsenstein. There I ogled in the owl's nest. What eyes he made at me!

A Voice. Why goest thou so quickly?

Another. He tore my skin. Seest thou not the wound?

Chorus of Witches.

>The path is wide, the path is long:
>What means this furious multitude?
>Goad with the pitchfork, and scratch with the broom......

Semi-Chorus of Wizards.

>Like the snail with his house we climb!
>All the women are before us;
>For whene'er the devil leadest,
>They take care to be to vanward!

Second Semi-Chorus.

>Women must take a thousand steps,
>For swift as she may wing her flight, behold,
>Man clears the distance at a single bound.

The Two Choruses.
>The wind is still, the star away;
>The sombre mist its course will stay!
>The magic mountain, humming loud,
>Throws forth of sparks a fiery crowd.

A Voice below. Halt! Halt!

A Voice above. Who calls from the cavern yonder?

A Voice below. Take me with you, take me! For three hundred years have I been climbing, and yet I cannot reach the summit.

The Two Choruses.
>The broom carries, and so does the stick;
>The pitchfork carries, and so does the ram:
>He who cannot mount to-day,
>A lost man will be for ever and aye!......
>When we gather round the summit,
>Then drag yourself along the earth,
>And cover all the far-off moorland
>With your swarm of witches.

Mephistopheles. How they press and push; how they murmur and tattle; how they hiss and eddy; how they pass and prate; how they shine and sparkle and stink and burn! A true witch-element is about us! Hold fast to me, or we shall soon be separated.

[*The dance of the wizards and the witches begins upon the Brocken. Faust's partner is a young girl.*]

Mephistopheles. Why dost thou quit the young girl who inspired thee in the dance by her pretty songs?

Faust. Oh, in the middle of her song, a red mouse leapt from her mouth.

Mephistopheles. A fine thing to be frighted at, truly! Here one does not mind such trifles. Enough that it was but a little one...

Orchestra (pianissimo).
>The clouds and the vapours
>Illumine the summits;
>The wind caresses the reeds and the foliage,
>And everything dissolves into dust.*

---

* At the end of this section, we subjoin Shelley's splendid version of the scene we have attempted to render into literal English.

Before going to sleep we reperused this wonderful piece of *diablerie*, and all the night we were disturbed by the most fantastic dreams.

Next morning we caused ourselves to be aroused at two. As on the preceding day, the clouds covered the valley in the direction of Ilsenberg; the cold was keen, and a lurid light rested on all the landscape around. We skirted the mountain-side for the purpose of re-visiting the masses of gigantic stones of which we had caught but a glimpse the day before. After following up a portion of the road which descends towards Schierke, we reached the principal platform just as the first rays of the rising sun enabled us to distinguish clearly objects at a tolerable distance. Our guide, who for some time had walked pertinaciously in advance, looking now to the right and now to the left, suddenly dragged me to an elevated point, from which I had the rare happiness of contemplating, for some seconds, the magnificent effect of mirage known as " the Spectre of the Brocken." Its aspect is very impressive. A dense fog,—what the Germans call *hochen rauch*,—which seemed to issue from the clouds like an immense curtain, rose suddenly to the westward of the mountain; a rainbow was developed; then certain vague forms outlined themselves:—at first, the great tower of the hostelry was reproduced in gigantic proportions, then the figures of ourself and the guide, more vaguely and less correct; all these suspended shadows were surrounded by the colours of the iris, serving as a setting for the fairy picture.

Towards noon we resumed our march; but prior to

our departure, the guide, in accordance with an ancient custom, had decorated our hat with the anemone of the Brocken; or, as the peasants call it, the "witches' flower."

The descent of the mountain offered no difficulties; and as the weather was clear, we enjoyed a very extensive view. We passed the night at Harzburg, and thence, on the following day, proceeded to Goslar, the ancient residence of the German emperors.

THE WALPURGIS-NIGHT SCENE IN "FAUST."

Hark how the tempest crashes through the forest!
   The owls fly out in strange affright;
The columns of the evergreen palaces
     Are split and shattered;
   The roots creak, and stretch, and groan;
    And, ruinously overthrown,
      The trunks are crushed and scattered
By the fierce blast's unconquerable stress.
Over each other crack and crash they all
In terrible and intertangled fall;
And through the ruins of the shaken mountain
     The airs hiss and howl—
    It is not the voice of the fountain,
   Nor the wolf in his midnight prowl.
      Dost thou not hear?
      Strange accents are ringing
    Aloft, afar, anear;
     The witches are singing!
The torrent of a raging wizard song
    Streams the whole mountain along.

Chorus of Witches.

    The stubble is yellow, the corn is green,
     Now to the Brocken the witches go;
    The mighty multitude here may be seen
     Gathering, wizard and witch, below.
    Sir Urian is sitting aloft in the air......

A Voice.
>Which way camest thou?

A Voice.
>Over Ilsenstein.
>The owl was awake in the white moonshine;
>I saw her at rest in her downy nest,
>And she stared at me with her broad bright eyne......

Chorus of Witches.
>Come away! come along!
>The way is wide, the way is long,
>But what is that for a Bedlam throng?
>Stick with the prong, and snatch with the broom!
>The child in the cradle lies strangled at home,
>And the mother is clapping her hands!

Semi-Chorus of Wizards, 1.
>We glide in
>Like snails, when the women are all away;
>And from a house once given over to sin,
>Woman has a thousand steps to stray.

Semi-Chorus, 2.
>A thousand steps must a woman take,
>Where a man but a single spring will make.

Voices above.
>Come with us, come with us, from Felsensee!......

Both Choruses.
>The wind is still, the stars are fled,
>The melancholy moon is dead;
>The magic notes, like spark on spark,
>Drizzle, whistling through the dark......
>Some on a ram, and some on a prong,
>On poles and on broomsticks we flutter along;
>Forlorn is the wight who can rise not to-night.

Chorus of Witches.
>Come onward, away! aroint thee, aroint!
>A witch to be strong must anoint, anoint.
>Then every trough will be boat enough.
>With a rag for a sail we can sweep through the sky.
>Who flies not to-night, when means he to fly?

Both Choruses.
   We cling to the skirt, and we strike on the ground;
   Witch-legions thicken around and around;
   Wizard-swarms cover the heath all over.
           [*They descend.*

Mephistopheles.
   What thronging, dashing, raging, rustling!
   What whispering, babbling, hissing, bustling!
   What glimmering, spirting, stinking, burning,
   As heaven and earth were overturning!
   There is a true witch-element about us;
   Take hold on me, or we shall be divided."

[Here we must pass over a long and striking passage, and come to the end of the scene and of our quotation.]

Mephistopheles. [*To* FAUST, *who has seceded from the dance.*]
   Why do you let that fair girl pass from you,
   Who sang so sweetly to you in the dance?

Faust.
   A red mouse, in the middle of her singing,
   Sprang from her mouth.

Mephistopheles.
   That was all right, my friend;
   Be it enough that the mouse was not gray.
   Do not disturb your time of happiness
   With close consideration of such trifles.

—*Shelley's Poetical Works,* edited by W. M. Rossetti, vol. ii., pp. 488–495.

A fine rendering of this scene is also given by Mr. Bayard Taylor in his translation of "Faust."

III.

The Pyrenees.

EVERYBODY is aware that the Pyrenees form a natural rampart, or mountain-boundary, between France and Spain, extending from the shores of the Atlantic on the north-west to those of the Mediterranean on the south-east. Their romantic and boldly-crested summits are clothed with snow; but just beneath this white and shining mantle their sides abound with luxuriant forests of pine, oak, chestnut, and beech; while their lower slopes and valleys luxuriate in perennial verdure. Occasionally the traveller comes upon a deep and shadowy glen, resounding with the din of a flashing torrent; or an extensive table-land of greensward, surrounded by rugged heights, and forming what is locally known as a *cirque*. The average breadth of the chain is between forty and fifty miles; and it is traversed, at a great elevation, by passes, *puertos*, or gates, of a singularly picturesque character. These are very barren and narrow; and if they afford the people of Spain the means of communication with their French neighbours, they also open up a passage to the winds, where they can indulge their fury uncontrolled. Of the Puerto de Venasque, near a town of the same name, the proverb says:—" In this defile no father will look back at his son, and no son will wait for his father." And no more favourable opinion can be given in reference to the other puertos. They are accessible, however, to equestrians; and the peasants traverse them with loaded mules. One of the most striking is the Brèche de Roland, near Mont Perdu, which, according to the legend, was excavated by the famous Paladin of Charlemagne, with his sword Excalibur.

The grandest aspects of the Pyrenees are presented on the Spanish side; where, too, they attain their greatest elevation. The Pic de Nethou, an eastern summit of Mont Maladetta, or the Accursed,—so called in allusion to its gloom and sterility, which make it look like "the ghost of some mountain belonging to a departed world,"—rises to the height of 11,426 feet. It was first ascended by a Russian officer, with a French companion and guides, in 1842. Of very striking appearance, as its name indicates, is the Mont Perdu; and scarcely inferior, in the eye of the artist, are the Pic du Midi and the Dent de Mulhacen. On these mountains, and in the forests generally, the hunter pursues the ibex and the chamois, the bear, the lynx, the wild boar, and the *lobo*, or wolf. The last-named is as sly as he is ferocious. He lies in wait in the rocky shelter of the passes, and when a caravan of mules approaches seldom fails to carry off a victim. "Who knows more than he?" said a shepherd to Mr. George Borrow. "He is acquainted with the vulnerable point of every animal. See, for example, how he flies at the neck of a bullock, tearing open the veins with his grim teeth and claws. But does he attack a horse in the same manner? I trow not." "Not he," said another shepherd; "he is too good a judge. He fastens on the haunches, and hamstrings him in a moment. Oh! the fear of the horse when he comes near the dwelling-place of the wolf!" "Yet," rejoined his companion, "the mares know occasionally how to balk him. See them feeding in the campo with their young *cria* about them; presently the alarm is given that the wolf is drawing near; they start wildly, and run about for a moment, but it is only for a moment; anon they gather together, forming themselves into a circle, in the centre of which they place the foals. Onward comes the wolf, hoping to make his dinner off horse-flesh. He is mistaken, however; the mares have balked him, and are as cunning as himself; not a tail is to be seen—not a hinder quarter; but there stand the whole troop, their fronts towards him, ready to receive him; and as he runs round them barking and howling, they rise successively on their hind legs, ready to stamp him to the earth should he attempt to hurt their *cria* or themselves."

But a better idea of the characteristics of the Pyrenees will be obtained by directing our attention to some particular peak, than by indulging in a purely general description. For this purpose, we cannot do better than undertake, in company with M. de Mirbel, an observant French traveller, the ascent of the Pic du Midi.

Pic du Midi d'Ossau.

The Maladetta; Puerto of Venasque in the Foreground.

1. *M. Perdu.*   2. *Cylinder.*   3. *Marboré.*   4. *Cirque de Gavarnie.*
5. *Brèche de Roland.*   6. *Taillon.*

THE PRINCIPAL SUMMITS OF THE PYRENEES.

THE PIC DU MIDI.

M. de Mirbel and his party numbered thirteen or fourteen persons, and on the day fixed for their enterprise started from Bigorre at four o'clock in the morning. Most of the travellers were on horseback; De Mirbel went on foot, with the tin case slung to his shoulders in which he preserved his botanical specimens. He was armed with a long iron-shod pole, and his shoes were provided with iron clamps.

They followed the valley of Barèges, along the Bastan, and in this way gained the slopes of Tourmalet. At its base opens, towards the north, a small lateral valley, watered by a shining brook which pours its tranquil waters into the impetuous Bastan. The *asphodelus ramosus*, a branched variety of king's-spear, somewhat softens the rudeness of its menacing declivities; its soil blooms with verdure, its sward is enamelled with flowers. The *veronica saxatilis*, hooking on its woody stem to the rocks which raise their sharp points above the turf, apparently desires to hide them from the traveller's ken. Its graceful deep-blue flowers, surmounted by two white anthers, are easily recognizable from a distance. Here, too, luxuriate the well-known yellow-flowered gentian and the Alpine plantain.

The valley which leads to the peak terminates at the Lac d'Oncet, where our travellers halted to take their breakfast. Those of our readers who know nothing of mountaineering, cannot conceive with what enjoyment the hardy climber devours his frugal repast, after a long and troublesome march, by the side of some limpid burn. Let them try a day among the Welsh mountains, or among the heights of Ballachulish and Glencoe! They will feel as if they had never before understood the true meaning of the word "appetite."

The shores of the lake smiled with the viola biflora, whose gilded flowers mingled with the glowing green of the prairie; here and there, on the lowest slopes, might be seen the yellow arnica, inclining its delicate head over the lake; and already the odorous daphne decorated the neighbourhood of the precipices with its creeping stems and rose-tinted blossoms, filling the air with balmy breath.

Westward of the lake, and springing abruptly from its waters, rose the lofty mountains. To the north, the rock was not practicable; but it sank towards the east, and exposed the bases of the Pic du Midi. This was the road to be taken by our travellers, and it ascended a gentle and even easy incline.

The sunrise was already flattering the mountain-tops with "gilded alchemy," and warning our little company that it was time to resume their march. Leaving by the lake-side a guide to take care of the horses, they set out, and slowly made their way towards the summit of the peak. The rarefaction of the air, the condition of the vegetation, the silence of Nature, the solitude of these places,—all indicated their approach to the upper regions. A dry, thin, slippery turf carpeted the rock; a few Alpine plants were scattered here and there. Among them were noticeable the *gentiana verna* and the *gentiana acaulis* (the gentianella of our gardens),

—those two inseparable companions, which, born in the same latitude, traverse the same regions, and indifferently flourish on the margin of the waters or the arid rock, the thick rich mould or the bare and naked rock. Sometimes, too, the eye rested delightedly on a few tufts of moss-campions; and near them the whitish-gray draba exposed its delicate leafage. Beyond, in the midst of landslips and ruin, monuments of the potency of Time, flourished in the chinks and fissures of the stones a few pale flowers, which found the nutriment of life in the bosom of destruction, and around which fluttered the bright-winged butterflies.

In an hour and a half our travellers gained the summit. The vapours of night were dissipated; the sky was serene; the sun poured forth his glory. The whole Pyrenean chain opened before them like an amphitheatre. To the right rose Neouvielle, a granitic mass crowned with eternal snows; to the left, the Brèche de Roland, the Tour de Marboré, and Mont Perdu—the distant summit of which towered above all the others. Letting the eye range in an opposite direction, it discovered an immense plain, the misty borders of which blended imperceptibly with the horizon. At one glance it seemed to include those mountains, those precipices, those glaciers, those antique snows, those aërial lakes, the immense and silent laboratories of Nature, and those fertile fields which the torrents, appeased and subdued, bedew with their fertilizing waters. The peaks which previously seemed to the confused traveller no better than an useless chaos, the result of the fantastic caprices of a blind Nature, then appeared like the sublime work of a Beneficent Hand. The traveller's gaze wandered over this wonderful world, the extent of which his imagination could scarcely measure, and the contemplation of which filled his soul with enthusiasm.

A few flowers enriched the table-ground. The Pyrenean antirrhinum inserted its slender roots into the fissures of the rock, and the bright blue of its flowers relieved the darker and purple-blue of the saxifrage. By its side expanded the golden corolla of the Alpine poppy.* The precipices sheltered this beautiful saxifrage,—the rare ornament of the mountains,—whose flower, of a dazzling whiteness, outrivalled the sheen of the snows.

THE BRECHE DE ROLAND.

A visit to the Brèche de Roland has been described by the same traveller:—

I should not have undertaken, he says, such an expedition, if I had not found in M. Jules Pasquier a man framed to participate in these labours, and ardently desirous of learning the secrets of Nature. He had admired the beauties presented by the Pic du Midi, but his enthusiastic soul was not satisfied. He knew that in the heart of the snows and glaciers some intrepid men had forced their way to the summit of the Pyrenean chain, and this was enough to provoke his emulation and incite him to scorn danger.

We set out from Barèges at six o'clock, on the 8th of August. On reaching Luz we engaged a guide, and continued our route towards the valley of Gavarnie. We trembled as we penetrated into it. There all is

* *Meconopsis Cambrica.*

grand, magnificent, sublime; and man, surrounded by solemn monuments, recognizes his weakness, and the almighty power of a Sovereign Hand. Such was my first thought on entering the valley; the second was more gratifying to my self-love. I could not see without admiration and pride this road suspended on the brink of an awful precipice, which the roar of the Gave rendered still more terrible. It is here that man has displayed simultaneously intelligence in his conceptions, strength and skill in his labours, perseverance in their execution. The valley mounts from north to south. To the east and west rise rugged rocks, composed of calcareous beds inclined from the perpendicular to the southward, and running from east to west. Frequently the rock, rising from the depth of the waters towards heaven, presents nothing but a naked wall which seems to defy human exertion; frequently, too, it is much inclined, and becomes so much the more difficult to traverse, owing to its long slopes, formed of schistous débris, stones detached from the higher summits, and loose masses of earth always on the point of rolling into the abyss. And yet, in such a spot as this, the skill of the engineer has succeeded in constructing a secure and convenient road, sufficiently wide to reassure the most timorous cavalier. It is impossible to see without astonishment this road rising and sinking as the mountain rises and sinks, here avoiding it, there returning to it, passing from one bank to another, and spanning the torrent with a bold and lofty arch, and opening up a communication through the rocks between France and Spain.

If the boldness of these works engages the curious attention of the traveller, he is still more strongly attracted by the various and original character of the surrounding scenery. The valley everywhere presents a diverse aspect. The verdurous lawns that ornament the rich basin of Luz, are prolonged to some distance in front of the mountain. Negligently spreading over gradual slopes which a vigorous vegetation crowns, which picturesque cottages embellish, they recall to the traveller's recollection the classic pictures of the famous valley of Tempe. But suddenly the greensward disappears; the rounded shoulders of the heights are succeeded by sharp and rugged crags; the tall robust trees give place to trunks, rent by winds and blighted by frost, which impend over the dizzy precipice. The Gave, imprisoned among the rocks, roars, and rises, and boils, and falls headlong back upon itself; the din of falling waters is heard on every side; and the threatening rock hangs suspended above the wayfarer's head.

When, says M. de Mirbel, I saw this valley for the first time, it seemed to me that I advanced from marvel to marvel; but what most impressed me was the view of the bridge of Sia.

Some time before you arrive at it, the banks of the Gave assume the rudest outlines; its waters slacken their course—they linger among the rich pasturages, in the shade of trees which weave together their green boughs like a pavilion, and hide them from the curious eye. You have scarcely advanced a mile, however, before you become conscious of a hoarse dull

VALLEY OF GAVARNIE.

murmur; and soon, as if by enchantment, you find yourself upon the bridge, which hitherto has been completely concealed. It is richly overhung with festoons of ivy. Its abutments rest upon the rock; and the Gave rolls its waters beneath the arch at a depth of upwards of one hundred feet. To the left, the mountain recovers its air of gloom and austerity; to the right, on the contrary, it retains its gracious aspect. In the foreground of the picture flashes the torrent; and, confined between the rocky banks, it gradually rises and swells, to fall with a mighty roar when the conformation of its bed no longer affords it a support, —and, after a while, having regained its tranquillity, to continue slowly its onward course.

We reached Gèdres in due time.

This romantic village lies at the foot of the Coumélie, —a mass of granite forming the point of division between the valley of Héas and the valley of Gavarnie.

......The nearer we approach the goal of our journey, the more imposing becomes the landscape in its character. Fantastic and irregular forms give place to grave and exact outlines, and vivid contrasts of colour to soft and uniform tints, which blend the airy summits of the heights with the cloudless blue of heaven.

We saw, in passing, the beautiful cascade of Savusa, falling in a shower of diamond-spray into the Gave. It might almost be mistaken for the folds of a robe of gauze agitated by the winds. Further, we come to the awful solitude of the Peyrade,—of which no one who has not seen it can form an accurate conception. But the reader may figure to himself, as best he can, a mountain whose shattered summits have crumbled one upon another, accumulating even in the lowest depth of the valley a labyrinthine pile of boulders and rocky masses, which astonish the eye and fatigue the imagination with their grandeur. The remains of the peak, which in some remote past experienced this terrible convulsion, have threatened for ages to bury the ruins we speak of under fresh accumulations. Enormous blocks are first precipitated into the torrent, checking the fall of the smaller crags, which remain piled one upon another in huge disorder. These blocks are separated by wide gaps, of which the engineer has availed himself in constructing the road.

It was not until two o'clock that we arrived at Gavarnie. We were not fatigued, however, and directed our steps immediately to the valley of Ossau, so that we might turn to advantage the evening hours.

This valley ramifies into several divisions; we chose the branch that strikes to the Lake des Espessières.

On the shores of the solitary basin were feeding numbers of young horses, which are always sent to the mountain-pastures during the summer season. Terrified by our approach, they abruptly ascended the declivities, and with light and rapid step crossed the steep summits, where they seemed to defy us to overtake them. We contrived to draw them to us in the plain by offering some handfuls of salt. While we were still engaged in caressing them, the Marboré and the Brèche de Roland wrapped themselves in a mantle of clouds; a violent peal of thunder re-echoed in the mountain-silences, and the foals, terrified, escaped from our hands. Trembling for the successful issue of our enterprise, we resumed the Gavarnie road. Happily, the sky soon cleared, the clouds dispersed, the setting sun tinted the peaks with a glowing purple, and the rainbow wreathed them with its unearthly colours.

At four in the morning we recommenced our ascent, conducted by an excellent guide, named Rondo. At five o'clock we began to discover the summits of Marboré. From a distance we mistook them for towers, so great is the regularity of their forms. After three-quarters of an hour's climbing, we found ourselves in front of the amphitheatre of Gavarnie,—the majesty of which literally defies description. At the first glance, one might be tempted to look upon it as the handiwork of men, on account of a regularity which is not very common in the great efforts of Nature; but the grandeur of the design, the richness of the forms, the enormous dimensions of the superimposed blocks, the magnificence of an architecture at once elegant and simple, and especially the luxuriance and variety of outline in the different parts, remind you, even while you remark the admirable symmetry of the whole, of the presence of a superior agent.

Immense strata, thrown back farther and farther according to the elevation of the mountain, form terraces or steps covered with snows and glaciers, whence issue a thousand waterfalls. On the left of the cirque, or amphitheatre, an impetuous torrent leaps from the mountains, strikes in its descent a projection of the rock, and thence falls back into the cirque. This glorious cascade was geometrically measured by Reboul, who calculated its height at 1266 feet. We should be tempted to doubt the accuracy of these figures, were it not for the confidence inspired by the calculations of so exact a mathematician. Nearly every stranger who visits Gavarnie thinks he exaggerates if he allows 300 to 400 feet to its cascade. Most of them, it is true, have never travelled in the mountains, and do not remember how each separate object effaces itself, or diminishes, in the presence of the imposing grandeur of the great whole. In this celebrated locality we see, perhaps, all that is most astonishing in the structure of the mountains. It offers the naturalist some grand problems for solution—some new systems for confirmation; to the painter, a sublime ensemble, in which he finds united grace and vigour of outline, vivacity and richness of colouring, and harmony and unity of parts.

The sun was already gilding the summit of the towers of the Marboré, when we took the route to the Brèche de Roland. Rondo led the way; M. Pasquier followed him; and as for myself, I was sometimes in front and sometimes behind, collecting plants, or examining the structure of the rock. I had told Lagunier, our guide from Luz, not to leave me, but to be at hand to help in case of need. It was necessary to climb the rocks in front of the cascade, and we advanced by a road the steepness of which was frightful! Formed by the fall of rounded and shifting stones, it ran along the side of the precipice, to which we clung with a desperate grasp. For fully half an hour we followed this

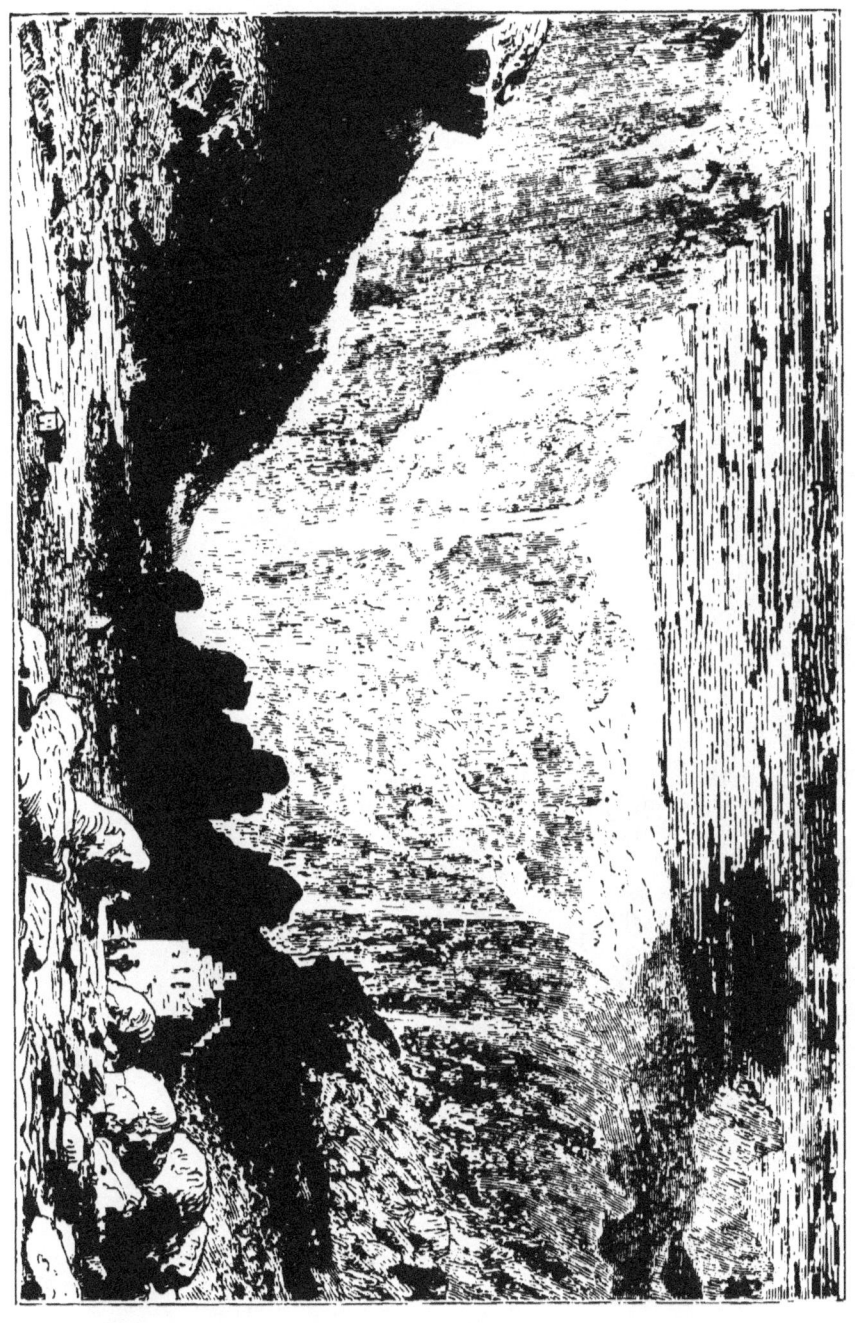

CIRQUE DE GAVARNIE

dangerous path, and then came upon another which was still more dangerous. The intrepid Rondo was the first to advance. The rock was exactly perpendicular; we drew up our body close against it, then we placed the point of the foot on the little projections formed by the degradation of the strata, and steadied ourselves by clinging with our hands to the projections above our head. This painful attitude had become almost insupportable, when Rondo was compelled to halt before new obstacles. Then each one of us, stiffening himself against the rock which seemed to bar his advance, remained suspended upon our frail and narrow platform, with a precipice several hundred feet in depth yawning beneath us. Happily this situation did not long endure. We soon arrived at a delightful table-land, where we found a numerous flock of sheep and goats, guarded by Spanish herds. They were enjoying their morning meal. Their dog ran up to us, and by his caresses seemed to invite us to share it. We gratefully accepted the milk which was cordially offered.

A few paces farther, we crossed a small ravine of snow, and saw before us the Brèche de Roland, which had long been hidden from sight by the summits intervening between it and ourselves. We were separated from it by great glaciers, and could discover no passage by which they might be avoided. Lagunier, equally terrified by the dangers he had already incurred, and the obstacles which remained to be overcome, plainly declared that he would not advance another step. We did not think it advisable to insist upon his following us, as, under such circumstances, he would have been rather a burden than an assistance.

We pushed forward into a new valley of snow, much larger than the first, and truly enchanting in appearance. To the north, the Taillon raises its perpendicular strata to a prodigious elevation. Southward, the first courses of the wall of the Brèche are likewise exposed; but, westward, the shining carpet of snow, resplendent in its "whitely" gleam, softly follows the sinuosities of the rock, sinking with it and rising with it, falling into a thousand undulations, and slowly mounting towards the region of eternal frost, where a bluish tint modifies its whiteness. While we were admiring the magic beauty of the scene, a troop of izards, with outstretched neck and elevated head, with nose to the wind, and foot firm and sure, leaped from a neighbouring rock, halted upon the snows, astonished at our presence, and suddenly, with the rapidity of the lightning, crossed the frozen plain, sprang from crag to crag, from summit to summit, appearing and disappearing before our eyes twenty times in a moment, to arrest their flight at length, tranquil and calm, on the precipitous ridge of the Taillon.

After having progressed for some time up the valley of snow, we bent our steps towards the glaciers which lay on our left. A Spanish contrabandista, or smuggler, accompanied us; and being more accustomed than we were to this kind of marching, he rapidly traversed the earlier ridges of the glaciers, and already had left us far behind him, when, the ice opening beneath his feet, he sank, uttering a piercing cry. Though we thought him lost, we ran towards him to render assistance if there were yet a chance. We found him clinging convulsively to the brink of the chasm, and hanging suspended over the depth, but contrived to release him from his danger —not without some serious reflections on the risk we should incur by the slightest imprudence. Rondo, however, was vigilant and prudent. With his hammer he broke up the ice, forming a series of steps, which every moment became more useful, as the ice increased in compactness, and offered a greater resistance to the iron points of our poles. We advanced in silence, carefully examining the place where we set our feet, and casting a glance from time to time at the gulf into which the slightest accident would have precipitated us, and on the journey we had still to accomplish. This painful ascent occupied us nearly a quarter of an hour, during which, at the most terrible passages, we could not completely overcome a slight shudder of dread.

At length we reached the goal of our labours.

The precipices are far distant from us; and if we still remember the dangers we have surmounted, it is to enjoy the more thoroughly our present security, and to value the more highly the sublime panorama unfolded before our eyes. Here we see the mighty rampart that rises between France and Spain; like the Marboré, it is composed of perpendicular beds and horizontal courses. A pass or gap, cut at right angles, opens a door of communication between the two countries. Standing on the threshold of this magnificent gateway, we distinguish, to the east and the west, the insurmountable barrier raised by Nature between the two peoples; and survey, from north to south, the lands subjected to their rule.

We need only add that the descent was safely accomplished, and that at ten o'clock at night the travellers were on their way back to Barèges.

MONT PERDU.

Our earliest knowledge of the characteristics of the Pyrenees is due to the indefatigable labours of the traveller Ramond, who spent many years in exploring their heights and valleys, and began that work of investigation which succeeding travellers have so fully accomplished. Prior to his time very little was known of this great mountain-range, except at the points where it was traversed by the roads between France and Spain; but now we are familiar with its every summit. Still, it seems due to the memory of this enthusiastic pioneer, that, in seeking to describe the most famous of the Pyrenean peaks, the mighty and magnificent Mont Perdu, we should avail ourselves of his assistance rather than of that of later tourists. We propose, therefore, to ascend Mont Perdu in the company of M. Ramond.

His first ascent was made in 1797, when he was accompanied by De Mirbel and Pasquier, who had just visited the Brèche de Roland, as already described, and by De Corbin and Marsey de Tarbes, two of his pupils, who were desirous of pursuing their botanical researches.

He and his companions—we have not enumerated all of them—ascended the Coumélie by a steep and winding pathway, which conducts the herds and flocks of

Gèdres to the pasture-grounds of the middle mountain-region. Numerous farms are scattered over these fertile fields, forming the three villages of Héas, Gèdres, and Gavarnie.

At one of these farms they passed the night, in considerable uncertainty as to the state of the weather. However, the south wind which had loaded the Marboré with the clouds of Spain, eventually gave way to the north, which came bringing with it the clouds of France. The latter are always elevated, and envelop the mountain-peaks; the former float in the lower atmosphere, and creep along the valleys. They gradually invaded the low grounds beneath us, forming an immense misty sea, pierced by the summits at which we had arrived, as ocean is by its reefs and isles of rock.

The greater part of the night was spent by Ramond in procuring guides. He had brought from Barèges two men in whom he placed great confidence,—one named Laurens, an old retainer, and Antoine Moaré. Both were mountaineers to the backbone, but the region on which they were now entering was as foreign to them as to their employer. At Héas, M. Ramond sought for a chamois-hunter who had been recommended to him as well-acquainted with Mont Perdu; though the event proved that the recommendation was altogether undeserved. Two villagers of Coumélie were also engaged, and their services happily proved of greater value; so that at daybreak the whole party were ready to set out, and took the route through the valley of Estaubé.

As soon as they began to face to the southward, they

were greeted by the imposing spectacle of the two valleys of Héas and Estaubé, girdled by enormous mountains, the forms of which, not less grand than simple, contrasted singularly with the hideous disorder of the ruinous and dismembered hills of granite they had left behind them. The lofty crest of Mont Perdu towered against the horizon. A very oblique and obtuse cone, all resplendent with eternal snows, it raises its huge bulk above the lofty walls of the Estaubé valley. M. Ramond pointed it out to his young companions; who, seeing it so distinctly, thought they were already at the goal of their pilgrimage. But to reach only the foot of the wall would occupy four or five hours of steady walking; and the experienced eye of the practised traveller measured with apprehension the steep escarpments of this wall, which would require to be climbed or turned.

Meantime they entered the valley of Estaubé, and in silence contemplated its tranquil solitudes. Here prevails the calm both of the upper and the secondary regions. Mountains which would appear of considerable dimensions even when not considered with respect to the elevation of their base, astonish by a simplicity of forms, which, commonly, they do not affect except on the threshold of the great chains, and in the vicinity of places where they degenerate into humble columns. The broadly and boldly moulded masses exhibit those flowing but majestic outlines which no capricious accident can take out of the category of the beautiful. Everything swells or subsides in just proportions.

Nothing interrupts the harmony of a design, the boldness of which is moderated by its severity; and a pure, transparent colour, a clear gray, lightly flushed with rose, sympathizing equally with the light and shade, whose contrast it softens, accompanies into the azure of heaven those soaring peaks which have beforehand clothed themselves with its transparent tints.

The débris is scanty, and the traces of recent ruin are very limited. Vegetation thrives in security up to the very foot of the precipices. Here and there it has encroached even upon some primeval rocks. A small stream—which lower down swells into a torrent—peacefully winds over a stony bed, while its banks are defined by the grassy sward. There the mountain-ash shelters the plant called Solomon's Seal, which in this locality attains an unusual size. On the slopes of the lateral mountains may be seen the red pine, which defies the woodman's axe. Every block is ornamented with floating plumes of the superb long-leaved saxifrage. On the untilled lands we meet sometimes with the Pyrenean thistle, sometimes with the beautiful eryngium, which occasionally changes its tint from amethystine blue to purple. The turfen patches are decorated with carline thistles; one of which, with acanthus-like leaves, is conspicuous through the golden glow of its calycinal crown.

Nothing can be more brilliantly sumptuous than the greensward adorned by the gold and silver of these two carlines. But it is the delicate shadings of the carpet enriched by this bright broidery which no botanical technology can hope to picture forth. If we speak of the meadows of the plain as green, how shall we qualify these lawns, by the side of which even the verdure of the lower valleys looks coarse and unreal?

Though enchanted by the rare and interesting objects which greeted them at every step, our travellers pressed forward gallantly and steadfastly; and at length found themselves at the base of the walls of Estaubé, which seemed to rise higher at every step they made to gain their level. They could make out the noble glaciers lying below the fields of snow with which they are chequered. At length, after a four-hours' march, they found themselves beneath the intermediary glacier, and halted to contemplate those massive ramparts which towered towards the heavens. This is the highest level inhabited by the shepherds. To their summer-stations they give the name of *couïlas;* and this one they designate the *Couïla* of the *Abassat-dessus.*

Here they fell in with two Spanish shepherds belonging to that not limited class who love to lead their flocks to the more elevated pastures, and hire them for that purpose. These men were lying by the side of a cabin built of stone, which was only just large enough to hold them when seated or lying down. But nothing more is required by these semi-savage nomades, who inhabit this bleak region only for a few days in the fine season. Even with this poor shelter they will readily dispense; and if they can find an overhanging rock, will not take the trouble to construct it.

Our travellers thought themselves fortunate in meeting with these two mountain-travellers, and immediately plied them with questions. But as they spend so brief a time in the region of eternal snow, their information proved to be scanty, and their answers unsatisfactory. However, a Spanish contrabandista appeared upon the scene, and turned out to be an authority. Compelled always to shun the beaten tracks, and trust to the hazard of the most dangerous paths, he had necessarily seen much of Mont Perdu; and, in truth, he had little else to tell us. While the great subject was under discussion between these Spaniards and the guides, our travellers took a little rest, and M. Ramond decided on a plan of his own. The result at length arrived at was, that they must pass the Puerto de Pineda, descend into the valley of Béousse, and reascend to the right by very steep acclivities,—which, however, were said to be practicable. But, to mount for two hours, to descend for one hour, and to climb these rocks, which would occupy four or five, was to gain the presence of Mont Perdu at the moment they would be forced to abandon it.

Now, M. Ramond had carefully examined the glacier beneath which the party had encamped. It was still covered with snow, and this snow would render it accessible. The incline was great, but not insurmountable; and the glacier led to a gap which seemed to open in front of Mont Perdu. He therefore declared himself ready to undertake the adventure. To the shepherds this appeared a freak of madness. They confessed that the snows were sometimes practicable, but would not believe that such was the case on the glacier, where some grayish spots indicated its actual surface. The contrabandista was the first to approve M. Ramond's resolve. Laurens next expressed his willingness to follow wherever his master led. The others simply smiled, and the local guides were at once the most incredulous and the least determined. It was necessary to settle the question. Ramond declared that he would ascend the glacier with any one who had the courage to follow him; and as decision always gets the better of irresolution, everybody agreed to his proposal. As for the contrabandista, he had already proceeded to manifest the courage of his opinions, and they soon lost sight of him.

They now made directly for the mouth of the glacier by a tolerably steep ascent, where the turf seemed to have been but for a short time freed from the burden of snow which lies upon it for seven or eight months of the year. It was blooming with its vernal verdure, and displayed all the luxuriance of the Alpine flora.

Soon, however, they approached the icy rampart, and the smallest objects acquired excessive dimensions. They gained at length the débris which the mountain ceaselessly pours down, and which, accumulating, forms the moraine of the glacier. They were forced to plant their feet upon the snow, and to look in the face the threatening pass, at the head of which rose Mont Perdu. The first short stage was a trifle; the snow was tolerably firm, and the slope gradual; and they sprang forward with all the confidence natural to those who have had no experience of mountain-climbing. This did not last long. The inclination became more and more abrupt, and could be seen to increase in what appeared a frightful degree. To the travellers it seemed as if a perpendicular wall rose above their heads. Steps slackened, heads bent down, limbs grew heavy and weary. A halt was called, and a consultation took place; though, as a rule, councils of war are as useless in mountain-climbing as on a battle-field. Ramond observed that La Peyrouse lingered far behind, and made him try the shoe-irons which he himself made use of—and his pupils also, following his example; but the help was as strange to him as was the region which compelled him to have recourse to it. In fact, after a man has attained middle life, no artificial means will supply the place of experience. A successful mountain-climber must begin while his limbs retain the suppleness and vigour of youth. He must undergo a special training like an athlete, or a competitor for the "championship of the river."

Nothing could be done with La Peyrouse but to leave him behind; and, accordingly, left behind he was, with Antoine for a companion,—the two seating themselves disconsolately on a rock, while the rest of the party continued the upward path through "snow and ice," like the youth in Longfellow's celebrated "Excelsior" ballad. After half an hour's climbing, they found the snow so hard that they left no footprints upon it; and they had to steady their steps by excavating holes in the ice with their hammers. They were, of course, ascending in a single file, and carefully placed their feet in the holes made by the leaders of the little column. In this way, for the first hour, all went "merrily as a marriage-bell." They took care to avoid the exposed part of the glacier; and by means of numerous skilfully devised zigzags, were eluding the inclination of a slope varying from thirty-five to forty degrees, when suddenly they descried a panic-stricken man clinging with all his might to a rock, and shrieking to them for help. It was the contrabandista! His story was written on the snow, where a long series of footmarks was just discernible. Without iron clamps, without hatchet, without any of the means of safety which people of his "profession" never fail to adopt, the unfortunate man had ventured on the ascent; and now he had slipped down more than two hundred feet before his fall was arrested by the rock. Had he missed it, nothing could have checked his ruinous and fatal course.

They would gladly have hastened to his succour; but it was imperative that they should proceed with great caution, or the whole party might have perished. After some efforts, however, they contrived to reach him, and placed him in their ranks. He had lost his hat, his waistcoat, his knapsack, and, what was even more valuable, his staff, which had fallen over the precipice, and could not be recovered. The other articles were scattered all around him, and with a little exertion the waistcoat and the knapsack were regained. The hat had fallen in a very dangerous corner, and though it was not twenty paces distant, a good quarter of an hour was spent in its recovery.

The poor man was placed in the middle of the little company; but he could not compose himself. In fact, Ramond's coolness had less influence upon him than his terror upon Ramond's followers. The countenances of two of the latter indicated a feeling of alarm and dread, the consequences of which might prove very dangerous to the common safety. At every step they begged their gallant leader to measure the inclination of the glacier; it had increased to 60°. The question was put forward: Should not the route be changed? Should not they resort to the rocks which bordered the glacier? This was not Ramond's opinion; but the general anxiety seemed to augment.

Twice the explorers struck earth, and the two guides from Coumélie attempted to scale it, but each time they were compelled to redescend. There was no resource but to stick to the glacier,—where, indeed, the path was safe enough, and the sole cause of fear lay in the evident discouragement of some of the party. It was true that at this point the incline was at its maximum, but then one more effort would conquer all their difficulties. Above this point they could see that the slope became more gradual, and the ice lay concealed beneath snow of a pure whiteness, which indicated the summit of the ridge, and defined it sharply against the intense blue of heaven. Triumph over this one obstacle, and, beyond, imagination revealed to them the soaring crest of Mont Perdu.

They collected all their energies for this final effort. They encouraged one another; animated themselves by mutual exhortations to supernatural exertions! And at every step they made they seemed to see the high boundaries of the valley gradually sinking. The gap which the projecting bulk of the glacier had long hidden from them, became visible in all its gigantic proportions, and they felt the cold wind sweeping through its colossal mouth. They hastened their steps; their limbs seemed filled with new strength; they leaped forward like young chamois; and, at last, they reached the wished-for goal. A shout of joy announced the welcome change of scene; and then a dead silence succeeded as the adventurers gazed upon the features of a new world, on the depths which separated them from it, on the glaciers which girdled and the clouds which covered it,—a spectacle, terrible and yet sublime, which overwhelmed all their faculties! A second, a moment, had developed it in all its majesty; but several moments, nay hours, would not have sufficed to bring it into harmony with their senses. "Behold Mont Perdu! Look yonder at Mont Perdu!" said one to the other; and yet no one could really distinguish it in that chaotic confusion of rocks, snows, and vapours. It was the all-wise and all-powerful God whose presence was *felt* rather than perceived, and who manifested Himself in everything that surrounded Him before He deigned to reveal Himself.

It was not without reason that they saw everywhere Mont Perdu; for all these belonged to it, all made part of it, even the ridge which they had reached, and which was separated from the principal summit only by a subsidence or erosion of a portion of its flanks. That huge summit rose grandly before them—a little to the left—white, but shaded with gray tints, and soaring out of the bosom of a dense mist that circulated slowly around it. To the right was detached the Cylinder,—more sombre than the cloud, more threatening even than

Mont Perdu itself, reared on its enormous pedestal at the same level as our explorers had already attained, and so near that it seemed as if they could touch it with their hands. Ramond had seen it a hundred times before; but what of that? Its apparition was only the more fantastic. Invisible always from any intermediate station, it had suddenly expanded into a colossus. That figure of a truncated tower which recalls known dimensions, contrasting with proportions to which nothing is comparable, its situation, its colouring, its proximity, the vapour which surrounded it,—all combined to make this enormous mass the most extraordinary object in the picture. Towards *it* every glance was constantly attracted; and *it* the guides persisted in pointing out as the Mont Perdu.

But what was still more unexpected, so to speak, than these strange aspects—what no anterior view had prepared us for; what, indeed, could be seen only from the summit of the observatory to which they had attained—was the indescribable appearance of the majestic support of these two summits. Hewn out by the same chisel which has moulded the stages of the Marboré, it presents a series of terraces, sometimes clothed with snow, sometimes bristling with glaciers, which overflow and pour down one upon another in great motionless cascades, to the very shores of a lake the surface of which, still frozen, but already disengaged from snow, shone with a gloomy splendour that enhanced the dazzling whiteness of its margin.

This lake, the desolate basin in which it reposes, the mass of ice that borders it on the south, the black walls

which surmount it, the peaks of the Cylinder and Mont
Perdu soaring into a storm-swept sky, and that bare,
precipitous, rent, and rugged rampart, from one of the
gaps of which the explorers contemplated the most imposing and terrific scene in the Pyrenees,—these defied
all comparison; there was no model or standard to
which the dimensions of so extraordinary a picture
could be referred, and they would have been reduced to
a vague calculation of heights and distances, had not accident furnished them with an object of definite proportions in a troop of chamois which wandered over the
surface of the lake, and sought to quench their thirst
in its crevasses. The adventurers shouted; and immediately they bounded away towards the ridges, leaving
them thenceforward alone in these vast deserts, the
extent of which they had unwittingly assisted in
determining.

The explorers were now called upon to decide in
what way they should reach the accessible parts of
the mountain. M. Ramond had already detected that
the route to the summits was absolutely shut up by the
disorder of their ice-masses and the precipitousness of
their sides. The very chamois had avoided them in
their flight, though it was their shortest way to escape
us, and had traversed the entire length of the lake, in
order to take refuge on the more accessible heights
which separate the Cylinder from the region of the
Marboré. But Ramond and his companions could descend into the basin. The incline, though exceedingly
rapid, was wholly free from danger. Once on the level

of the lake, its frozen surface opened up every communication, and nothing prevented them from following in the track of the chamois as far as the western ridge, which would lead them to the foot of the Cylinder and the last terraces of Mont Perdu. At the same time, it was necessary to give a thought to the question of *returning;* for it was now noon, and the aspect of the sky plainly pointed to a change of weather. If they spent the rest of the day in the ascent, they had no longer the choice of retreat; and their sole resource would be to regain the valley of snow they had so recently traversed. But those of Ramond's companions who had paled before the perils of the *ascent*, could not safely be exposed to the much more real peril of the *descent*. Ramond, in this difficulty, recollected the escarpment of the valley of Béousse, which the Spanish shepherds regarded as the natural road from the lake. According to them, it communicated with the Puerto de Pineda on the other side. True, the circuit was a long one; and if undertaken, any new enterprise must be renounced for the present. But, on the other hand, the contrabandista declared that the rocks were really practicable, and that he had crossed them himself on his way to the valley of Fanlo. Ramond, therefore, might reascend to the lake next day by the same route, and perhaps carry with him La Peyrouse into those extraordinary localities where he already regretted his absence bitterly.

Ramond decided immediately to inform him of his march. He wrote a few lines, directing him to cross without delay the Puerto de Pineda, and wait for the adventurers in the valley of Béousse—at a hut which he indicated, from information supplied by the contrabandista. He acquainted him with his intention of reascending to the lake on the following day, and his hope of being able to take him also; and this missive he placed in the hands of one of the guides of Coumélie, who decided to return to La Peyrouse, if possible, by the track through the valley of snow. The departure of this messenger was not the least touching incident of the expedition. They could see him creeping over the snow, using his hands, and cautiously lengthening his body so as to place his foot in the holes already excavated. The slowness of his course was not a good omen for the success of his mission; and so the event proved. M. Ramond did not carry La Peyrouse with him to the summit of Mont Perdu.

In bestowing a last look on the rocks of the mountain-gap, Ramond's attention was drawn to the small number of plants which resist the keen experiences of winter at an elevation of nearly 10,000 feet above the sea-level. The northern exposure offered only one specimen; but this was the *ranunculus glacialis*—so rare in the Pyrenees, that Ramond had not met with more than a couple on the summit of Neouvielle. Here it was abundant and superb, but suspended to rocks so steep, and these suspended on a precipice so formidable, that to reach them needed all the zeal of the most enthusiastic science. Mirbel and Pasquier were the first to climb them, and their example gave encouragement to the others. They had not yet crossed so hazardous a bit, and none had been crossed with so much readiness.

From the bosom of the lake rises a belt of rocks so as to form a long promontory. Its configuration indicated a perfect similarity between its structure and that of the bases of the Cylinder; it offered, therefore, an object of comparison by which M. Ramond could settle all his doubts.

He lost no time in effecting a descent. The lake was covered with a thick ice, which rendered the passage of the crevasses easy, and he soon gained the promontory. It proved to be divided into horizontal strata, like the terraces of the Marboré, like the walls of the Brèche de Roland, like the Cylinder and its platform. But were these strata layers or beds? The first stroke of the hammer answered this question; they were simply layers, and the beds were vertical. Ramond was on the point of dealing a second blow at the solid stone, when he remarked a reddish projection on the surface. Looking more closely, he recognized a piece of a polypid. Again he looked; and he saw the upper valve of an oyster, then some fragments of a madrepore, and then some other zoophites so broken that he could not distinguish the species.

A shout of joy, and his companions gathered round him on those rocks all thickly incrusted with the débris of the organic kingdom. Ramond pointed out to them the fossil remains, which, on the flanks of Mont Perdu, acquired a remarkable importance. They spread themselves over the promontory; they eagerly gathered everything which could be distinguished from the substance of the stone; and Ramond enjoyed, while working with fresh ardour in the midst of these zealous labourers, a happiness which none could share with him—that of having opened up to his successors an ample field of observation, where they would one day discover what the condition of scientific knowledge in his darker age did not permit him and his companions to see.

But if, says Ramond, it was gratifying to see the pupils of two newly-founded schools in possession of a country the discovery of which would be a source of envy to the whole scientific world,—if I could not regard without emotion these young disciples drawing from a first success the passion for inquiry and the thirst of knowledge,—they themselves, on their side, experienced the full influence of the scene, and abandoned themselves to transports bordering upon delirium. Let us remain here, they said to me; to-morrow, perhaps, we shall succeed in our attempt upon Mont Perdu.—But how guard against the coldness of the night? Oh! what is a single night compared to such a prospect of success! —We are without provisions! Oh! we can do without them!—Fatigue, fear, danger—all was forgotten; preparations, precautions—all were in default. No longer was there anything frightful in the ice-masses; no longer was there anything ominous in the dense clouds which girdled the peaks; when suddenly, from the very bosom of that cloud, issued an awful peal which the echoes of the desert multiplied. The most resolute paled before it; they thought it indicated the outbreak of the tempest in these frightful solitudes whose issues it would speedily close up. But it was nothing more than a waterspout which had burst on the upper terraces of the mountains. However, the impression was made; and my companions now thought of nothing but their departure.

The explorers had not long passed the lake when they came upon the brink of a singularly terrific precipice. It seemed as if the earth vanished suddenly from beneath their feet. In whatever direction they looked, they saw nothing but precipitous escarpments and lofty walls. To the left the mountains of Estaubé, to the right Mont Perdu, plunging together to an immense depth, furnished two long parallel chains, formed of the same rocks, moulded in the same fashion, and enclosing between enormous ramparts the valley of Béousse, over which the travellers dominated, like gods in the upper regions of Olympus.

But how charming *was* that valley, in the midst of the formidable mountain-belt which sheltered it with its precipices, and fertilized it with its snows! Luxuriant with the luxuriance of nature, and beautiful with a wild beauty, it shone with all the splendour of the young earth before man had furrowed it with laborious plough. The travellers sought in vain for the traces of frequent footsteps; neither path nor hospice was visible; the inhabitants had apparently concealed themselves; the visitor had fled before that magnificent nature which the former had been unable to subdue, which the latter had not dared to contemplate; and the last person to approach it would probably think himself the first who had descried it.

It is grand to see these pastures without cattle, these shady groves which no human hand has planted, these forests still virgin; these long lines of thriving box-trees, which no skill has traced; and that torrent, born of Mont Perdu,—the Cinca, which, proud of its origin, impetuous and indomitable, marks out its uncertain course at the bottom of that deep cleft, where the ruins accompanying it keep back the verdure at a respectful distance. The eye, beguiled to follow, wanders afar with it into the extensive desert which it traverses without obstacle and almost without witness. It speeds, it flies, like swift Camilla; and one cannot quit it; on the limits of the horizon the eye seeks the last glimmer of its waves; the attentive ear eagerly catches the last murmur borne on the passing wind. Finally, it escapes from both eye and ear into the profound valleys which conduct it afar off; but imagination pursues it still to the remote shores where the Ebro receives these waters, the everlasting sources of which lie in the mountain's bosom.

But what then is the secret charm of this wilderness? What deep, involuntary, masterful sentiment detains the traveller in a desert where human industry has failed to gain a footing? What irresistible inclination incessantly draws thither his thoughts and his footsteps, detains him there, and amuses his fancy with the vain desire of erecting his hut, and concealing himself and his loved ones in its depths? What is the value of civilization, if still in our hearts survives the imperishable regret of our former independence? What is the use of society, if man, who has moulded it to his liking, and is bound to it by all the ties of habit and necessity, cannot for a moment escape from the crowd that surrounds him without bestowing a tear on the need that compels him to return?

Ramond renewed his attempt upon Mont Perdu in the following September. His companions on this occasion were Mirbel and Pasquier, who had abundantly proved their address and resolution in the first adventure; and M. Dralet, an agriculturist of some eminence, and a devoted student of natural history. Though unused to mountain-climbing, he preserved throughout the enterprise an admirable presence of mind. At Barèges the explorers engaged the services of two men: one, Ramond's old and trusty guide, Laurens; the other, a "new hand," whose experiences, it will be seen, were hardly such as to tempt him again to an essay in mountaineering. He was, however, a vigorous fellow, and skilful enough among the crags and precipices; he failed only when the travellers penetrated into the upper region with its snow and ice. On their arrival at Gèdres, they added to their party a peasant named Rondo, known as one of the nimblest and most adventurous men in the country. The dangerous passes of the Marboré were his familiar paths. There was not a mountaineer throughout the Pyrenees so thoroughly acquainted with the snows of every season. Such a reinforcement was indispensable to the successful conduct of an expedition necessarily more perilous than the preceding one; and M. Ramond has left on record a high testimony to the skill and courage of the humble mountaineer.

In order to gain time, and employ to useful purpose the whole of the following day, they resolved to spend the night as near to Mont Perdu as possible. Therefore, they determined on taking their rest at the bottom of the Estaubé, in the hut of the *Abassat-dessus;* and arrangements were made to ensure their reaching it at an early hour. They were well supplied with "wraps," and carried a stock of fuel; though these precautions proved scarcely sufficient to protect them from the cold they experienced at so considerable an elevation and in a season so far advanced.

On this occasion, as Ramond desired to revisit its eastern slopes, they ascended the Coumélie by its anterior face. Thence they passed through the valley of Héas to gain the *Passet des Glouriettes*, which mounts directly to the valley of Estaubé. As they mounted higher and yet higher, the freshness of the air and the serenity of the sky were accepted as good omens of favourable weather; but at every step they left behind them some of the plants of summer. Autumn, with her brow of dusky gold, and robe of many colours, awaited them on the heights, and with finger on her lip pointed to the frowning shadow of Winter as already darkening on the summits.

The hut was reached before sunset. It was empty; for the pastures were blighted by the nocturnal frosts, and the shepherds and their flocks had descended to the lower grounds. M. Ramond took possession of the asylum thus open to him and his companions, and occupied the calm of a lovely autumnal night in studying the surrounding mountains.

A lovely night, indeed; a night calm and cloudless, but very cold. The adventurers kindled a great fire, and lay down around it, rolled up in their coverlets. At daybreak they were on the road to the Gap. The character of the soil, and the structure of the strata, were indications that they had reached the bases of Mont Perdu. Everything already announced, and bore the impress of, his majesty. The precipices, issuing from an immense accumulation of ruin and snow, tower to the very clouds, and seem to describe an arc of a circle, each extremity of which is flanked by a huge glacier. The higher of these occupies a kind of niche in the vicinity of the Puerto de Pineda; the larger and grander lies on the opposite side, where it is prolonged towards the Brèche d'Allany, and corresponds to those visible from Gavarnie on that advanced body of the Marboré which there bears the name of Mont Perdu. In the middle of the cirque, two ascents or causeways, loaded with snow, rise to the very summit of the precipices. Of these the western is absolutely inaccessible; and at its base two huge conical rocks are planted like boundary-marks which may not be overpassed, columns of Hercules, which really indicate the boundary-line of the known and the unknown! The other causeway, so to speak, is broader and not so steep: this, too, has its bound, which is even more remarkable than the other in form, as it is more imposing in dimensions; but it will not delay the advance of the enthusiast, who thinks nothing of possible peril in comparison with the pleasure of seeing Mont Perdu in the most striking of its aspects.

> "Ah, that such beauty, varying in the light
> Of living nature, cannot be portrayed
> By words, nor by the pencil's silent skill;
> But is the property of him alone
> Who hath beheld it, noted it with care,
> And in his mind recorded it with love!"

The impressive features of such a scene as we have attempted to describe, of this mountain amphitheatre with its two great rivers of ice, and its ever-changing effects of light and shade, cannot be adequately presented to the reader's mind in words. We must leave it to his imagination to inspire with the glow of life the dull framework, which is all we can set before him.

Our travellers approached the giant causeway, and for some time contemplated the glacier with anxiety. It had undergone much alteration since M. Ramond's first attempt. There was no snow; its surface was absolutely bare, and did not offer a single point where the traveller's foot could leave its imprint. The middle of it was hollowed out. Two great crevasses traversed it from top to bottom; and at about two-thirds of its height could be seen a transversal depression, which considerably increased the inclination of the upper portion. To attempt the front was impossible; it was scarped at the extremity, and presented simply a series of clean, sharp cuttings, opening into the crevasses. Compelled to ascend at the side, they soon found that at the slightest inclination it was already dangerous. The clamping-irons did not "bite;" and though the travellers leaned on their iron-shod poles with all their strength, they scarcely indented the hard frozen surface.

However, they had furnished themselves with suitable instruments for splitting the ice, and to these they now had recourse. Rude and arduous was the work; which, moreover, they could not regulate as they would have liked. As we have said, the glacier hollowed in the middle, like a gutter, and was riddled with crevasses and holes; therefore they were compelled to keep away towards the sides, and yet not to approach these too closely; following, in fact, almost a straight line between the Scylla and the Charybdis prudence warned them to avoid. It was like mounting a ladder of ice; no zigzags could be adopted to lessen or disguise the incline, which continually increased in proportion as the precipice deepened.

For upwards of two hours they continued the laborious ascent, and yet had accomplished only the least difficult portion of their task. They then drew near the protuberance formed by the glacier above the depression of which we have spoken previously. How to attack this eminence they knew not; they had exhausted all their expedients. Rondo proposed to double upon it by mounting the border they had hitherto so carefully avoided. Let us describe this border or bank. It was a knife-like ridge, separated from the mountain-mass by a broad gap, which opened, funnel-like, into the cavity of the glacier. An hour before the adventurers would have rejected Rondo's proposal as a foolish jest; but now it was accepted as suggesting the only mode of issuing honourably from their perilous enterprise. A dozen steps, hewn out almost perpendicularly, conducted them to the ridge, which they had to level before they could find standing-room, and to test by heavy blows to determine if it would bear them. Continually levelling and sounding, they succeeded in accomplishing about thirteen paces in twenty minutes; balancing themselves on the slippery edge, with the precipice in their rear and on either side. We do not know that the annals even of Alpine adventure offer a more dangerous position, or one better calculated to try the nerve of the coolest and most courageous. However, at the end of these thirteen paces they were forced to halt, and again take counsel together.

The guide they had hired at Barèges now declared that he felt dizzy, and should tumble headlong. He was one of the vanguard, and nothing could be done but to put him in the middle of the little company; an operation both difficult and perilous on a line without breadth, a line exactly fulfilling the definition of Euclid. In the movement thus occasioned Ramond's telescope and compass fell from the bag carried by Laurens, and rolled down into the chasm that separated them from the rock. Rondo gallantly offered to descend in search of the precious articles, and would listen to no dissuasion. He slipped down into the cleft, and penetrated into the foremost ice-cave, where he found the compass. The party above then lowered a rope, which he fastened round him, and they proceeded, with no slight effort, to haul him up to the ridge. The cold at the bottom of the ravine was so intense that he had been unable to search for the telescope. Laurens, however, insisted on descending. He was hauled up in the same manner;

and certainly those who gave were not in a less critical position than those who received the help. Laurens brought back nothing. The result was that Ramond had lost an excellent telescope; but then the little band of adventurers had gained from the effort a fresh confidence in their energies and strength, and pushed forward another thirty paces, scarcely taking the trouble to level the ridge as they advanced.

And yet that troublesome ridge exposed them every moment to new risks. Twice they were arrested by angles of the rock which projected in front of them, and barred the way. They could neither ascend nor descend; they could only twist themselves round the projections, at the imminent hazard of losing their balance and falling headlong into the chasm. Soon it became utterly impossible to move forward, and they had no other refuge than the very rocks which, at first, had appeared inaccessible. They are broken up into steps or stages, it is true, by the intercrossed cuttings of their beds and layers; but, to understand the disposition of these stages, let the reader figure to himself, in the first place, a flight of steps, each of which shall almost always be higher than it is broad, and which are built up in such a way that the angle of inclination increases by one-third; next let him add to this idea that of all the irregularities and all the degradations which such a construction must necessarily occasion in such a structure; the uncertainty felt by our travellers as to the nature of the prospect before them; the foreboding excited by the previous fruitless attempt on the part of the guides of Coumélic; and he may judge with what feelings they regarded the last resource that remained to them.

Nothing could be done but climb, step by step, the repellent rocks. The foremost adventurer was pushed forward by the second in order, and, having made good his footing, lent a hand to assist his friend. The risk was equal on both sides; or if there were any disadvantage, it was experienced by the later comers. Those in front could not make a false step without compromising the rest of the party, nor dislodge a stone which did not fly over their heads. Ramond himself was rather seriously wounded by one of these accidental missiles, against which he could only stiffen himself, as his position prevented him from avoiding it.

This last escalade lasted upwards of an hour, and the dangers incurred by our adventurers sufficiently show that the ascent of Mont Perdu by this route is practicable only in summer, when the glaciers are still covered with snow. A month before, they had accomplished it in two hours; and, in truth, experts in mountain-climbing would have regarded it as a bagatelle. Now it occupied five, and in these five there was not a minute in which they did not run the risk of their lives.

At length they reached the summit of the ridge; there were but a few more steps to climb, and the more regular arrangement of the strata already conduced to the diminution of the gradient. Ramond looked at his companions; none seemed afraid, but none seemed particularly elated. Depressed by fatigue and prolonged anxiety, no one could rouse himself to a conception of the recompense prepared for him by beneficent Mont

RAMOND'S ASCENT OF MONT PERDU.

Perdu. After so many inclined planes, and precipitous crags, and treacherous slopes of ice, they felt no desire for anything more than a little level ground, where they could plant their feet without deliberation; but this level spot,—no sooner did they touch it than the scene suddenly changed, and everything was forgotten! From the summit of the rocks they contemplated with dumb surprise the majestic spectacle which awaited them at the passage of the Brèche, or Gap. They knew nothing of it, had never seen it, had no idea of the incomparable splendour with which a sunny day invested it. On their first visit the curtain had been but slightly uplifted; the shroud suspended from the peaks flung a shadow of gloom even over the objects it did not cover. But on the present occasion there was nothing veiled,—nothing which the sun did not illuminate with its fullest glow: the lake, completely thawed, reflected a firmament of azure; the glaciers glittered; and the summit of Mont Perdu, all resplendent in celestial radiance, seemed no longer a thing of earth.

But it were vain to attempt to paint the magical appearance of this glorious picture. Drawn by a Divine hand, realized by a Divine will, clothed in colours of wonderful intensity, who can hope to set it forth in words? To such scenes not even the memory of the spectator, in after-years, can do anything like justice. It retains but a vague and lifeless image of what was formerly so full of life, so exact in outline, so unrivalled in brightness. It retains little more than a sentiment of beauty or grandeur as associated with some particular landscape. And so M. Ramond, when he comes to write down his reminiscences of Mont Perdu, is compelled to resort to general terms, from which the reader can derive nothing accurate and real. "In vain," he writes, "should I attempt to describe what this apparition possessed of the unexpected, the astonishing, the fantastic, at the moment when the curtain dropped—when the gate was thrown open—when we stood at last on the threshold of the gigantic edifice. Words linger far behind a sensation swifter than thought; we cannot believe our eyes; we seek around us a standard of comparison; everything simultaneously refuses it; one world finishes, and another begins—a world governed by the laws, as it were, of a different existence. How deep the repose in that vast enclosure where centuries pass with lighter feet than do the years in our lower world! How profound the silence on these heights where every sound, whatever its nature, announces a grand and rare phenomenon! How absolute the calm of the atmosphere, how perfect the serenity of the heaven which floods us with its glory! Everything is in harmony—air, sky, earth, water; everything seems to don its bravest livery in the presence of the all-glorious sun."

Comparing the vast symmetry of the cirque with the hideous chaos it presented when a dense fog lingered round its terraces, our travellers found it difficult to recognize the localities they had then visited. It was no longer the colossal bulk of the Cylinder which exclusively attracted the attention. The limpid purity of the air rectified the appearances which had confused the interposition of the cloud; the main summit had regained its rights; and thus brought into unity and order the various parts of the mighty chaos. Never before had such a scene greeted the travellers' wondering gaze! Ramond tells us, in a rapturous strain of excitement, that he had seen the upper Alps—had seen them in his early youth, when "a young man's fancy" sees everything invested with even a supernatural beauty and grandeur—but that which he had not seen was the magnificence of the loftiest summits worn by a mountain of the secondary order. These simple and austere forms, these bold clean cuttings, these firm and solid rocks with their broad strata arranged like courses of masonry, curve into an amphitheatre, mould themselves into terraces, soar aloft as towers to which the hands of giants seem to have applied the plummet and line,— these are features the explorer vainly looks for in the abode of eternal frost, vainly seeks in the primitive mountains with their flanks elongated into spires and pinnacles, and their base concealed beneath piles of wreck and ruin. Whoever is satiated with their savage aspects, will find strange and novel phases in the Pyrenees. From Mont Blanc the lover of Nature should pass on to Mont Perdu; after surveying the chief of the granitic peaks, then he has still to explore the chief of the limestone mountains.

IV.

Norway: The North Cape.

PECULIAR interest attaches to the extremities of earth, the frontier-buttresses of islands, continents, and peninsulas, the great capes or headlands which year after year defy and endure the shock of "warring waters." Somehow or other, the imagination loves to dwell upon these limits, these boundary-marks of the world, which separate, as it were, man's long-known and long-occupied territory from that ocean which he can never hope to subdue; it invests them with an ideal grandeur, and generally associates them with many a wild fable and picturesque legend. Few travellers, we suspect, are insensible to the influences of this association when they stand on the rugged summit of the Land's End, where the billows of the Atlantic ceaselessly beat on the furthest shore of Great Britain. To the voyager, Cape Horn, as the extreme limit of the New World, and the Cape of Good Hope, as the termination of the continent-peninsula of Africa, assume a special and remarkable interest. It usually happens that these great promontories are

romantic in themselves, in their natural features, their height, their massiveness, or their boldness of outline; and such a circumstance does not fail to increase their attraction. We have referred to the Land's End: few spots in Great Britain are more sublime in character, or present a scene of grander confusion. So, too, Cape Horn is distinguished by its wildness of aspect, its chaos of basaltic and lava rocks, which, in their general outline, suggest to the mind the idea of "a sleeping lion, facing and braving the southern tempests." But no one of the earth's chief promontories surpasses in these respects that remote boundary-mark of Europe which is known as the North Cape. Its elevation is so considerable that it may justly be included among the "mountains," and a pilgrimage to it lies, therefore, within the scope of the present volume.

A glance at a good map of Norway will show the reader that voyagers "in these parts," on issuing from the Strait of Havoe pass a small and rather low island, the green Masoe, formerly inhabited, but now abandoned to the sea-birds; and then come in sight of the notorious Stappen, a group of black reefs rising like towers out of the yeasty waves.

We now see before us the dread expanse of the Polar Ocean, of that rolling and tumultuous sea which has witnessed the wreck of so many hopes as well as some of the finest deeds of human daring. The seething waters, as they fling high into the air their crests of foam, indicate the immediate neighbourhood of that promontory so dreaded by the navigator, the North Cape, which might justly be called the Cape of Storms. For, in truth, the sea in this vicinity is never tranquil,—not even in the calmest and sunniest days of summer. The eddies of all the tempest-tossed tides of the Atlantic, of the Frozen Ocean, and the White Sea expire at the foot of this rocky peninsula, which projects between the continents of America and Northern Asia.

A contrary wind, let us suppose, forces us to tack, so that we have an excellent opportunity of contemplating at our leisure the severe and impressive spectacle of its rocky mass. Elongated like a ship's bows, it seems to challenge an encounter with the powerless billows, which have vainly spent their fury against it for countless ages. But at length we succeed in making the shore, and drop anchor to the east of the Cape,—in a small curve or hollow, which, from its peculiar outline, has received the name of *Hornvig* or Horn Bay.

On landing we are agreeably surprised, I think, to find ourselves surrounded by a sub-Alpine meadow-land of the most extraordinary richness. Tall thick grasses rise to our knees; and here at the extremity of Europe bloom the flowers which adorn the floral world of Switzerland and the Alps. As vigorous these, as bright, and as full-blossomed, as on their native mountains. To the right rises the imposing bulk of the North Cape, black, scarped, inaccessible. In front of us, however, a sharp but verdurous ascent will carry us to the summit by doubling the base of the promontory. First, let us gather specimens of this Boreal botany around us. A peculiar charm surely attaches to these flowers as more robust and adventurous than their European

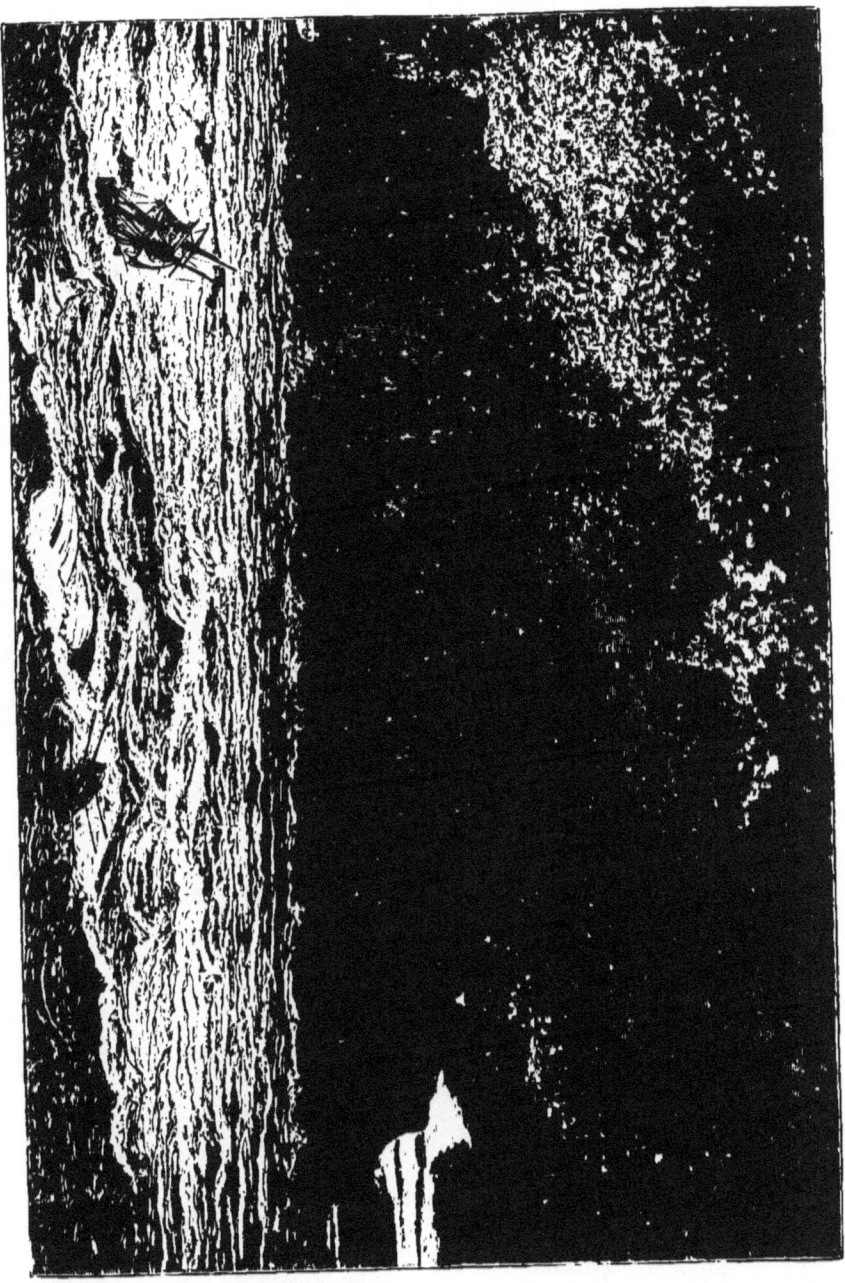

THE NORTH CAPE

sisters. We are tempted to ask of them why they have quitted the sheltered banks and pleasant glades of their native regions for this savage and desolate locality, where cold winds blow, and the roar of the melancholy ocean mingles with the scream of the migratory birds.

On reaching the crest of the ascent we find ourselves on a naked and barren table-land, strewn, as it were, with pools of water. Afar off, until lost to sight, are unrolled successive plains and grand undulations of a slightly broken ground, separated by bays and marshy shallows; the whole scene being cold, motionless, desolate. While a delightful calm prevails in the rich meadow-land below, the north wind sweeps furiously the table-land of the Cape, so that we can scarcely stand against it. Nevertheless we press forward to its very margin. Oh! the gloomy grandeur of the spectacle which there presents itself to the spell-bound gaze! Before us, the vast Frozen Ocean, whose limits touch the Pole, heaving and rolling beneath the burden of clouds which rests heavily upon it; to the left, a long, low, narrow point of land, fringed with cream-white foam; to the right, some rocky islands, nameless and uninhabited. We lean cautiously over the brink of the precipice which forms the seaward face of the promontory, and see the wild waves struggling and wrestling at its base, fully one thousand feet below. From the height at which we are placed, the enormous waves coming direct from Greenland, Spitzbergen, or Novaia Zemlaia, form, as they break, but a thin white line of foam; such as is made by the ripples of a little lake when driven shoreward by a light breath of wind.

The most elevated summit of the North Cape is estimated by Charles Martins to be 308 mètres (about 984 feet) above the sea. It is crowned by a small rocky boulder, on which the voyager hastens to engrave his name. He will find among the memorials of former visitors that of Parrot, so celebrated for his adventurous travels in the Alps, the Ararat, and the Caucasus. Even this topmost crest is not wholly devoid of vegetation. Small round clumps of foliaceous lichens, black as the rock, flourish upon it; and a microscopical moss hides in its fissures. A few meagre, wind-withered plants cling to the rough surface of the table-land, or seek a refuge behind the undulations of the soil which may shelter them from the perpetual gusts that beat upon the North Cape.

The following description is borrowed from Louis Ernault's "La Norwége," an interesting and agreeable record of Northern travel :—

The North Cape is distant twelve or fifteen miles from the Giestvar fiord. We crossed this short interval in calm weather, using our oars much oftener than our canvas. On our left was the open sea; on our right, the shore of the island of Mageroe—of which, and not of the mainland, the North Cape is a promontory. The entire shore resembles a lofty wall, formed of perpendicular strata : at its base, reefs and breakers; at its summit, a straight and narrow crest, sometimes broken by sharp peaks. In the midst of this rocky rampart we perceived, afar off, a great square tower projecting boldly, and flanked by massive bastions : it was the Cape.

Instead of landing immediately, we stretched a point out to sea, for about a quarter of a mile, to obtain a better view of the general effect. The enormous mass rose precipitously from the bosom of the sea; sombre, dreary, repellent, unapproachable. Unmovable as the buttress of a world, solid as the bulwark of a continent, it impresses the spectator with the idea of a power that cannot be shaken. Europe sleeps in peace behind that advanced sentinel, who defends her against the floods and tempests of the Polar Sea.

We doubled the point, and penetrated into a second bay; a bay of small dimensions, hollowed out and rounded by Nature in the very heart of the mountain. The vast shadow of the Cape here fell upon us. Around the bay a semicircular girdle of rocks sharply defined its outlines. Sometimes those blackened masses crumble like lavas which a shock would have ground into dust on their issue from the crater. Sometimes they split up among themselves into broad sheets, like leaves of slate or tablets of marble. Between them and the sea, a layer of vegetable mould is gay with turf and flowers; with the andromeda and the Arctic ranunculus, the small wood-violet, the crane's-bill, the angelica, and the forget-me-not—which seems to bloom in this remote solitude as if to recall the memory of old familiar faces. Over a stony bed, among the flowers and grasses, a small silvery streamlet murmurs and sparkles.

We soon began the ascent of the Cape.

It forms a mountain, about one thousand feet in height, cut down to a precipice on the seaward side, and almost inaccessible everywhere. Its declivities are all steep, abrupt, and rugged; frequently rendered dangerously slippery by belts of humid moss, short, compact, elastic, and spontaneously repelling the foot, which can find no support or resting-place. At other times the explorer is called upon to struggle over heaps of rolling stones, which fall away at the lightest touch; or up masses of rough, rude rocks, that can be conquered only by escalading them. Here and there, in the hollows which retain a little vegetable earth, some dwarf birches essay to raise their disconsolate heads; but speedily fall back upon the ground, where they creep, and writhe, and vegetate, and die. At intervals, a gull, perched on some distant crag, regarded us with its clear and piercing eye; but reassured by our pacific air, continued its reverie, without again turning towards us its motionless head. Croaking hoarsely, the crows skimmed the soil in black whirling clouds; while, in the pure empyrean, the eagle and the falcon wheeled swiftly in immense circles.

At length we attained the topmost ridge, a terrace-like table-land covered with yellowish mould, for which mosses and lichens contend,—and where, on strata of gloomy granite, gleams the whiteness of the quartz.

When I recognized that I stood upon the farthest point of the old European continent, I experienced a deep and almost overpowering emotion. Behind, was the ancient world, its civilization, and its history; in front, the unknown ocean that struggles onwards to the Pole through a region of ice and snow, buried in cloud and mist!

It was a quarter of an hour past midnight. The sun had risen above the horizon. The lower rim of its disc scarcely skimmed the ridge of the empurpled waves. There the indefatigable luminary pursues a four months' course without repose, prior to sinking into the sea. Only, it does not seem to follow its accustomed march. Instead of tracing above our heads a luminous arch, one point of which reposes on the east, the other on the west, he glides softly along the insensible curve of a disproportionately elongated ellipse.

But let it be noted that the amount of light is not uniform; it varies in intensity and colour according to the position of the luminary from which it emanates. If the noonday orb launches, as with us, a flood of ardent beams,—if, towards ten o'clock, its oblique disc plunges into waves of purple which overspread one half the firmament,—often, at midnight, when it touches the line of the horizon, its light, decomposed by an invisible prism, flickers and degrades itself into the yellow and greenish half-tones of a limited but infinitely varied gamut. Then every object assumes a fantastic tint; and, however clear may be the atmosphere, we do not fail to feel that this is not the true daylight, the daylight adapted for action and movement. Sometimes, during the prolonged day, the moon disputes possession of the sky with the greater luminary—or rather, each orb reigns over a part of the horizon. And in proportion as the sun advances in his glory, all streaming with gold and fire, the moon, always beautiful in her roseate paleness, hastens to withdraw her sphere, though she remains dimly visible through the pearly veil of the clouds.

Not unfrequently, the North Cape becomes an impassable witness of those great convulsions of Nature which revolutionize the face of the globe. The north and north-west winds, on their path from the Pole to the Equator, rage headlong with ungoverned fury, and produce the most terrible commotions. Upheaved in liquid mountains, the billows, driven before the gale, simultaneously assail the promontory on every side, and expend their violence upon its immovable walls of granite.

Such is the North Cape, the advanced post of Arctic Europe.

V.

The Peak of Teneriffe.

"A summer-isle of Eden glowing in a purple sphere of sea."—TENNYSON.

OFF the west coast of Africa, in long. 18° and lat. 27° to 29° N., lie a beautiful group of islands,—the Canaries,—which the older geographers loved to clothe in the radiant colours of fable. These were the Happy Isles of the Blest, where angry winds never blew; where the bright seas were never shaken by storms; where man drank of the fountains of eternal youth, and his serene life was free from the shadow of worldly cares or human ambition. When they came to be visited by European navigators, the contrast between the wild Atlantic and their verdurous groves and glades was so great, that they lost little of their ancient repute, and to adventurous spirits they seemed to offer a delightful retreat, when they should grow weary of the intrigues of European courts. It is now known that their natural advantages, though great, are hardly such as to justify the glowing language in which they were formerly described. Yet they possess a warm and genial climate, and, being all of volcanic formation, are generally fortunate in a fertile soil. When viewed from the sea, they seem so many oases of verdure, cradled in the bosom of ocean; and this is especially true of Teneriffe, which raises its pyramidal bulk, 12,236 feet in height, out of a wonderfully luxuriant girdle of vines, laurels, pines, and junipers. Lanzarote is little else than a mass of lava and ashes, with a crater which burst into activity as recently as 1824. But Ferro, anciently reputed the westernmost point of the Old World, is pleasantly green and fertile; and Palma and Gran Canaria—the latter fully forty miles in circumference—rejoice in an abundant and various vegetation.

We shall here confine our attention to Il Pico, or Teneriffe, the great volcano of which is in every respect remarkable. While within three thousand feet of the full height of Mont Blanc, its sides are as richly clothed as those of Etna, and its form is as sharply defined as that of Stromboli. It rises from the sea like a huge pyramid, and at sunrise and sunset its black pyramidal shadow stretches for fifty miles across the deep, so that the contiguous islands seem to repose in a melancholy twilight. Its declivities exhibit a well-marked succession of zones of vegetation, each differing in character, and assuming more and more of the sub-Alpine features as they approach the summit, —that singular sugar-loaf peak, or Piton, which crowns the mountain-top, and springs out of a dreary sea of volcanic ashes.

The ascent of the Peak has often been accomplished, and between the narratives of different explorers it is difficult to chose. We shall select, however, that of the French *savant*, M. Berthollet,—as being, in all probability, the least known to English readers.

He tells us that it was on the 8th of July he resolved to undertake the ascent of the Pic de Teyde, or, as it is generally called in Europe, the Peak of Teneriffe. It was his design to ascend on the south side; for though he knew that no former traveller had attempted it, and that the paths leading thither were almost impracticable, he was fired by the hope of discovering some rare plants which had escaped the researches of Brousonnet and Charles Smith. His starting-point was Chasna,—a village picturesquely situated to the south of the Teyde, at an elevation of 4700 feet above the sea, though not more than three leagues distant from the southern shore of the isle. His companion was Mr. Macgregor, then British Consul at the Canaries; and, attended by a couple of guides, the two friends started at five in the morning. Two hours' steady walking brought them to the base of the central mountain. The pines of the Canaries, which had covered nearly the whole of the district they had been traversing, now became much rarer; as they advanced into the gorge of Oucanea they insensibly disappeared, and were replaced by resinous brooms. Oucanea is a place worthy of a pilgrimage: a volcanic eruption, attended in all probability by violent commotions, by formerly overthrowing the base of the central mass, created the great ravine which now exists. The principal crater is easily recognized; it poured forth a torrent of vitrified lava which inundated all the surrounding tract, and flowed over a space of upwards of two leagues in the direction of the sea-coast. The wild confusion of the scene is further increased by the presence of enormous rocks or boulders, which seem to have been detached from the neighbouring acclivities.

On emerging from the ravines of Oucanea, our travellers continued to climb the mountain before them; the white brooms, several clumps of which they had already met near the crater, now appeared in great abundance, and soon formed a zone of vegetation which dominated exclusively round the bases of the peak.

The station at which they had arrived is called the *Degollada* of Oucanea. The Teyde rose right in front of them: they could count the black lava-torrents which furrowed its slopes, and discover all the central mountains of Teneriffe; for it is from this point only that it is possible to embrace with a single glance the whole group of volcanic peaks. This is a very striking and imposing spectacle, of which no language can give any just idea. The mountains of the Canary archipelago, which perhaps in some remote antiquity formed a completely circular chain, are now intersected by several broad passages, whose rent and convulsed approaches sufficiently bear witness to the violent causes that produced them. The lofty crests rise upwards of 9500 feet above the sea; the whole space enclosed within the line of circumvallation of these trachytic mountains constitutes an immense crater, of earlier origin than the peak itself,—which, indeed, the geologist Escolar aptly entitles *el hijo de las Canadas* (the son of the Canaries).

PEAK OF TENERIFFE

It is nearly in the centre of this elliptical crater, the major diameter of which measures about five leagues, that the Teyde, with its cloud of smoke, raises its elevated crest. The vast circuit around it is designated at Teneriffe under the name of the "gorges of the Peak" (*Canadas del Teyde*, or simply *Canadas*).

The track ascending to the Degollada of Oucanea, in the depth of the gorges, is exceedingly rugged; the counterscarp of the mountain is almost perpendicular, and at several places breaks up into precipices not less than nine hundred and fifty feet in height. When M. Berthollet and Mr. Macgregor descended into the interior of the Canadas, they could scarcely conceive how they should manage to reach the bottom; however, they succeeded. The level of these gorges is 2730 mètres (8860 feet) above that of the sea, and the summit of the Teyde rises other 985 mètres (3230 feet). On one side stretched the vast acclivities of the great cone, and on the other the mountain-chain which they had just descended, the almost perpendicular cutting of which had formerly served as the wall of this immense crater of elevation. What an astonishing spectacle! And if the imagination transports itself into the ages of geological revolution when this formidable volcano was in all its activity, it cannot conceive without terror of a fiery gulf more than nine leagues in circumference and nine hundred and fifty feet in depth! Then only is it possible to form an idea of the condition of fermentation of that epoch of incandescence, and the formation of the Teyde in the middle of this gulf will seem but a secondary effect.

After having contemplated these great volcanic catastrophes, and before advancing farther towards the base of the Teyde, our travellers betook themselves for a few minutes' repose to the fountain of La Piedra, for they were suffocated by the heat. In this elevated region the air is always calm and transparent, the sky always of a brilliant azure, and the lightest cloud never comes to disturb the "pure serene." The intensity of the solar rays in these ravines, their refraction on the expanses of glittering white tufa, their dazzling scintillation on all the fragments of pumice-stone and obsidian which strew the soil, are so many causes productive of a high temperature. From this elevated point one seems to rule the clouds, and therefore none of those beneficent mists which, at the lower levels, come to refresh the atmosphere, bedew earth and revivify vegetation. The inhabitant of the plains cannot traverse this zone without speedily feeling its influence. The extreme dryness of the air closes up the pores, arrests perspiration, and cracks the skin; an immoderate thirst incessantly torments him, and he frequently seeks in vain for the concealed spring which can quench it only for a moment. It is in vain too that, to escape the burning arrows of the sun, he attempts to take refuge under the clumps of flowering broom or in the shadow of some projecting rock; everywhere the earth is burning, everywhere the heat is insupportable, everywhere prevails that dead tranquillity which disheartens him, and he is speedily forced to abandon a shelter that no breath of air can reach.

The fountain of La Piedra yields a deliciously fresh

water; the goats, which are allowed to wander freely in these ravines, and the bees whose hives are situated in the neighbourhood, frequent it to quench their thirst; all around it the white broom flourishes: this useful shrub is the ornament of the Canadas; the goats browse on its stems, while the bees incessantly plunder its balmy flowers. Without the broom, which all-provident Nature has so abundantly spread in this valley, how could those herds and precious swarms subsist, which form for the inhabitants of the south of Teneriffe one of the most important branches of rural economy?

Our travellers next continued their ascent through the defile of the *Canada blanca;* afterwards, their guides led them across a torrent of lava to enter another defile, which opened into a third. The tracts thus invaded by the volcanic eruptions are called, in the language of the natives, *mal pais.* As they advanced, the obstacles seemed to increase in difficulty; every moment they were called upon to climb the heaps of scoria and masses of obsidian which blocked up the passes. For upwards of two hours they dragged their weary limbs over this terrible soil. Then their guides, who had already halted several times for the purpose of holding council, seemed uncertain as to the route which should be followed. At length one of them informed the travellers that they had lost the track, and the enterprise must be abandoned. Such, however, was not the opinion of our travellers; they had advanced too far to be willing to return; but they owned that it was necessary to extricate themselves from their difficult position, for night was approaching. The locality into which their ignorant guides had plunged them was assuredly discouraging: lavas, accumulated in great blocks, everywhere surrounded them; beyond, they appeared to spread out in vast sheets; in what direction to bend their steps, our explorers could not determine. At last, by dint of sheer hard work and exertion, they contrived to make a way for the unfortunate horse which carried their provisions, and had narrowly escaped destruction some ten times in the course of the journey.

They were worn out with fatigue when they arrived at the base of a mountain of pumice-stone heaped up perpendicularly. When they had overcome this obstacle, their boots were reduced to shreds; but as they had already reached one of the slopes of the Teyde, they took courage, and prepared for further efforts. M. Berthollet, who had visited the spot in 1825, recognized its features; and, certain now of his path, led the little company, without further difficulty, to the *Estancia*, where they arrived about nine o'clock, by the light of a cloudless moon. Notwithstanding the great elevation of this station, they found the temperature very endurable; the air was exquisitely pure, and occasionally some light gusts of the north wind brought them the resinous odours of the broom. The guides, immediately on their arrival at the station, levied a contribution on the surrounding bushes, kindled an immense fire, and proceeded to roast an unfortunate goat which they had killed in the Canadas. Soon after supper, they grouped themselves around the temporary hearth, and fell asleep.

M. Berthollet was not so fortunate; the day's march had fired his blood, and his system was in such a state of irritation that he could enjoy only a few fitful snatches of slumber. The spectacle before his eyes had, moreover, too powerful an attraction for him; the serenity of the sky, the solitariness of the scene, the fantastic groups of rocks piled around the bivouac, the solemn shadows reposing on the gorges from which the travellers had just escaped, formed a strange, a weird, and an imposing spectacle.

It was three o'clock in the morning when they abandoned their bivouac, and resumed their adventurous march towards the summit of the peak.

The path which at first they followed was sufficiently steep, yet by no means impracticable; but on approaching the *Altavista*, they found the chaotic condition of the soil, through the accumulation of volcanic matter, a formidable difficulty,—and it was only with the utmost caution they could thread their way through a labyrinth of crags and crevasses. After having got clear of this *mal pais del Teyde*, as the guides called it, they reached the platform of the *Rambleta*. All the indications in this place point to the existence of a crater anterior to that of the peak, for it is from thence have issued the numerous lava-rivers which in past times inundated the Canadas. The Teyde will have had its intervals of repose, and it was probably after one of these that a fresh outbreak produced the peak. This volcanic "capital," which covers the ancient gulf, rises, in fact, in the middle of the Rambleta; hence it crowns the mountain, and the fissures of its crest, which were plainly discernible to the adventurous explorers, were lighted by the first rays of the sunrise. They already "began to be aware" (as old writers say) of sulphurous odours; they touched the goal of their enterprise; but they had still to climb the declivities of this little cone, the height of which is estimated at about 475 feet. The pumice-stone and the fragments of scoria rendered this ascent particularly fatiguing; however, after resting several times to take breath, they finally gained the summit.

The prospect enjoyed by the traveller from this tremendous elevation is necessarily very majestic; it would be impossible to formulate any accurate idea of its various features, or to describe the conflicting emotions which it awakens in the mind of the spectator. He is half-dizzy with surprise, wonder, awe; admiration compels him to a breathless silence. From this grand natural watch-tower, which the volcanic eruptions have raised to a height of nearly 12,300 feet above the sea, his glance embraces the seven verdurous oases of the archipelago: to the east, the lofty summits of Canaria pierce through the sunlit clouds; beyond, Lanzerote and Fortaventura sleep in their girdle of blue waters; to the west, the deep shadow of the Teyde stretches in an immense triangle as far as Gomera; and close at hand lie Palma and Ferro. Beneath him he sees the green slopes of Teneriffe, with the bold outline of its coasts, its mountainous ramifications, its table-lands, and its picturesque valleys. Long wanders the enraptured gaze over the multitude of ridges and hollows indicated by the play of light and shade; and every moment it discovers some new beauty, some fresh object of interest and attraction.

The panorama, charming as it was, lay at too great a distance from our travellers for them to distinguish every detail. They were forced to be content with the general outlines of the picture, and its splendid masses of colour; and, indeed, could they have seized all its points, the impression of grandeur and supernatural beauty would have been weakened. It was not possible for them to appreciate even the heights and the distances, for the mountains seemed to be dwarfed by the colossal shadow of the Teyde. The immensity of the spectacle overwhelmed them with admiration; but it quickly changed its aspect. As the sun advanced on its westward path, the vapours rose on every side, and gradually gathered into condensed masses, floating around the hills and over the valleys. A wreath of clouds soon encircled each lofty peak; and before long the whole surface of the island was shrouded in a pearly mist, over which the eye of the spectator wandered as over a cloudy sea.

As the descent of the peak presents no features of interest, we shall take leave of our adventurers upon its majestic summit.

VI.

The Peter-Botte.

(ISLAND OF MAURITIUS.)

T some distance from the east coast of Madagascar, in the warm waters of the Indian Ocean, and in latitude 20° S., lies the fine island of Mauritius. It owes its name to the Dutch, its original discoverers,—who so christened it in honour of their great statesman, Prince Maurice of Holland. From them it passed to the French, who renamed it Ile de France, and held it for about a century, when it was conquered by the British. Its possession was confirmed to us by the treaties of 1814 and 1815; and we restored to it its old title. Thickly wooded and copiously watered, with a healthy climate and a fertile soil, it forms a valuable colony.

The Mauritius is traversed by several mountain-chains,—the culminating point of which, named the Peter-Botte, rises 2874 feet above the sea. For a long time this singular peak, with its round and barren crest, frequently hidden by impenetrable mists, defied the efforts of the most enthusiastic mountain-climbers, and remained one of the virgin summits of the world. Unless, indeed, we accept the tradition which connects its name with that of a mysterious traveller who ascended it without assistance. Having arrived, says the story, at the upper contraction of the peak, which is called the *col*, he carried over it, by means of an arrow armed with a long piece of line, a rope strong enough to sustain his weight; but the unfortunate adventurer, in the course of his descent, was precipitated into the ravines that border the mountain, and his corpse was never found.

Various attempts were made at various times to accomplish the ascent of this formidable mountain, but none proved successful until the month of September 1832.

In the previous year, Mr. Lloyd, an engineer, had attained a point near the *col*, where he had raised a ladder against the perpendicular face of the rock. Although it did not reach more than half-way up the precipice, he came to the conclusion that it was possible to overcome this first obstacle; and, consequently, in the following year he resumed his efforts, accompanied by Lieutenant Taylor and several other officers.

The bold adventurers started on the 7th of September. After having crossed a ravine which intersects the lower portion of the peak, they made rapid progress to the point where Mr. Lloyd had left his ladder in the preceding year. Here they found themselves on a ridge not more than seven feet wide,—which on the one hand was dominated by a wooded gorge, and on the other was abruptly terminated by a precipice rising upwards of 1600 feet above the plain. One of the extremities of this ridge was similarly terminated by a precipice of equal depth; the other abutted upon the mountain, and there raised itself with numerous gaps and projections, like the blade of a knife broken into notches of different size. After extending to the mountain-neck, or *col*, it joined on to a narrow ledge which ran around the mountain, and above which rose, in disdainful haughtiness, the summit of the Peter-Botte.

The travellers now addressed themselves to their task: they reared the ladder which Mr. Lloyd had left there the year before, and firmly planted its foot against a projecting crag. Then a negro servant of Mr. Lloyd mounted to the summit; where, boldly trusting to his agility and presence of mind, he climbed along the perpendicular rock, clinging to it after the manner of the apes, with hands and feet, and availing himself of every projection, though a single false movement would have precipitated him into the depths below. His daring, however, was crowned with success. He gained the topmost point, and uttering a loud *hurrah!* exclaimed, "All goes well!" A rope which he had carried with him he firmly secured, and then the rest of the party, four in number, hauled themselves up by it. In this way they gained the mountain-neck, sometimes on their knees, sometimes straddling across the top of the ridge; being able, as Lieutenant Taylor afterwards said, to fling at one and the same time their left shoe into the wooded ravine, and their right into the plain which lies on the other side of the mountain.

The head of the peak, as we have said, consists of an

THE PETER-BOTTE, MAURITIUS.

enormous rock, about six feet and a half in height, which, owing to its bulging form, extends considerably beyond its base, like a pear set erect upon its stalk; the ledge which circles round its neck is about seven feet wide, and everywhere terminated by a precipice, except at the point of access discovered by our explorers.

How should they cross this head and its expansion? Fortunately, one of the faces, though jutting beyond the base, rises perpendicularly on the prolongation of the lower precipice, instead of exceeding or overpassing it like the others; and, to add to the good fortune of our party, it corresponded precisely to the point at which they had arrived. This being ascertained, they established a communication with the lower part of the mountain by means of a double rope, and in this way hauled up their equipment,—such as a crow-bar, a hammer, additional ropes, and the like.

They had prepared some iron arrows, attached to the end of a rope; the difficulty consisted in launching them over the head of the Peter-Botte, since the latter projected beyond the base on which they were established. Mr. Lloyd, having wound round his body a stout rope, one end of which was held by his companions, cautiously passed to the other side of the mountain; and there, armed with the arrow-loaded gun, inclining over the abyss, supported by the cord around his loins, and his feet forming a prop or buttress against the brink of the precipice, he fired. Twice the arrow missed; he then had recourse to a stone fastened to a cord, and balancing it diagonally, like a sling, he attempted to make it pass over the rock. Vain hope! Disappointment seized upon the travellers; when, at a last effort, a momentary gust of wind beat back the stone upon the rock, so that it fell on the other side! Immediately the ladders were arranged and made fast; a good cable served as a balustrade; and the engineer, Lloyd, was the first to haul himself to the summit of the rock, with joyous shouts and loud hurrahs. The others followed; and the Union Jack, waving freely and gracefully on the crest of the vanquished Peter-Botte, was immediately saluted by a frigate lying in the roads, and by the land battery. Then the hardy adventurers broke the neck of a bottle of good wine, and standing erect on this elevated pinnacle, baptized it in the name of King William,—drinking to His Majesty's health, and hailing

"The flag that has braved a thousand years
The battle and the breeze"

with hearty acclamations.

It is satisfactory to state that the descent was safely accomplished, and that the adventurers returned that same evening to Port Louis, where they met with the reception due to their courage. That the ascent of the Peter-Botte added anything to the sum of scientific knowledge cannot, indeed, be asserted; but we think it may be said that every fresh manifestation of intrepidity and resolution is a decided gain to humanity.

VII.

Mount Athos.

A GLANCE at the map of Greece will show the reader that the coast of Macedonia throws off into the "blue Ægean" three narrow peninsulas, like the prongs of a trident. The easternmost of these is the only one of special interest. It is the *Hagion Oros*, or Holy Mountain of the Greeks,* the *Monte Santo* of the Italians, otherwise Mount Athos; though, strictly speaking, the last-named appellation belongs only to the high peak which forms its seaward termination. This peninsula is a mountain-mass, about forty miles long by four miles broad, connected with the mainland of Macedonia by a low, narrow isthmus, through which Xerxes, warned by the wreck of the fleet of Mardonius on its difficult shores, cut a navigable canal. From the isthmus the ground rises rapidly into a steep central ridge, which traverses the peninsula like a backbone, and is broken up laterally into deep romantic gorges, clothed with forests of beech and chestnut on the higher slopes, and on the lower

* The ancients called it *Acte*.

with oaks and plane-trees, the olive, cypress, arbutus, catalpa, and a rich undergrowth of heath and broom; in addition to which, as if the hand of a benignant Nature never wearied of pouring forth its stores, abundant creepers trail over the trees, and wreath the branches with their gay festoons. The peak itself, says Mr. Tozer, is, from its height (6400 feet) and solitary position, its conical form and delicate colour, a most impressive mountain. It rises far above the region of firs, in a steep mass of white marble, which, from exposure to the atmosphere, assumes a faint, tender tint of gray. "I have seen," he adds, "its pyramidal outline from the plains of Troy, nearly one hundred miles off, towering up from the horizon, like a vast spirit of the waters, when the rest of the peninsula was concealed below. So great is the distance that it is visible only at sunset, when the faintness of the light allows it to appear. From its isolated position it is a centre of attraction to the storms in the north of the Ægean; in consequence of which the Greek sailors have so great a dread of rounding it in winter, that it would be no unreasonable speculation for an enterprising government to renew the work of Xerxes."

Mount Athos was formerly the station of a fire-beacon, intended for the guidance of the mariners of the Ægean. The Greek sculptor Deinocrates conceived the magnificently extravagant idea of carving it into a statue of Alexander the Great, holding a city in his hands.

A few names of towns—such as Uranopolis, Diuna, Olophyxos, and Cleones—are nearly all that antiquity has left us in the sacred peninsula. At the extremity were the promontories of Nymphæum and Akrothoon. But if antiquity has done little for it, Nature has done much. Its scenery is everywhere of the most striking character, and includes the finest imaginable combinations of those three essential elements of a romantic landscape,—rock, wood, and water. In every view is found the deep blue stretch of the classic Ægean; and on the horizon, to the north and east, tower the heights of Mount Pangæus, and the bold and varied outlines of the historic islands of Thasos, Samothrace, Imbros, and Lemnos. Turning to the slopes of the Holy Mountain, the traveller sees a softer but not less pleasing picture. They are dotted with farms and monastic buildings, around which the blooming corn-fields bear witness to human industry skilfully exercised. Striking inland, he comes upon dells filled with spreading planes and chestnuts, and embowered with creepers,—"a wilderness of leafy shade,—places which Shelley would have delighted in," which he has described in his "Alastor;" and from the openings in the luxuriant foliaged screen the majestic peak is frequently visible, its lower declivities melting into purple haze, while its summit assumes an unearthly, ethereal, delicate tint of violet.

In the centuries immediately following the coming of Christ and the proclamation of the gospel, the imperial persecutions compelled a great number of Christians to withdraw into the deserts. While many sealed with their blood their witness to the truth, others, less confident in their moral strength, preferred to escape from the conflict, and, in imitation of the disciples of St. John, in retirement from the world, to lead an austere and devout life. Thus it came to pass that thousands of Christians peopled the solitudes of Syria and the Thebaid. It was probably about the same time that some fugitives from Pagandom sought out a refuge upon Mount Athos,—the peninsular form and abrupt declivities of which offered many opportunities for a secure retreat. The exact date of this hegira cannot be determined. Several of the monasteries possess relics and works of ancient art which are described as presents from the Empress Pulcheria; others attribute their foundation to the time of Constantine. At all events, hermitages and saintly retreats existed here at a very early period; and when the Moslems overran Egypt, their number would be increased by the monks who fled before the baleful Crescent.

Owing to this remote antiquity, and to the exemption it has enjoyed from the storms of war, Mount Athos possesses at the present day many features of almost unexampled interest. Nowhere in Europe, it is said, can such a collection of ancient jewellery and goldsmith's work be found as is presented by the relics treasured up in its monasteries; nowhere else can the peculiarities of the Byzantine school of painting be so advantageously studied; and some of the illuminated manuscripts are masterpieces of scriptorial art. With the single exception of Pompeii, the monastic buildings are the oldest specimens extant of domestic architecture; and within their walls the life of the Middle Ages is in constant course of reproduction, with all its manners and customs, its dress, and its modes of thought and belief, absolutely unchanged.

If Athos offers a delightful field of exploration to the traveller, it is with this exception,—he must visit it unaccompanied by wife, sister, mother, or children. St. Kevin was not more jealous of the presence of the "other sex" on his holy island, than the monks of their intrusion into the sacred shades of the peninsula. Not only, says Mr. Tozer, are women prevented from landing on its shores, but no cow, ewe, she-goat, sow, hen, or other creature of the forbidden sex, is, under any circumstances, admitted. "This restriction, absurd as it seems at first sight, is in reality a singular parallel to some of the ordinances of the Mosaic law—such, for instance, as those in Leviticus xix. 19, where garments of mixed linen and woollen texture are forbidden to be worn; the object in both cases being to enforce the main precept by keeping it before the minds of the people in a number of minor analogous cases." And it may be observed that the prohibition was justifiable on the grounds of policy; the presence of woman would have been incompatible with the peace and serenity of a monastic community. Even the Turkish governor, during the term of his residence, must forego the domestic pleasures of the harem. This officer, the representative of the Porte, and the only Mohammedan allowed to live here, is in reality of very little influence in the affairs of the monks, and his duties are chiefly limited to the collection of taxes. The defensive force of the district consists of about twenty-five Christian soldiers,—who are under the direction of the Holy

Synod, a federal representative body, to which each of the twenty monasteries sends a delegate (ἀντιπρόσωπος). The independence and privileges of Athos are of very ancient date. Shortly before the conquest of Constantinople, the monks of the peninsula agreed to submit to the rule of Mahomet II. on his guaranteeing them all the rights and liberties they then enjoyed; and this guarantee has been observed with much fidelity by the Turkish sultans.

The monasteries of Mount Athos now number twenty; or, as some authorities say, twenty-three. They are scattered all over the mountain, at a short distance from the sea. Eleven are situated on the eastern slope. Among the most ancient may be named those of Aghia-Labra, or the Holy Monastery; Vatopedi; Iveron; and Xilandari. Aghia-Labra occupies the summit of the Cape of Monte Santo, the *Akrothoon* of the ancients. This monastery, which now contains about four hundred monks, was founded by St. Athanasius early in the fourth century; and to this origin it owes a peculiar consideration—as, indeed, its designation indicates.

The convents on the western slope are all of later date, and consequently of inferior interest.

Between the two declivities, and on the culminating point of the mountain, stands the small church of the *Metamorphosis* (or *Transfiguration*). There are also a town and some small villages on the peninsula. Its metropolis, so to speak, is the town of Caryes, or "the Hazels," which occupies a central position, and is surrounded by groves of the trees from which it takes its name. It consists mainly of one long street, with open shops, forming a kind of bazaar; and is inhabited entirely by monks.

Mr. Tozer remarks that one of the greatest sources of interest in a visit to Athos consists in this,—that it exhibits in one view all the different phases of Eastern monastic life. First, we are introduced to the hermits, who, like St. Anthony, the first anchorite—though free from his peculiar temptation—dwell here in complete solitude, and practise the severest exclusion. In the καθίσματα, or retreats, we meet with small associations of monks, living together in retirement, and labouring together, on the communistic principle, like the early Christians: "And all that believed were together, and had all things common" (Acts ii. 44). Then, when several of these retreats are grouped round a central church, they compose a skete, or ἀσκητήριον, which in some cases differs from a monastery only in not possessing an independent constitution. And, finally, we find the regular monasteries; each with a corporate existence of its own, possessing land on the mountain, and the right of representation in the Synod. These must be subdivided into two classes: first, the *Cœnobite*, with one hegumen or warden, a common stock, and a common table; second, the *Idiorrhythrine*, in which "each man is a rule to himself," and the constitution is based on republican principles, the government being vested in the hands of two superiors, annually elected. Here the inmates usually take their meals in their own cells, and enjoy considerable freedom, both as to the disposal of their time and the accumulation of private means.

The Idiorrhythrine rule is, as Mr. Tozer remarks, a departure from the original form, and of comparatively recent introduction; and it is worthy of note that the majority of the monasteries on the eastern slopes have adopted this less rigorous system of discipline, while those in more secluded positions, under the rugged precipices of the western side, have, with only two exceptions, remained Cœnobite. The lands which these monasteries possess out of Athos lie partly in Macedonia, partly in the Ægean Islands, and still more largely in the Danubian principalities,—having been bestowed upon them in the old time by the Hospodars of Moldavia and Wallachia.

The number of monks on Mount Athos exceeds 3000. There is also a population of 3000 to 3500 $\kappa o \sigma \mu \iota \kappa o \iota$, or seculars; some of whom reside permanently in the convents as servants or labourers, but without taking monastic vows, while others accept engagements for a limited period. The number of monks in the separate monasteries varies from twenty-five to three hundred, but one hundred may be regarded as the average.

The following account of a visit to the Aghia-Labra is from a French source:—*

I set out from Athens, he says, accompanied by a dragoman, or interpreter. The wind was favourable, and we were soon far distant from the Piræus. The brig cast anchor off Cape Sunium,—the headland rendered classic by Falconer's poem of "The Shipwreck," and Byron's well-known description in "Childe Harold."

* M. Papety, in the "Revue des Deux Mondes."

The famous temple of Pallas Athene is situated on the summit of the promontory, which rises precipitously from the sea. Nine of the columns of the neos, or nave, are extant, while three others surround an angle of the façade which faces towards the east. These are of the Doric order, and constructed of gray marble. But it must have needed the "eagle eyes" of a Greek sailor to descry, as Pausanias assures us, at this distance of thirty-six miles, the lance of the statue of Pallas, which formerly dominated over the Athenian Acropolis.

We doubled the island of Andros and the extremity of Eubœa, whose rich vegetation forms a striking contrast to the barrenness of the scenery around it. Next day we came in sight of the isles of Ipsara and Scio, and also discovered the island of St. Estrata. The watchful vision of the seamen could now make out the cloud-like Athos. I recollect with pleasure the evenings I spent on the quarter-deck, in the midst of all this beautiful panorama of sea and land. The pilot, with much shuddering, related the story of the Vrakopoula, a kind of vampire, from which one can save oneself only by piercing him to the heart at midnight—that is, at the moment when he issues from his tomb. He told us also that in Milo, his native isle, every night might be seen three white phantoms, who fluttered along the shore, and spell-bound the belated fishermen. I felt myself thrown back to past ages on hearing him call those shadows *sirens*.

On the third day after our departure from Athens, we saw Mount Athos before us. We perceived its convents, like small white specks, or a girdle of detached forts.

Immediately on disembarking, I directed my steps towards a pathway almost covered with flowering hawthorns and carob-trees, which, after a quarter of an hour's climbing, conducted me to the convent of Aghia-Labra.

The convent-church is rich in the possession of one of the most complete and authentic specimens of the Byzantine school of painting. The cupola is entirely occupied with a colossal image of Christ, represented under the pure and majestic traits afterwards adopted by the artists of the Renaissance. His complexion, to use their expression, is *wheat colour* ("couleur de blé"). With one hand He points to the gospel, which, with the other, He holds to His heart. He has fair long hair, but the beard is black, and so are His eyebrows, which thus communicate to His half-closed eyes an expression both of power and tenderness. The painters of the Byzantine school proportioned the size of their figures to the importance of the rôle which they attributed to the personages represented; thus the saints increase in stature according as they are placed nearer and nearer to our Lord; while He himself so completely overtops them, that nothing but His bust is ever seen.

At the bottom of the cupola are erect figures of archangels, clothed in golden dalmatics, and holding great sceptres, surmounted by an image of Christ, in their hands. The brilliant colours of their costumes are "brought up" by the black background on which they are defined. Their attitude breathes a tranquil majesty. Above them may be perceived some small angels, who like pure spirits, seem, as they approach the Saviour throned in the centre, to disengage themselves more and more from the material. These angels borrow nothing from the human form but the head; the body is replaced by a greater or less number of wings. They might be described as flames floating in the azure of heaven, and it is in the midst of these asteroids that, on a ground of gold, the image of Christ, immense, and dominating the whole church, appears. Wherever one kneels in prayer, one kneels immediately in the eye of God.

The pendants represent the four evangelists writing to the dictation of an apostle. The remainder of the church is covered with subjects drawn from the Old and New Testaments. In the two arms of the cross are figured the saints of the Church Militant and those who protected the rising Christianity. They are all represented erect, and full front, having among them no bond of composition, and outlining themselves, as it were, upon a black ground. The same arrangement is noticeable in all the other convents; where, in conformity with the immutable rules of the Byzantine art, we find exactly the same subjects treated in exactly the same manner, and exactly the same personages in exactly the same attitudes.

Towards the lower end of the nave, on the left, a painting, accompanied by an almost illegible inscription, would seem to represent one of the French princes who carved out for themselves a domain in Greece on their return from the crusades. He wears the head-gear of the Merovingian kings, and a dalmatic which, as well as his crown, is ornamented with *fleurs de lis*. In his hands he holds the façade of a church, which probably he had erected at his own cost. In front of him stands his son, similarly attired.

Under the exterior portico are figured, in the attitude of prayer, the *ascetes*, or anchorites,—who, in imitation of the fathers of the desert, inhabit the mountain-caves, preserving the most absolute seclusion. These solitaries, reduced by excessive abstemiousness almost to the condition of skeletons, have no other clothing than a girdle of leaves. Their beard, pointed, descends to the ankle. By the side of these figures runs the inscription:—"Such was the life of the ascetics!" It is, in truth, the ideal of an ascetic life, which the artist has here set forth within his narrow limits. Art itself is for the hermits nothing more than the expression of that life, whose frightful austerity reflects itself in the paintings with which they embellish the various monasteries. These hermits also carve small wooden crosses, masterpieces of patience, which preserve to this day the character of their ancient frescoes.

By the monks of Aghia-Labra its very remarkable paintings are attributed to a monk named Manuel Pauselinos; but they do not know at what date he flourished. The figures are executed on fresco by small hatchings, so fine as to be invisible at a distance. The tones are very pale, and make no pretension to imitate or rival reality. The whole is rather coloured than painted.

I had to expedite my visit to other parts of the mountain, and a longer sojourn at Aghia-Labra would have taught me nothing. I therefore quitted the monastery. On the road to Caryes, I caught sight of several ruined towers. This tract of the mountain is finely wooded, and contains game in abundance; a useless luxury, for the monks never hunt. Beyond, we crossed a dilapidated bridge, and arrived at a hermitage, where new cenobites arrive daily, and where the scene is so agreeable as to seem destined, at some not distant date, for the site of a new convent.

Continuing my pilgrimage without halting at the convents of Caracallon and Philotheon, which are in no way remarkable, I arrived by abrupt paths at the convent of Iveron. The buildings composing it are grouped with more attention to order than those of the other monasteries. Access to the cloister is obtained by a single gate, which is closed every night, for fear of attack or surprise. On entering, we observe some booths where the religious sell the rudely-imprinted images they obtain from Caryes; various utensils fabricated in the convents; amulets of horn and copper—the former chiselled by a knife, the latter struck out by a wedge; monastic vestments, and tunics woven from bark tissues, imported from Constantinople; veils, likewise of Turkish manufacture, but embroidered by the monks with wonderful skill, and intended for the service of the altar.

Caryes is situated in the centre of Athos, and overlooks a wooded valley. The aspect of the town is that of a cluster of Turkish pleasure-houses. The twenty-three convents of Athos send each, to represent them in the protalion at Caryes, a senator or *epistate*, who is generally the ex-superior or *igoremenos* of the preceding year. To each senator is allotted a separate house.

His functions last but a twelvemonth. From these twenty-three representatives is annually chosen the head of the little republic. The great council administers the revenues of the convents, and inflicts the punishments incurred by the monks for transgressing the statutes. At Caryes also resides, as already stated, the Agha who represents the Turkish Government.

The appearance of Caryes is sufficiently curious. The town is divided into several streets almost entirely occupied by gloomy booths or shops, with very low fronts. The articles sold in these are imported from Salonika, and among them are found all kinds of utensils, carved in wood, and images of saints and Madonnas sculptured out of horn. A printing-press is one of the attractions of Caryes; it turns out a large number of rude engravings exclusively representing religious subjects, or views of convents, chiefly remarkable for not bearing the slightest resemblance to the places they are said to represent.

The total absence of women, common to all parts of Mount Athos, becomes more marked at Caryes by the movement of an agglomerated population, where one sees only *caloyers*, merchants, purchasers, vendors, promenaders. Caryes offers the spectacle, unique in Europe, of a town of monks exercising themselves in all the labours of civil life. At intervals in the streets the traveller comes upon wooden benches, occupied by monks and novices sitting cross-legged, and threading through their fingers their rosaries of mother-of-pearl.

I had visited the most interesting portions of Athos,

and nothing remained for me but to rejoin the commander of the *Argus*, who was waiting my return to set sail. A boat was sent to carry me to the part of the isthmus near which the brig was anchored. An incident which almost immediately followed on our departure, showed me that the population of Athos is not exclusively composed of pacific monks. We had embarked some hours, and were skirting the coast, when, towards midnight, we were silently accosted by a boat, the rowers of which attempted to board our own; the sight of our arms made them beat a retreat, and we got quit of them with a violent shock; a noise of oars indicating a rapid flight was the only reply vouchsafed to our indignant questions. Had our military equipment disconcerted a hostile project, or simply frightened away some curious visitors? I do not know, but the former hypothesis appears to me the more probable. Since the Mohammedan conquest, in fact, pirates have never ceased to infest these waters.

At sunrise we found ourselves near the narrowest part of the isthmus, where some traces of the canal excavated by Xerxes are still visible. I crossed the isthmus to the so-called "Gates of Cassandra," where we lighted a fire, the preconcerted signal. A boat came for us, and we steered towards Athens.

This visit to the monasteries of Mount Athos had enabled me to seize more accurately and clearly the different phases of the Byzantine school, and its real influence on the destinies of Art. Originating at a period when the human race, abandoning its exhausted traditions, sought to translate into the language of the past the new thoughts and feelings which were about to dictate the law of the future, the Byzantine school rendered to Christianity, and to the art which was its expression, the most eminent services. While the intellectual heritage of antiquity was at its disposal, the Byzantine artists adapted to their use all the elements they could borrow from it. Their art reached its apogee about the third century, and continued to flourish until the seventh; the protection of the Constantinopolitan emperors encouraged its progress and sustained its flight. Withering, in the centuries which followed, under the invasions of the barbarians, obscured and sophisticated in its technical portion during the long intellectual night into which Europe was plunged, this art nevertheless survived; and the school preserved these traditions which, transmitted at a later date to the Western nations, were, under more favourable circumstances, to receive so magnificent a development. This honour suffices to immortalize it; but there stopped the services it was able to render. The prolonged influence of this transitional art, confined to principles of dogmatic inflexibility, finished by suffocating—by crushing the life out of—the more elevated and perfect art which was called to replace it. There was wanting to the Byzantine school that principle, as indispensable to man's intellectual as to his moral development,—liberty. This principle our Christian art received from Italy, and thenceforth drew from it a marvellous vitality in the combination of every individual force and every spontaneous inspiration.

Thus far, M. Papety. But a few notes from Mr. Tozer's valuable narrative are essential to complete our sketch of Mount Athos and its monks.

The general features of the church attached to the Athos monasteries may be understood from a description of that of Iveron. Entering at the west end, we find ourselves in the proaulion or porch,—a corridor, externally supported by light pillars, and running the entire width of the building. Here are represented Apocalyptic scenes,—more particularly the punishment of the wicked; and in one place we may examine some pictures of the Œcumenical Councils—that of Nice being specially interesting. For observe: the great Athanasius figures as a young man stooping down to write the Creed, while Arius is seen between his two opponents, Spiridien and Nicholas, vigorously contending: to the right of this animated group a band of Arians, in philosopher's garb, are entering the council-chamber to recant their heresy, or are being driven into a prison by a man armed with a club.

Next we pass into the first narthex or antechapel, which contains representations of various forms of martyrdom; on either side of the entrance are figures of SS. Peter and Paul. In the second narthex are frescoes of saints and hermits, who frown from the walls in austere gloom. "These narthekes, which are divided by walls from one another and from the body of the church, seem originally," says Mr. Tozer, "to have been intended for catechumens and penitents, and must have been introduced into the monastic churches more for the sake of maintaining the usual type, than with a view to actual use: as it is, they are employed for the celebration of the more ordinary services; and when the body of the church is too small for the number of worshippers, they serve to provide additional room."

We now enter the main body of the church, which is in the form of a Greek cross, with a central cupola supported on four pillars, symbolical of the four Evangelists. At the east end and in the transepts are semi-cupolas; but the sanctuary is wholly concealed by the cionostase, —a wooden screen reaching nearly to the roof, and most elaborately carved and gilt, with pictures in carved settings of our Lord and saints. The position of two of these frescoes is always the same in every monastery: in the cupola, a colossal figure of the Saviour; and over the western entrance-door, the Repose (κοίμησις) of the Virgin. The walls elsewhere are blazoned with Scriptural subjects; and generally in one of the transepts may be seen a group of young warrior-saints, with St. George conspicuous among them. How singular the irony of fate, which has made this favourite hero of the Eastern monks the patron-saint of "merry England"!

A graceful brass coronal hangs from the drum of the cupola, and to this are suspended silver lamps, small Byzantine pictures, and ostrich eggs: these are symbolical of faith, in allusion to the curious but beautiful fable, embodied by Southey in his "Thalaba," that the ostrich hatches its eggs by gazing steadfastly at them. The floor is partially ornamented with *opus Alexandrinum*,—a kind of inlaid work, or mosaic, of white marble, porphyry, and *verd antique;* and at suitable places lecterns, elaborately enriched with mother-of-pearl and tortoise-shell, are erected. Around the sides are ranged the stalls, which are duly provided with *misereres*, though the monks mostly stand during the whole service.

Having completed our examination of the church, we return to the *proaulion*; where are two *semantra*, or instruments for summoning the brethren to prayers. One of these is a flat long board, narrow in the centre, so that it may be held by one hand while the other strikes it with a wooden mallet. The second is of iron, resembling a piece of the tire of a wheel; and this is operated upon with a hammer. At dead of night the monotonous sound of these strange rude instruments, summoning the caloyers to prayers, has a very peculiar and impressive effect.

Outside the west end of the church, a graceful cupola, supported on pillars, protects the stone basin in which is blessed the holy water used in the Epiphany ceremonies and other rites of the Greek Church. Opposite is the refectory (τράπεζα), a building in the form of a Latin cross. Along its interior walls are arranged small stone tables, one of which at the upper extremity is placed so as to form a high table. The pulpit, attached to the wall, stands at the angle where one of the transepts joins the nave: here, during meals, is read a homily. Most of the refectories are decorated with frescoes of saints along the side walls, and a representation of the Lord's Supper over the high table.

Over the entrance of the refectory rises a bell-tower, in the lower story of which has been constructed a new library. Among its contents is a curious Greek translation of Goldsmith's "History of Greece." Of the contents of the monastic libraries generally, a full and interesting description is given in Mr. Curzon's "Monasteries of the Levant."

The monks of Mount Athos are described as "pale grave men, with long beards and flowing hair, dressed in dark-blue serge gowns and high caps." Few of them are clergy; few, teachers or missionaries; while none are students or literati. Yet they realize the "primitive idea of monasticism" in a way in which it is nowhere else realized. When St. Anthony and his disciples retired to the Thebaid, it was not for the purpose of study or for the benefit of their fellow-men; but simply to withdraw themselves from the dangerous temptations of the world, and to devote their lives to religious exercises and spiritual meditation. This is the monastic ideal still favoured in the Eastern Church; and, accordingly, as in the days of St. Anthony no distinction of monastic orders existed, so here only one rule is followed, and that is the rule of St. Basil. The services of the Church consume six or seven hours of every week-day, and a still greater portion of the Sunday; which, in truth, is a startling exemplification of the Horatian phrase:—

"Partem solido demere de die."

On some of the greater festivals not less than from sixteen to twenty hours are devoted to religious exercises. The life of these enthusiasts is one of the strictest bodily mortification. They abstain wholly from meat in the

Cœnobite, and almost entirely in the Idiorrhythrine convents. Nearly half the year is spent as fast-days, when exhausted nature is scantily supported on a single meal of bread, vegetables, and water; and during the first three days of Lent, those whose constitutions can bear the strain go absolutely without food. Further: such a boon as a "sound night's rest" they never know, their slumber being broken in upon by the first services between one and two A.M. The remainder of the time not occupied in public prayer is spent by the superior in administering the affairs of the community, and by the lower monks in such menial duties as are exacted from them.

Mr. Tozer says that the most thoroughly monastic group he met with during his excursions, was in the small secluded Cœnobite monastery of Constamonita. Here, on his arrival, he was shown into the guest-chamber, a small and gloomy room, and cordially welcomed by the hegumon. While they were conversing, entered to them (as the old play-books say) a very old man, of so venerable appearance that the most indifferent person would instinctively have risen in his presence. Snowy white was his flowing beard; while his body was so frail and spare, that he looked like a resuscitation of one of the ancient hermits. The man who waited was not unworthy of the group: a tall, gaunt caloyer, with stern features, like those of a Covenanter. He spoke fervently of the protection afforded to them by the sacred relics, of the devoted lives of some of the hermits, and their prophetic power; of the need of mastering and keeping down the passions, in order to gain an insight into the higher spiritual mysteries,—until at length he resembled one inspired, and his utterance was confused and broken by his ardour. The sight of those three men together in the dark monastic chamber,—shut out from all the joys and innocent sanctities of domestic life,—was one not to be readily forgotten.

And now for a few last words. We ascend to the summit of the Holy Mountain, the narrow area of which is entirely occupied by a small chapel, dedicated to the Transfiguration. On the north side the rocks descend in tremendous precipices, while to the south lies a narrow platform of rock, a few feet wide, from which again the cliffs abruptly fall away. As our English traveller approached from the east, he caught the solemn tones of chanting from the sacred interior, and on coming round to the platform in front was rewarded with a singularly picturesque scene. The moonlight fell clearly and fully on the weird, ghostly figures of the monks, with their long dark beards and unshorn locks drooping over their sombre robes: some sat close to the window of the chapel, where service was being held; some lay about in groups, dimly perceptible in the heavy shadows, or outlined sharply against the white rocks.

"There were about sixty of them," writes our authority, "besides a number of Russian pilgrims. We were not less an object of wonder to them than they were to us. They even forgot the usual salutations. 'Where do you come from?' ($\dot{a}\pi\grave{o}$ $\pi o\hat{v}$ $\epsilon \hat{i}\sigma\theta\epsilon$) was all that they could say. We told them that we were Englishmen, and that we came from the Lavra [the nearest monastery]; on hearing which they brought us to the wood fire they had lighted, and made some coffee for us. In connection with the fire, the classical reader will remember that this peak was one of the stations of the fire-beacons which carried Agamemnon's telegram to Clytemnestra. At intervals, as we sat there, the priest came out, arrayed in gorgeous vestments, and swung the incense about us; until at last, as the vigil service lasted the whole night, I betook myself to a small crevice in the rock, where I slept, wrapped in my plaid, for a couple of hours; after which I lay awake, gazing up into the bright heaven, and feeling the strange sensation of being elevated on such a rocky pinnacle, with nothing but sea and sky around—*cœlum undique et undique pontus.*

"At dawn the service ceased, and the monks kissed one another, and were sprinkled with holy water. When the sun rose, the shadow of the peak was projected over sea and land to the west, in a distinctly-marked pyramid; but daylight added little to the view, as the greater part of the peninsulas of Athos and Sithonia had been visible during the night, and the distance was hazy. Eight of the monasteries, however, could be distinguished, and the expanse of sea was an extraordinary sight. On a clear day, both Ida and Olympus may be seen. Half an hour after sunrise, the Eucharistic service—the Liturgy, as it is called—commenced; and at its conclusion a bunch of grapes was brought in and blessed—this being the first day on which they are allowed to be eaten. Then they descended the mountain by the zigzag path in companies, singing psalms; and, after breakfasting on the grass by the Chapel of the Virgin, we dispersed to our several destinations."

An old tradition relates that before the birth of Christ a heathen image—perhaps an altar to Zeus—had existed on the summit, but was destroyed by St. Athanasius. Another makes it the scene of our Lord's temptation. And a third, of modern date, declares that just prior to the Greek Revolution in 1821, a luminous cross was seen here by the monks, with the historic words,—" In this conquer."

VIII.

Mount Etna.

> " 'Tis the last
> Of all the woody, high, well-watered dells
> On Etna; and the beam
> Of noon is broken there by chestnut-boughs
> Down its steep verdant sides; the air
> Is freshened by the leaping stream, which throws
> Eternal showers of spray on the mossed roots
> Of trees, and veins of turf, and long dark shoots
> Of ivy-plants, and fragrant hanging bells
> Of hyacinths, and on late anemones,
> That muffle its wet banks; but glade,
> And stream, and sward, and chestnut-trees
> End here; Etna beyond, in the broad glare
> Of the hot noon, without a shade,
> Slope behind slope, up to the peak, lies bare:
> The peak, round which the white clouds play."
> MATTHEW ARNOLD.

MOUNT ETNA, one of the most remarkable of the European volcanoes, is situated on the east coast of the island of Sicily, between Taormina (the ancient Tauromenium) and Catania (the ancient Catana). Its elevation above the sea, into which it strikes its roots, is 10,874 feet, though liable to some changes after eruptions. A highroad winds round its lower slopes with a total circuit of 93 miles; but if we take the sea, and the rivers Simeto and Cantara, as defining its natural boundaries, we must reckon its total circumference at 120 miles; and even this limit will not include the whole of the district over which it pours its lava-floods. Its Greek name is probably derived from Αἴθω; its modern Sicilian designation, Mongibello, from the Latin *Mons* and the Arabic *Gibel*—both words signifying "mountain," and the compound being intended to indicate pre-eminence,—the "mountain of mountains," which Etna assuredly is, so far as the Mediterranean basin is concerned.

The ascent of Mount Etna is peculiarly interesting, because it conducts the traveller through three distinct zones of climate and vegetation, which graduate, so to speak, from the semi-Oriental to the Alpine. The lowest of these zones is named *Piedimontana*, in allusion to its position, and *Colta*, as descriptive of its fertility. It stretches up the acclivities of the mountain to a distance varying from two miles on the north, to ten or eleven miles on the south. Its soil, consisting of decomposed volcanic matter, yields abundant harvests of corn, and wine, and fruit. The air is soft and bland; the winds breathe warmly, as if influenced by the subterranean fires; the slopes laugh with flowers, and are decked with groves of chestnuts and Oriental planes; orchards and vineyards seem to yield their treasures almost spontaneously; while the landscape everywhere echoes with the music and brightens with the sunshine of copious streams. Villages and convents are numerous: the former are reckoned at sixty-five, with a population of 300,000; and their condition generally appears peaceful and prosperous.

Every picture, however, must have its shade; and

MOUNT ETNA, FROM TAORMINA

here, as in other parts of Etna, the slopes are furrowed by the black channels of ancient lava-streams, bearing significant witness to the terrible power of the subterranean fires, and conveying to the mountaineers a warning of possible calamity which they regard with supreme indifference.

From the Piedimontana we pass into the *Regione Nemorosa,* or *Selvosa,* or *Il Bosco,*—the wooded region, or forest,—the characteristics of which have been described with so much accuracy and beauty in Mr. Matthew Arnold's poem, "Empedocles on Etna." The botanical aspects of the forest differ, however, in different districts. At Bronte, pines of goodly stature abound. At Paternò, the oak, the beech, the ilex, and the fragrant lime. Poplars mingle with the oaks and pines near Matello; while hawthorn and cork-trees, fir, beech, and oak intermingle their shades in the district extending from Nicolosi to Zaffarana. Between Mascali and Piraino, a "woody tract" known as the Carpinetto, groves of oak-trees and of immense chestnuts afford a delightful shelter to numerous flocks and herds. Here is found that botanical marvel, the "Castagno di Cento Cavalli," which can receive a hundred horsemen beneath its leafy canopy. The scenery of this region is rich in picturesque effects, which recall the old poetic descriptions of the classic Arcady. It is diversified by occasional cones, the craters of extinct volcanoes; some of which are still bare and rugged; but most rejoice in the adornment of luxuriant groves. The forest recesses are the home of game and wild animals of almost every description: the wild boar, the roebuck, the fox, the badger, the porcupine, wild cats, weasels, ferrets, the eagle, the falcon, the partridge, and a host of song-birds. And here, too, the Etnean flora, which includes 477 species, may be examined in all its beauty.

We pass on to the Desert Region, *Il Diserta, Netta,* or *Discoperta*, the upper part of which is fitly called the "Abode of Snow." It begins at an elevation of about 6279 feet. At first the traveller meets with a few stunted plants and lichens, as in the frozen wastes of Greenland; but soon he leaves even these scanty traces of vegetation behind him, and climbs a dead ascent of ashes, scoriæ, and lava to the great cone, itself some 1100 feet in height, which incessantly pours forth a cloud of sulphureous vapour. From June to October this region is bare and black; but during the rest of the year Nature conceals its desolation with a thick mantle of snow. The air is chill and piercing, and the eye nowhere lights on a sign of life or motion. Even the eagle does not mount to a solitude so inhospitable; and it is wholly abandoned to the discordant voices of the thunder and the storm.

We must not omit to allude to what Sir Charles Lyell has aptly and justly called the grandest and most original feature in the physiognomy of this remarkable mountain—namely, the number of comparatively small cones scattered over its declivities, especially in the Regione Nemorosa. These, in relation to the colossal bulk of Etna, are like the protuberances on the rind of an orange; but in the levels of Lincolnshire they would

THE CASTAGNO DI CENTO CAVALLI.

THE VAL DEL BOVE.

pass for lofty hills. About eighty of these minor volcanoes are found at different parts; cones of eruption, with rent and broken craters, which now in general form the most romantic wooded basins imaginable, but in some instances retain their original ruggedness and naked desolation. On the western and northern slopes lie fifty-two, and on the eastern twenty-seven. Monte Minardo, near Bronte, is upwards of 700 feet in height; Monti Rossi, near Nicolosi, a double cone, is 450 feet high, and two miles in circumference at the base.

Another remarkable feature of Etna is the great depression on the eastern side, known as the *Val del Bove*, which may be reached either from Aio Reale or Catania. Commencing near the summit of the volcano, it cuts right through the Wooded Region, in a vast circular chasm from 3000 to 4000 feet deep, until it touches the edge of the Piedimontana, or cultivated zone, near the coast. On one side it is prolonged by another and narrower valley, the Val di Calanna; which opens into a third ravine, the Val di San Giacomo, extending to a point near the village of Zaffarana. Everywhere it is surrounded by precipices of lava, tuffa, or breccia, traversed by vertical dikes of blue basalt or trachyte, and diminishing in height from 4000 feet to 1000 feet. A description of this chasm has been attempted by almost every traveller, but none is more faithful or eloquent than that of the late eminent geologist, Sir Charles Lyell.

Let the reader picture to himself, he says, a large amphitheatre, five miles in diameter, with precipices surrounding it on three sides. The plain thus enclosed has been flooded by repeated streams of lava; and though apparently level, when seen from a distance, is even more rugged in reality than the surface of a billowy sea. Further: in one part the valley is broken up by a ridge of rocks; two of which, Mersara and Capra, are very prominent. They are of gigantic dimensions, and from many points seem almost isolated. The face of the surrounding precipices is picturesquely diversified by vertical dikes of lava, which usually stand out in relief like bold cliffs, are very various in outline, and of immense altitude. In the autumn their black forms may often be seen relieved by clouds of fleecy vapour which settle behind them, and do not disperse until mid-day; so that they fill the valley with pearly mists, while the sunlight is pouring on every other part of Sicily, and on the higher regions of Etna. The desolation of the scene is enhanced, rather than mitigated, by the strips of green herbage and forest-land which here and there contrast with the black, hard lava-tracts that have failed to overspread them. A profound silence prevails; for no torrents dash from the sterile rocks, no "musical lapses" of waterfalls fill the echoes of the valley. Every drop of rain from the heavens, every drop of moisture from the melting ice and snow, is instantly absorbed by the porous lava; and the dearth of springs is so great that the herdsman is compelled to supply his flocks, during the hot season, from stores of snow laid up in the hollows of the mountain during winter.

The scenery is so stern in character, so severe in its

grandeur, that no poet would ever select it for a valley of enchantment. It would accord far better with one of Dante's circles in the "Inferno," or that well-known picture of the nether world so powerfully painted by Milton. If, as Sir Charles Lyell says, we can imagine ourselves spectators, in the night's deep darkness, of one of those fiery currents which have so often traversed the great valley, we may easily recall

> "Yon dreary plain, forlorn and wild,
> The seat of desolation, void of light,
> Save what the glimmering of these livid flames
> Casts pale and dreadful."

The circular form of the Val del Bove, and its vertical dikes of lava, reminding the spectator, only on a gigantic scale, of the Atrio del Cavallo, on Vesuvius, points to its former existence as a vast crater; and Sir Charles Lyell recognizes the existence at some remote period of a double axis, or two points of permanent eruption, to Etna, with a "saddle" or intercolline area between them. These may either have been contemporaneous, like Kilauea and the summit crater of Mauna Loa, in Hawaii; or successive, like Somma and Vesuvius. The one is represented by the present cone, Mongibello; the other, by that of Trifoglietto, in the Val del Bove, about three miles to the south-east of the former, which has attained a complete ascendency, and continues in full vigour. The expansion of the Val del Bove to its present size, and the removal of the matter which formed the Trifoglietto cone, Sir Charles Lyell attributes partly to the subsidence of the ground, partly to the effects of aqueous erosion, and partly to lateral and paroxysmal explosions unaccompanied by any outburst of lava.

ASCENT OF MOUNT ETNA.

The ascent of the mountain is generally undertaken from Catania, which is about 29 miles from the summit. A carriage-road proceeds to Nicolosi (12 miles); thence, in summer, mules will carry the traveller to the Casa degli Inglesi, at the foot of the cone; in winter, to the Grotta delle Capre only, 8 miles from Nicolosi, in the upper part of the Wooded Region. From the Casa degli Inglesi to the summit, 2 miles, the traveller must be content to foot it.

It is customary to start from Catania soon after noon, in order to be in time for sunrise on the summit; this "effect" being the great attraction of the ascent. In about four hours the traveller drives to Nicolosi, whence he may make a short excursion to Monti Rossi, the twin-cones formed by the eruption of 1669. At ten P.M. he will push forward to the Casa degli Inglesi, where he will pass the night. Then he will ascend to the summit, view the sunrise, pay a visit to the Torre del Filosofo, and catch a glimpse of the yawning chasm of the Val del Bove; after which he will return to Nicolosi, and, by such stages as he thinks proper, to Catania. So much for "generals;" now for "particulars."

On leaving Catania we begin at once to ascend, passing through a landscape which presents a strange combination of the attractive and displeasing. The villages are surrounded by "purple orchards;" the wayside cottages peep out smilingly through a screen-work of trellised vines; corn-fields wave with golden crops on either hand; and delicious odours come from the depths of groves of almond, orange, and olive trees. But these delightful features are painfully contrasted by tracts of black and hideous lava, often overhanging the road in low precipices, often traversing the fields in huge barren dikes. With these significant memorials of a terrible past before his eyes, the traveller finds it difficult to enjoy the prosperity of the present, which seems to him darkened by the shadow of a possibly disastrous future, for he knows that the volcanic fires have lost nothing of their fatal force.

He passes successively through the villages of Pasquale, and Gravina, which is near the Monti Rossi, and Mascalucia, which may almost be called a town,—enjoying, as he ascends, some glorious prospects of the island-scenery, with glimpses of azure sea beyond. Between Torre di Grifo and Nicolosi, however, the scene changes, and the radiant landscape is replaced by a dreary expanse of lava and scoriæ, which clumps of dwarf oaks and broom do but little to relieve. This expanse marks the course of the lava-flood of 1537, which, poured out of the Monti Castellani, in the Bosco of Paternò, divided into two branches, flowing, the one to Torre di Grifo and the other to Borello.

Nicolosi is "a frightful assemblage of low huts," at an elevation of 2264 feet above the sea. In a place where terrible earthquakes are of frequent occurrence, architecture cannot be expected to flourish; and the "low huts" of Nicolosi are rudely built up of lava and scoriæ. A little to the north is situated the vine-embowered convent of S. Nicola dell' Arma, now used as a hospice, but retaining the character originally given to it when founded by Simone Count di Policastro in 1156. In its vicinity rise the finely-wooded and romantic cones of Serrapizzuta and Santo Nicola.

We now cross the boundary of the cultivated region, and enter the dells and glades, cool and leafy and well-watered, of the forest zone. This may be defined as beginning at the Casa di Rinazzi, about four miles from Nicolosi. Traversing the ferny growth and turfen slopes, we reach, at eight miles from Nicolosi, the Casa del Bosco, 6233 feet above the sea, and on the verge of the open or Desert Region. Here, on the left, rises the cone of Monte Vittoria; on the right, that of Monte Nero; and near at hand is the natural rocky arch of the Grotta del Capre.

The difficult part of the ascent now begins, and for nine miles the way lies over rugged lava or loose shifting ashes, seldom brightened by any considerable patches of vegetation. A pile of lava-blocks marks the mid-point between the Bosco and the summit; and to the right stretches the long rude volcanic ridge of Montagnuola; thrusting its roots down into the Val del Bove on the east. We pause for breath on the narrow area, comparatively level, of the Piana del Lago, so called in memory of a small lake filled with lava by the eruption of 1607; and then betake ourselves to the welcome shelter of the Casa degli Inglesi,—a lava-built hut,

MOUNT ETNA.

erected by the English officers stationed in Sicily in 1811. An inscription over the door reads thus:— "Ætnam perlustrantibus has ædes Britanni in Sicilia, 1811." The altitude of this small but substantial asylum is 9592 feet above the sea, and the surrounding atmosphere is Arctic in its rigour.

Here we abandon our mules, and trust to our physical energies to carry us up the steep summit-cone which rises so boldly and abruptly out of a "rugged sea of lava and scoriæ." The base of the cone is at an elevation of 9760 feet, and the summit at an elevation of 10,874 feet.

"The lower part of the cone," says Mr. Dennis, "composed of ashes intermingled with blocks of lava, is comparatively easy to mount; it is when the lava ceases, and you enter on the mass of sulphur, ash, and fine dust, sprinkled with *lapilli*, which forms the upper part, that the great difficulty begins. In no case is it easy to climb a steep which rises at an angle of 45° or more, but here the difficulty is greatly increased by the looseness of the ash, which yields beneath the feet at every step, so that you often lose ground in the attempt to advance; and by the hot vapour charged with hydrochloric acid which gushes from the sides of the cone, blinding the eyes, disgusting the nose and palate, almost suffocating the lungs, already sufficiently oppressed by the rarefaction of the atmosphere, and disturbing the stomach sometimes to the extent of inducing sickness. Happy is he who to these difficulties has not to add that of a strong wind; to contend with which, under these circumstances, is a severe trial of strength. After resting a while on the summit the disagreeable sensations wear off, and the mind is left to the full enjoyment of the glorious scene around and beneath." As Mr. Arnold says,—

> "Through the black, rushing smoke-bursts
> Thick breaks the red flame ;
> All Etna heaves fiercely
> Her forest-clothed frame.

On reaching the summit our attention is necessarily attracted, in the first place, by the yawning depths of the crater, with its ever-rolling clouds of vapour and smoke, sometimes of a snowy whiteness, sometimes lurid and ghastly, sometimes kindled into brilliancy by the jets of fire and flame. The sides are rugged and uneven, and of as many colours as the rainbow, owing to their incrustations of ammonia, vitriolic salts, and sulphur; but a glowing orange predominates. Such considerable changes are yearly effected through the force of the subterranean action, that an accurate description of the size and aspect of the crater is impossible. In one day its circuit has been enlarged from three miles to six; but its ordinary measurement is two and a half miles. Let the reader conceive of this huge abyssmal pit as filled with wreathing clouds of sulphurous vapour; or sometimes, as in 1839, when it was visited by Mr. Gladstone, with seething lava.

Having satisfied our curiosity with a prolonged examination of the crater, we may spare a glance to the sunrise, as its flush of dawn comes up from the Ionian Sea, and touches isles, and capes, and peaks with an unearthly light. Then we see that the mountain defines itself on the panorama of the island-plain in a pyramidal purple shadow, and also reflects itself in a diminished but perfect image on the mists of the western horizon. At times, the sun, instead of soaring *above* the ocean's rim, seems to emerge from the waters beneath it, and upwards and upwards to force its way through the liquid mass, until its full-orbed glory fills the radiant sky.

The view from the summit of Mount Etna is necessarily very extensive, and it is not less diversified. It includes every characteristic of a striking landscape; the sublime, the picturesque, the softly beautiful. Rising from the plain in undisputed prominence, without a neighbouring peak to question its grandeur, Etna looks forth, as it were, from its lofty pinnacle over a subject world, and sees woods and plains, cities and villages, rivers and seas, lying at her feet. Not only the whole of Sicily, but the Mediterranean and the Italian shores are within the gorgeous panorama, which, from morn to night, kindles with a succession of glorious colours. To the east the spectator's gaze wanders along the range of the Corleone heights, and catches the wreath of vapours which encircles the brow of Mount Eryx, formerly celebrated for its Temple of Venus, "Erycina ridens." Beyond this limit extends the shining sea on every side, as if to enclose and preserve this glorious picture of nature. To the west rise the mountains of Palermo; and to the north lie in the tranquil haze Milazzo and the islands of Lipari, and the black volcanic pyramid of Stromboli; while the eye marks every undulation of the soil, and every break and curve in the coast-line along the Straits of Messina and the rugged shores of Calabria. To the south it lingers over Augusta, and the historic Syracuse, and the headland of the ancient Pachynus, now Cape Passaro; and finally endeavours to pierce the clouds that rest in luminous folds upon the ruins of Agrigentum and the modern town of Girgenti.

Admiral Smyth has estimated the radius of vision from the summit at 150 miles; hence the circumference must amount to about 937. But when the horizon is clear the spectator can detect Malta, at a distance of 130 miles; and even Monte S. Giuliano, and the Ægadian Isles, at a distance of 160 miles; and the Marquis of Ormonde asserts that he saw the glow and shimmer of the Gulf of Taranto, and the dark outline of the mountains of the Terra di Lecce, which are fully 245 miles off!

Mr. Dennis remarks that Etna itself, when viewed from its crest, presents a very interesting and impressive appearance. The snow-wreaths, according to the season, stretch to a greater or less distance down the slopes, sometimes shrouding the whole Desert Region in their white pall, and descending even into the woods beneath; sometimes, as in summer, lying only about the base of the cone. The belt of forest girdles the volcano with verdure, out of which rise the wooded cones in picturesque confusion; while streams of lava strike across it in every direction, like black roads, "the highways of destruction to the country beneath." But the grandest view in all this panorama is where, on the east, lies the awful chasm of the Val del Bove, with clouds of smoke issuing from its still active cones.

Mr. Gladstone, who ascended the mountain in 1839, has left on record a descriptive narrative, from which we borrow the following passage:—

To ascend the highest peak, he says, our choice lay between a precipice and a corner of a crater. We went over the lava in a very warm atmosphere; sometimes, on passing a rift, too hot for a moment or two to breathe. We got upon the back of the peak, and worked up through the sulphur-clouds, which here alone were seriously disagreeable. We here gazed upon the eastern view, embracing the Messina mountains and the fine kindred outline of the Calabrian coast, as described by Virgil:—

> " Haec loca, vi quondam et vasta convulsa ruina,
> (Tantum aevi longinqua valet mutare vetustas)
> Dissiluisse ferunt, cum protenus utraque tellus
> Una foret; venit medio vi pontus, et undis
> Hesperium Siculo latus abscidit, arvaque et urbes
> Litore diductas angusto interluit aestu."
> *Aeneid*, iii. 414.

From thence it stretched all along the southern coast to Cape Passaro. But our chief object from this point was the crater of the opposite side, into which, having now reached a position higher than any part of it, we had a considerable insight. We enjoyed keenly our full clear sight of the volcanic action, and even at the moment I could not help being struck with the remarkable accuracy of Virgil's account. The great features of this action are the sharp and loud clap which perceptibly shook from time to time the ground of the mountain under our feet; the sheet of flame, which leapt up with a sudden momentary blast, and soon disappeared in smoke; then the shower of red-hot stones and lava. At this time, as we found on our way down, lava masses of 150 or 200 lbs. weight were being thrown to a distance of probably a mile and a half; smaller ones we found even more remote. These showers were most copious, and often came in the most rapid succession. Even while we were ascending the exterior of the cone, we saw them alighting on its slope, and sometimes bounding down with immense rapidity within perhaps some thirty or forty yards of our rickety footing on the mountain-side. They dispersed like the sparks of a rocket; they lay, beneath the snow, over the mountain, thicker than even the stars in heaven; the larger ones ascended as it were with deliberation, and then descended first with speed and then with fury. Now they passed even over our heads, and we could pick up some newly fallen, and almost intolerably hot. Lastly, there was the black gray column, which seemed smoke, and was really ash, and which was shot from time to time out of the very bowels of the crater, far above its edge, in regular unbroken form.

IX.

Mont Blanc.

"Mont Blanc is the monarch of mountains,
They crowned him long ago."
BYRON.

THE Alps form the most important European mountain-system, and contain the loftiest peaks. They strike across the north of Italy, from the shore of the Mediterranean, and extend to the borders of Hungary. Geographers divide them into distinct groups or masses, to which distinct names are attached. Thus, from the borders of the Gulf of Genoa to Monte Viso, along a line of about 100 miles, stretch the so-called Maritime Alps; from Monte Viso to Mont Cenis, about 60 miles, the Cottian Alps; from Mont Cenis to the Col de Bonhomme, about 50 miles, the Graian or Graiæn Alps; the Pennine run from the Col to Monte Rosa, 60 miles; the Helvetian, from thence to Mont Bernardine, 50 miles; from Mont Bernardine to the Drey-Herren-Spitz, or Three Lords' Peak, in the Tyrol, 140 miles, the Rhætian; and from thence to the neighbourhood of Vienna, about 200 miles, the

Noric Alps. Those lower ranges which lie in the Austrian provinces of Carinthia, Carniola, and Dalmatia, and connect the Alpine system proper with the ranges of the Balkan, are respectively designated the Carnic, Julian, and Dinaric Alps.

The loftiest heights and the most extensive glaciers are found in the Pennine group,—which includes Mont Blanc, 15,750 feet; Monte Rosa, 15,152 feet; and the Matterhorn, 14,837 feet.

Next come the Helvetian, which send their roots far down into the heart of Switzerland, and include the Grabenhorn, 15,440 feet; the Finsteraarhorn, 14,111 feet; and the Jungfrau, 13,718 feet.

The highest passes practicable for pedestrians are the Col de Géant, 11,172 feet, and the Mont Cervin, 11,096 feet, both in the Pennine group. Four carriage-roads cross the Helvetian, and two the Rhætian chain; one of which, through the Stelvio Pass, 9174 feet, is the highest carriage-road in Europe. A railway now crosses the Graian Alps, by means of a tunnel through Mont Cenis.

The culminating summit of the Alps is Mont Blanc, which,—

> "On a throne of rocks, in a robe of clouds,
> With a diadem of snow,"—

has long reigned supreme among European mountains. Its position is remarkable, for it is almost equidistant between the Pole and the Equator. A huge pyramidal mass, elongated from north to south so that it resembles the hump of a dromedary, girt round with soaring *aiguilles* or pinnacles, furrowed by enormous glaciers, and shrouded perpetually in ice and snow, it presents a remarkably majestic aspect, and impresses the spectator with a wonderful feeling of sublimity and power. Hence it has long exercised a strange fascination over the minds of men, and its ascent has become one of those enterprises which offer a peculiar attraction to the adventurous. Its summit was first reached by Paccard and Jacques Balmat in August 1785; in the following year it was attained by De Saussure, who made some interesting scientific experiments. Since that time ascents have entered into the ordinary holiday programme of the bolder class of tourists; though the undertaking is one which requires considerable strength, endurance, and resolution, and the direction of efficient guides. Several ladies have accomplished it, however: among others, Mademoiselle Paradis, 1809; Mademoiselle d'Angeville, 1838; Mrs. Hamilton, 1854; Mademoiselle Formaren, 1856; Miss Walker, 1862. The ascent and descent usually occupy the best part of three days; but in 1875, a Mr. C. H. Taylor, of Chicago, achieved the task in a little over eighteen hours. He started about 12.30 A.M. on Tuesday, July 27th, and returned to his hotel before 8 P.M. on the following evening. He was accompanied by only two guides, a Swiss and a German. A famous dog, named Tschingel, after the first glacier, had succeeded in the attempt in the previous week,— having started on Thursday the 22nd, in the company of his master, Mr. W. A. Coolidge, and his master's aunt, Miss

Brevoort, reached the summit on Saturday, and descended in the course of the same day. Tschingel deserves special commemoration in a volume devoted to Mountain-Climbing, for he has ascended Mont Blanc half a hundred times, as well as the Jungfrau, and numerous lesser peaks.

The ascents of Mont Blanc have not always been made from a thirst for adventure or to gratify a commonplace curiosity, but in the highest interests of science; and to those accomplished by Saussure, Agassiz, Forbes, Tyndall, and Charles Martins, we are indebted for much of our knowledge of glaciers and glacial phenomena. In the annals of Science no mountain occupies a more distinguished place; while it has furnished the artist with inexhaustible sources of inspiration.

The story of these ascents, however, has been so often told, that it is impossible to enliven it with any novel interest, and we should gladly have omitted it from these pages, had we not felt unwilling to incur the reproach of placing *Hamlet* before the reader with the part of "Hamlet" omitted. It must be confessed that a book on Mountains and Mountain-Climbing, which took no special notice of the monarch of the European peaks, would be open to severe criticism. Yet, for the reason we have given, we shall confine ourselves to a narration of only two or three of the more remarkable and interesting episodes in its annals.

We begin with the ascent by M. de Saussure in 1787; and we shall allow that courageous man of science to tell his own story:—

On my way to Chamounix, he says, in the early part

MONT BLANC, FROM MONT BUET.

of July, I met at Sallenche the courageous Jacques Balmat, who was bound for Geneva to inform me of his recent success,—he had ascended to the top of the mountain with two other guides. It was raining when I reached Chamounix, and bad weather continued for four weeks. But I was determined to wait until the end of the season rather than miss the favourable moment.

At length this long-desired opportunity arrived, and I started on the 1st of August 1787; accompanied by a servant, and by eighteen guides, who carried our scientific instruments and all the apparatus of which I had need. My eldest son ardently desired to go with me, but I feared that he was not strong enough, nor sufficiently accustomed to this kind of labour. I begged him, therefore, to abandon his intention; and he remained at Prieuré, where he made with much care similar observations to those which I was making on the summit.

In order to feel perfectly free in my selection of places where to pass the nights, I took with me a tent; and on the first evening I reposed under its canvas roof on the summit of the peak of La Côte. This part of the journey is without difficulty and danger; we are always upon turf or rock, and it is accomplished easily in five or six hours. But from thence to the summit the route lies wholly over ice or snow.

The second day's march is not the easiest. You must first cross the glacier of La Côte, to gain the foot of a small chain of rocks which lie embedded in the snows of Mont Blanc. This glacier is both difficult and dangerous. It is intersected by broad, deep, irregular crevasses; and often you can traverse these only upon bridges of snow, which are sometimes very slight, and suspended over formidable abysses. One of my guides nearly perished here. The day before, in company with two others, he had gone to reconnoitre the route; fortunately they had taken the precaution of tying themselves together with ropes: the snow gave way beneath him in the middle of a broad deep crevasse, and he remained suspended between his two comrades. We passed very near the opening which had formed under him, and shuddered at the sight of the peril he had incurred. So difficult and so tortuous is the passage of this glacier, that we spent three hours in climbing from the top of the Côte to the foremost rocks of the isolated chain, though the distance, as the crow flies, does not exceed a quarter of a league.

After reaching these rocks, we kept away from them at first, in order to mount by a winding path to a snow-loaded valley, which runs from north to south to the foot of the loftiest summit. The snow was cut at intervals by enormous and superb crevasses, the sharp clean section of which showed the snow arranged in horizontal layers, each layer representing a year's formation. However wide the crevasses, you can nowhere discover their bottom.

My guides were fain to have spent the night near one of the rocks which we fell in with on this route; but as the loftiest were still from 3600 to 4200 feet below the summit, I wished to ascend to a higher point. For this purpose, it was imperative that we should encamp in the middle of the snows; but I had much difficulty in reconciling my companions to such a course. They imagined that during the night an absolutely unendurable degree of cold prevailed in the upper regions of the snow, and seriously feared lest they should perish there. At length I told them that, for myself, I was determined to go forward with those companions on whom 1 could rely; that we would dig deeply in the snow, and cover the excavation with the canvas of the tent; beneath which we would all ensconce ourselves, and we should not suffer from the cold, however rigorous it might prove. This arrangement reassured them, and we pushed ahead. At four o'clock in the evening we reached the second of the three great table-lands of snow we had to traverse. And there we encamped, at an elevation of 8750 feet above Prieuré, and 11,970 feet above the sea, or 540 feet higher than the Peak of Teneriffe. We did not proceed to the final plateau, because it lies open to the avalanches; and the first plateau, by which we had just crossed, is not exempt from this danger. We had traversed two of these avalanches, which had fallen since Balmat's last journey, and covered the valley throughout its extent with wreck and ruin.

My guides at once set to work to excavate a place which might form our quarters for the night; but they quickly felt the rarefaction of the air. Robust as they were—men to whom the seven or eight hours' marching they had just accomplished was as nothing—scarcely had they thrown out five or six spadefuls of snow before they were compelled to abandon the task; it was necessary to relieve one another every minute.

A guide who had gone back a short distance to procure some water from a crevasse we had noticed in passing, was taken ill as he went, returned without the water, and spent the evening in severe agony. Even I myself, accustomed as I was to the mountain-air,—who feel better in it than in the air of the plains,—was exhausted with the fatigue of preparing my meteorological instruments. Our physical uneasiness filled us with a burning thirst, and yet we could obtain a little water only by melting some snow; for the water we had seen in our ascent proved to be frozen when we returned to it, and the small charcoal chafing-dish we carried with us did but satisfy very slowly twenty thirsty persons.

From the middle of this plateau, enclosed between the topmost peak of Mont Blanc to the south, its lofty eastern terraces and the dome of the Goûté on the west, we could see nothing but snow; snow spotlessly pure, of a dazzling whiteness, and on the higher summits forming a very singular contrast with the intensely blue, nay, the purple-black sky of these elevated regions. No living being was visible, no appearance of vegetation; it is the abode of cold and silence. When I pictured to myself Dr. Paccard and Jacques Balmat first arriving at close of day in these dreary deserts, without shelter, without succour, without knowing even whether men could easily exist in the localities to which they directed their steps, and yet persevering in their intrepid enterprise, I could not but admire their strength of mind and courage.

My guides, constantly preoccupied with fear of the cold, closed so carefully every chink and crevice of our tent that I suffered greatly from the heat and from the air corrupted by our breath. In order to breathe freely, I was compelled to go out into the night. The moon shone with the greatest splendour in the midst of a sky as black as ebony. Jupiter, all radiant, emerged from behind the loftiest peak to the east of Mont Blanc; and the light reverberated from all this vast amphitheatre of snow was so dazzling, that I could distinguish only stars of the first and second magnitude. At length we began to sleep; when we were awakened by the crash of a great avalanche which covered a part of the slope we had ascended the day before. At dawn the thermometer marked 3° below freezing-point.

We did not start until late, as we had first to melt the snow for our breakfast and for our refreshment on the march. It was drunk up as fast as it was melted; and my guides, while scrupulously respecting the wine I had given them to carry, were continually stealing the water I had set apart for future consumption.

We began by ascending to the third and last plateau; then we diverged to the left in order to gain the loftiest rock lying east of the topmost peak. The acclivity is exceedingly abrupt,—as much as 39° in some places; everywhere it abuts upon precipices; and so hard was the surface of the snow, that those who went in advance could not steady their steps until they had broken it with a hatchet. We spent two toilsome hours in climbing this acclivity, which measured about 1500 feet in height. Having reached the summit-crag, we turned to the right,—that is, to the westward,—in order to ascend the final incline, the perpendicular height of which was nearly 900 feet. This incline was only at an angle of 28° to 29°, and offered no danger; but owing to the excessive rarefaction of the air, a man's strength is very readily exhausted. Near the summit, I had to stop to take breath at every fifteen or sixteen steps. At intervals, indeed, I experienced a weakness which compelled me to sit down; but always as my respiration recovered itself my physical energies revived; and, on resuming my march, I felt for the moment as if I could dart like an arrow to the very crest of the mountain. The guides, in proportion to their strength, were in the same condition; some better, some worse. Hence, it took us two hours to climb from the last rock to the summit; and when we arrived there it was eleven o'clock.

M. de Saussure's first looks and thoughts, in the moment of victory, were given to Chamounix, where he knew his wife and sisters, with their eyes fixed to the telescope, were following his steps with an anxiety which might, perhaps, be exaggerated, but was not the less distressing; and he owns that he felt a tender and consoling sentiment when he saw the fluttering folds of the flag which they had promised to hoist as soon as their fears were to some extent relieved by seeing him safe at the summit.

He was then free to give himself up to the enjoyment of the magnificent spectacle before him. A light vapour suspended in the lower regions of the air concealed from view the lowest and remotest objects, such as the plains of France and Lombardy. But this was not much to

GREAT CREVASSE AT THE FOOT OF MONT BLANC

be regretted; for he saw what he had come to see,—the aggregate and mighty whole of all those lofty peaks, the organization of which he had so long desired to know. He could hardly believe his eyes; it seemed to him a dream, when beneath his feet he beheld those majestic summits, those formidable spires and pinnacles,—the Midi, the Argentière, the Géant,—even to the bases of which he had found it so difficult and so dangerous to make his way. He eagerly embraced their relationship to one another, their connection, their structure; and a single glance dissipated the doubts which years of study could not have removed.

Meanwhile, the tent was pitched, and the little table made ready on which he intended to essay his experiments. But when he began to arrange his instruments, he found himself interrupted every moment by the excessive difficulty of respiration. The air on the topmost peak of Mont Blanc—

"The difficult air of the iced mountain top,"

as Byron calls it—has only half the density of our ordinary atmosphere, and hence the traveller has to make up for this want of density by the frequency of his respirations. Now, this frequency necessarily accelerates the circulation, and all the more because the arteries are no longer counterbalanced from without by a pressure equal to that which they usually experience. Consequently our adventurers suffered from an access of fever.

So long as Saussure remained perfectly quiet, he felt no very great uneasiness, simply a slight palpitation of the heart. But after the least exertion, or if he fixed his attention on any particular subject for several consecutive moments, and especially when, by stooping, he contracted his chest, he was forced to rest, and draw his breath steadily for two or three minutes. The guides experienced analogous sensations. They had no appetite; and, in truth, their provisions, which had all frozen on the route, were not calculated to excite it; they did not care even for wine or brandy. And, indeed, it was found that strong liquors increased the uneasy sensations, undoubtedly because they still further quickened the already accelerated circulation. Nothing but fresh water relieved them or gave them any pleasure; and it was not without a considerable expenditure of time and labour that they kindled a fire and melted some snow, in order to procure the welcome boon.

With true scientific zeal and courage, De Saussure remained on the summit until half-past three—in all, four hours and a half; but though not a moment was wasted, he could not complete all the experiments which he had frequently made in three hours on the sea-shore. He performed with care, however, those which were most essential.

On quitting this magnificent watch-tower, or observatory, Saussure, in three-quarters of an hour, reached the rock which forms the eastern shoulder of the summit. The *descent* of this incline, the *ascent* of which had been so painful, was easy and agreeable. The snow was neither too hard nor too soft, and as the physical movements which they made in descending did not compress the diaphragm, they failed to embarrass the respiration, and our adventurers were not incommoded by the rarefaction of the air. Moreover, the declivity being wide, and distant from the precipices, it presents nothing to alarm the traveller or delay his progress. But this was not the case with the descent which, from the top of the shoulder, led to the plateau where De Saussure had passed the previous night. The rapidity of this descent, and the insupportable glare of the sun, reflected by the snow, dazzling their eyes, and rendering more formidable in appearance than they even were in reality the precipices which it revealed beneath their feet, proved very serious obstacles. Again : as the hardness of the snow had made their morning march very difficult, so now its softness, due to the action of the sun, gravely inconvenienced them; because, beneath its yielding surface or upper crust, they always found the bottom hard and slippery.

Sooth to say, all the little company dreaded this part of the descent; and some of the guides, while De Saussure was making his experiments on the summit, had sought in vain for an easier route. However, it was accomplished in safety, and in less than an hour and a quarter. They passed near the spot where they had slept, or at least reposed, on the preceding night, and pushed forward fully another league, to the rock near which they had encamped on their ascent. There De Saussure resolved to halt for the night; and their tent was pitched against the southern extremity of this rock, in a very curious situation. It stood on a foundation of snow, and on the brink of a steep declivity which strikes down into the valley beneath the Dôme de Goûté, and is terminated, southward, by the massive summit of Mont Blanc. At the bottom of the slope yawned a broad and deep crevasse, which separated them from the valley, and in which everything was swallowed up that fell from the vicinity of De Saussure's tent.

This position was chosen in order to be out of reach of avalanches; and because, the guides being able to shelter themselves in the hollows of the rock, the tent was not so inconveniently crowded as on the night before.

De Saussure tells us, in his interesting narrative, that he occupied himself in watching the masses of cloud that floated above the valleys and mountains, but beneath his feet. These clouds, instead of presenting smooth and even surfaces, as we see them from the lower levels of earth, were broken up into a variety of exceedingly fanciful forms,—towers, castles, giants,—and seemed to be uplifted by vertical winds, issuing from different points of the countries underneath them. Above all these clouds the horizon was embroidered by a girdle composed of two bands: the lower, a dark red; the upper, much clearer, and throwing off apparently a beautiful flame of rosy dawn, unequal, transparent, and variously tinted.

De Saussure's thoughts were not unnaturally as rose-hued as the horizon on which he gazed; for he had the pleasure of knowing that he had successfully carried out a project on which he had brooded for seven-and-twenty years—that is, since his first journey to Chamounix, in 1760; a project frequently abandoned, but always resumed, though it had been a source of continual anxiety and disquietude to his family. His preoccupation, indeed, had assumed the character of a disease; his gaze had never rested on Mont Blanc, which was visible from so many points of the district where he lived, without his experiencing a painful sensation. And now as, in the silence of the night, after having recovered in some measure from his fatigue, he recapitulated the observations he had collected, and retraced the magnificent panorama of mountains he had seen, his satisfaction was without alloy.

On the 4th of August, the fourth day of the expedition, the adventurers resumed their march about six o'clock; and in less than an hour they reached the cabin. Afterwards they descended a snowy incline at an angle of 46°, and traversed a great crevasse on a bridge of snow only three inches thick. Another hour's descent, and, to avoid the crevasses which continually interrupted their route, they descended a slope of 50°. When they struck the glacier which they had to cross, they found it so changed in four-and-twenty hours that they could not recognize their former track. The crevasses had widened, the bridges had fallen in; often, finding no means of issue, they were compelled to retrace their steps; still more often they had recourse to their ladder to bridge the crevasses,—which, without this assistance, would have been impassable. At half-past nine, however, they gained the solid rock, having triumphed over every obstacle; and about three hours later they arrived in safety at the Priory of Chamounix.

Thus was accomplished the first scientific ascent of Mont Blanc.

ASCENT BY M. CHARLES MARTINS.

An ascent of Mont Blanc was successfully achieved by M. Charles Martins, author of the very valuable and interesting record of travel, *Du Spitzberg au Sahara*, in 1844; when he was accompanied by Auguste Bravais, a lieutenant in the French navy, and Auguste Lepileur, a physician.

The three explorers quitted Geneva on the 26th of July. On foot they followed the cumbrous four-wheeled car which carried their equipments, and arrived at Chamounix on the 28th. They spent some days in the necessary preparations. With the view of sojourning at the highest possible elevation on Mont Blanc, they had brought from Paris a military tent, with its pegs and uprights, some goat-skin overcoats, sheep-skin bags, coverlets, and other necessaries. Numerous physical and meteorological instruments were required for the projected experiments; and three days' supply of provisions. In all, the baggage weighed eight hundredweights and three-quarters, to be transported to a height of 10,000 feet above the vale of Chamounix; yet each porter can carry only thirty-three pounds, besides his rations.

No wonder, then, that M. Charles Martins and his friends found themselves at the head of a retinue of forty-three persons; three being guides,—Couttet, Mergnier, and Balmat,—thirty-five porters, and two young people of the valley, who had asked permission to accompany them. On the 31st of July, at half-past seven in the morning, they quitted Chamounix. The weather was beautiful, though, as the wind blew from the south-west, and the barometer had slightly sunk, the travellers had not much confidence in its continuance. Along the right bank of the rushing Arve, and through green and smiling meadows, wound the gallant procession. On arriving opposite the hamlet Des Pélerins they turned to the left. The last house in the village is that of Jacques Balmat, the courageous peasant who first scaled the virgin snows of the mighty peak, and afterwards perished miserably (in 1834) in the glaciers which overhang the valley of Sixt.

On emerging from the purple vineyards which surround the hamlet Des Pélerins, our adventurers entered the forest; it is composed of tall firs and aged larches, the withered branches of which are festooned with long wreaths of gray lichens. In the preceding spring an enormous avalanche, loosened from the Aiguille du Midi, had dug a deep furrow across the forest, like a colossal ploughshare. Uprooted trees now strewed the soil which they had formerly shaded; others had been split in twain, and their shattered crests lay at their feet; some, with roots laid bare, hung inclined towards the valley. These results are due to the pressure of the air impelled before it by the avalanche, to the local wind it creates, and partly to its own mass.

The caravan separated in the wood, and each man sought out his own path. A narrow track skirts the precipice, washed by the torrent of the Pélerins, and leads to the moraine of the Glacier des Bossons; then it mounts in the midst of the heaped-up crags which compose it, and reaches the Pierre de l'Echelle, an enormous rock, under which is concealed the ladder always employed in crossing the crevasses of the glacier. This stone or cliff is 8050 feet above the sea-level, or about the same elevation as the Hospice of St. Bernard. There the daring climber bids farewell to earth,—he quits it to set foot upon the glacier,—and thenceforward, even to the summit of Mont Blanc, he meets only with a few isolated rocks, rising, like islands, out of a sea of eternal snow.

On the occasion of the ascent of M. Martins, the *cirque* of the Glacier des Bossons was—as it always is—a chaos of *séracs*,* aiguilles, and pyramids of ice, into the midst of which plunges the eastern wall of the Grands Mulets. The vertical layers of which these walls are built up differ considerably in height, and form, as it were, a series of steps, by means of which it is possible to climb to every point. The rock, decomposed under the influence of the atmospheric agents, accumulates between the layers; and in this rude soil, sheltered by the cliff, warmed by the sun which it reflects, and moistened by the snow, flourish some charming Alpine plants. In a few weeks these accomplish all the phases of their vegetation. Of phanerogamic plants M. Charles Martins estimates there are twenty-four species, and to these must be added twenty-six species of mosses, two hepaticas, and thirty lichens, bringing up to eighty-two the total of the plants which grow on these isolated rocks, in the midst of a sea of ice, deprived apparently of every kind of vegetation. But more: these plants serve as the nourishment of a rodent, the *campagnol des neiges*, which of all mammals lives at the highest

---

* Cubical masses of compact snow, resembling the *séracs*, or Swiss cheeses.

PIERRE DE L'ECHELLE.

level in the Alps, though nearly all its congeners are inhabitants of the plain.

Bravais had undertaken the task of measuring the variations of the magnetic intensity with the height. For this purpose he employed a compass in which a needle is suspended horizontally to a thread of raw silk. This needle is made to oscillate during a series of perfectly equal intervals of time, and by the number of oscillations is computed, after infinite and minutely careful corrections, the relative intensity of the magnetic force of the place compared with that of Paris, which is taken as equal to unity. The reader will appreciate the importance of these measurements when we remind him that it is hoped they will one day reveal the still mysterious laws of the currents which circulate around the terrestrial globe—that colossal magnet, the two poles of which do not coincide with the two extremities of the ideal axis around which the earth describes its daily revolution.

Meantime the sun approached the horizon. Already he had disappeared behind the mountains of Vergy; the valleys of Sallenche and Chamounix had long slept in the shadow, while the neighbouring granitic points seemed to glow red-hot, like iron just taken from the furnace; soon, too, the Aiguille of Varens and the rocks of the Fiz were extinguished, and the gloom spread to the glaciers of Mont Blanc. The snow, so luminous but a moment before, assumed the ghastly livid tint of a corpse; the death-chill seemed to invade those regions along with the advancing obscurity, and to reveal all their horror. The Aiguille of the Goûté, and the Monts Maudits, paled in quick succession; only the crest of Mont Blanc remained illuminated for some time longer, until its living rose-tint also gave way to the livid hue, as if life had deserted it in its turn. Towards the horizon, above the sea of clouds, the sky appeared of a bright green colour, resulting from the combination of the yellow rays of the sun with the blue of the celestial vault; the contours of the isolated clouds were circumscribed by an orange border of the greatest splendour. In those lofty regions that soft gloaming-light which has such a charm in the leas and vales is wholly unknown; night abruptly follows day.

Our explorers sheltered themselves behind a wall of stone which had been raised in front of a cavity. Their guides were grouped on the terraces of the rock, around small fires which they laboriously kindled with juniper-wood brought from the vicinity of the Pierre de l'Echelle; they sang in unison some slow monotonous songs, which derived from the scene and time a melancholy sweetness. Gradually the voices ceased, the fires died out, and no sound could be heard but that of the avalanches down-thundering from the neighbouring heights. Before long the moon arose behind the Monts Maudits, and silvering, though unseen by our travellers, the Dôme du Goûté, illuminated the snows with a strange phosphorescent radiance. When it had passed the Aiguille du Goûté it was surrounded by a greenish aureole, which shone defined upon a sky as black as ink; the stars sparkled brightly; the wind did not subside, but blew in strong and abrupt gusts, succeeded by a moment of perfect calm. Everything betokened bad weather on the morrow, and yet not one of M. Martins' party breathed the word "return:" all wished to exhaust their last chance, and not to give up until it was absolutely impossible to continue the ascent.

Next morning, while they were engaged in readjusting the burdens of the porters, M. Martins suddenly caught sight of an old man, unknown to the exploring-party, who was slowly ascending the acclivity leading to the Petit Plateau; stooping upon the snow, and sometimes supporting himself by his hands, he progressed slowly, but with the firm and measured step which indicates the trained mountaineer. This old man proved to be Marie Couttet, aged eighty, who in his youth had acted as guide to De Saussure. Formerly his surprising agility had procured him the sobriquet of "The Chamois." And he well deserved it. No one excelled him in intrepidity. One day he accompanied an English tourist on a difficult journey. The Englishman preserved throughout the air of cool indifference characteristic of the true "gentleman," and the most rugged and perilous passages drew from him neither a gesture of astonishment nor a word indicative of the slightest hesitation. Irritated by his imperturbable composure, Couttet bethought himself of a venerable pine which projected horizontally over the edge of an escarpment three hundred yards in depth; he marched boldly along the trunk, and on gaining the extremity sat down upon it, and then suspended himself by his feet above the precipice. The Englishman looked on without emotion, and when Couttet returned to his side, gave him a piece of gold on condition that he did not repeat the exploit. Such, in his youth, was the man who preceded M. Charles Martins up the lower slopes of the Petit Plateau. His intellect had grown feeble before his body: he thought he had discovered a new route to the summit of Mont Blanc, and recommended himself to every tourist who attempted the ascent. Though his offer was refused, he would still go as a volunteer, up to a certain elevation, in order to demonstrate the excellence of the new route he had discovered. Knowing the old man's monomania, we had carefully concealed from him the day of our departure; but having learned that we were at the Grands Mulets, he had started on the same evening, crossed the glacier, and towards midnight arrived at our bivouac, where he took his place around the fire with our guides. At dawn he was the first to start, to point out the track.

The Grand Plateau is a vast *cirque* of snow and ice, the bottom of which is a plain slightly raised towards the south. But M. Martins had scarcely time to determine the configuration of places, the clouds having completely enveloped him and his companions, and the snow whirling in dense showers around their heads. There was no time to hesitate; either they must immediately redescend or erect their tent. Two porters, Auguste Simond and Jean Cachat, offered to remain with the three travellers and the guides. The others flung their loads down upon the snow, and hastily made their way towards the Petit Plateau: they disappeared like shadows in the mist, which every moment increased in density. Left alone, the little band of courageous souls began by removing the snow, to the depth of thirteen or fourteen inches, over a rectangular space thirteen feet long by six and a half feet wide; then, guided by a rectangular cord which had been previously prepared, each knot of which corresponded to one of the stakes of the tent, they planted in the snow some long, strong, wooden plugs, of which the head was furnished with a hook. This done, the tent was raised on the cross-beam and two supports which formed its framework, the buckles of the ropes being passed around the head of the plugs. The adventurers then hastened to get their instruments under cover, and next their provisions. And well was it they lost no time, for several bottles of wine left outside could not afterwards be recovered, being buried deep by the falling snow in less than an hour. Beneath the tent they improvised a kind of flooring, by placing some light planks of deal upon the snow. At one end reposed the guides, and at the other their employers; and so narrow was the space that no one could stand upright —he must remain seated or recumbent. The "kitchen" occupied the centre. The first step was to melt some snow in a vessel warmed by the flame of a spirits-of-wine lamp; for at such an elevation coal burns very badly. Bravais hit upon the lucky idea of pouring the hot water on the tent-pegs; and as the water froze immediately, instead of being sunk in shifting snow, they were soon embedded in masses of compact ice. Besides, a rope fixed to the bolt which joined the horizontal main-beam to one of the vertical supports, and attached like a shroud to the side from which the wind blew, was stoutly moored to a couple of stakes thrust into the snow. These precautions taken, our explorers had nothing to do but to wait. All observations were impossible, except those of the barometer in the tent, and of a thermometer outside,—the former marked $2°.7$ below zero on their arrival; at two o'clock it had sunk to $-4°.0$; and at five, to $-5°.8$. Meanwhile, night had gathered in, and they lighted a lantern,—which, suspended above their heads, illuminated the little "interior." The guides, huddled together, conversed in a low voice, or slept as tranquilly as in their beds. The wind redoubled its violence; it blew in gusts, interrupted by those moments of profound calm which had been a source of astonishment to Saussure in similar circumstances. The wind raged furiously in the vast amphitheatre of snow, on the edge of which their little tent was placed. A veritable avalanche of air, the wind seemed to crash down upon them from the summit of Mont Blanc. Then the canvas of the tent expanded like a sail filled by the breeze; the supports bent and vibrated like the strings of a violin; and the horizontal main-beam yielded in a curve. Instinctively they supported the canvas with their backs while the gale lasted, for their safety depended on the solidity of this comparatively frail asylum. By stepping outside, they could easily form an idea of what would become of them if it were carried away. M. Charles Martins remarks that until now he had never been able to understand how travellers, full of health and vigour, had perished at only a few paces from the spot where the storm had surprised them; but his experience on this occasion assisted him in comprehending it.

Within the tent, the cold was insupportable. The thermometer oscillated between 2° and 3° above zero. Their goat-skin clothing and sheep-skin bags protected them sufficiently, though the hair of the pelisse was glued by the ice to the canvas of the tent. During the night the wind diminished in violence. Unfortunately for our mountain-climbers, the temperature continued to decrease, and at half-past five in the morning the thermometer marked -12°.1. The freshly-fallen snow was twenty inches thick; but the canvas of the tent was not covered with it, the wind having swept it away as fast as it fell; and it continued to drive horizontally great clouds of hail and snow from the Grand Plateau. The barometer remained as low as on the preceding evening. During a brief interval of calm, the summits of Mont Blanc, the Monts Maudits, and the Dromedary became visible, all terminated by a white crest in a north-easterly direction: this was the snow which the south-west gale had driven through the air.

It was impossible to ascend to the summit; even on the Grand Plateau the adventurers were doomed to inaction. Recognizing the uselessness of struggling against adverse circumstances, they arranged their instruments in the tent, and closed up its entrance with snow. This was at seven A.M., when the thermometer still indicated seven degrees below zero. The recently-fallen snow having hidden every chink and crevasse, they fastened one another to the guiding-rope, and descended rapidly to the Grands Mulets. After a few minutes' rest, they traversed the Glacier des Bossons. The narrow pathway leading to the Pierres-Pointues, covered by the fresh snow, had become slippery and difficult. The snow had fallen still lower down,—as low even as the place called the Bacures Dessous, which is only 2500 feet above Chamounix. Their return reassured everybody; for bad weather had prevailed in the valley as on the summits, and a rumour had got abroad that the adventurers had perished.

On the 25th of August, however, the weather changed to fair; the barometer rose steadily, and a north-west wind blew gently in the upper regions of the atmosphere. M. Martins knew that his tent was still standing on the Grand Plateau—he had sighted it from the ridge of the Brevent; but it seemed to be buried deep in snow on the south-west side, while the opposite was swept completely clear. Assured, therefore, that they would find their instruments in good order, they started again on the 27th—the three enthusiasts of science—at half an hour after midnight. The moon brightened their march; and at half-past three they reached the Pierres-Pointues. The sky was serenely pure; only a few isolated clouds resting on the Col de Balme and the Monts Vergy. A fresh and steady breeze, and the subdued scintillation of the stars, were signs of favourable weather. Castor and Pollux beamed with a tranquil light above the Aiguilles of Charmoz.

On reaching the upper precipices, our travellers closed up their line, and were careful that the angles formed by their zigzags should open fifteen degrees at least. They sank to their knees in the snow, the temperature of which was uniformly $-11°.0$ at a depth of four inches. The rarefaction of the air and the thickness of the snow, from which they were every moment compelled to extricate their limbs, forced them to move slowly; at every twenty paces they halted suffocated, with their feet painfully cold, and on the point of freezing. During their brief halts, they struck them with a stick to warm them and restore the circulation. This portion of the ascent was very fatiguing. However, an unclouded sun and a tranquil atmosphere favoured their exertions; but on reaching the declivity which separates the Rochers-Rouges from the Petits-Mulets, they suddenly caught sight of the heights to the south of Mont Blanc, and, beyond these, the plains of Italy. But they had no longer any shelter; the north-west wind, previously imperceptible, carried off Mergnier's hat; and M. Martins says that, though he was thickly clad, he suddenly felt as if stripped to his skin, so cold was the wind and so penetrating. Striking obliquely to the right, they soon reached the Petits-Mulets, some protogenic rocks situated at 500 feet below the summit.

And now they were near their goal; but they marched slowly, with heads drooping, chests panting, like a convoy of invalids. The rarefaction of the air made itself painfully felt: every moment the procession halted. Bravais tried how long he could push forward, using his utmost speed; at the thirty-second step he was brought to a stand-still, incapable. At length, at a quarter to two, they attained the eagerly-desired summit, which consists of a ridge running east-north-east to south-south-west; this ridge was not, as Saussure had found it, a narrow knife-like edge, but fully sixteen to twenty feet in width. On the north side it abutted on an immense snow-slope, with an inclination of from 40 to 45 degrees, which terminates at the Grand Plateau; southward it is continued with a small smooth level surface, parallel to the crest, inclined about 12 degrees, and some 330 feet in breadth. This surface is prolonged towards the south, where it connects itself to a rapid slope, abruptly interrupted at the level of the great rocky precipices which overhang the Allée-Blanche. After recovering their breath, they hastened to enjoy the magnificent panorama spread out before them in all the rich colouring of the cloudless day. Its details we have already described in our sketch of De Saussure's ascent.

It does not appear that the height of Mont Blanc has varied materially since it was first measured by Schuckburgh in 1775. This uniformity is certainly astonishing, when we remember that the summit is composed wholly of ice and snow, to a depth, according to De Saussure, of nearly 220 feet. It appears evident that Mont Blanc, like the neighbouring Aiguille du Midi, is a pyramid. The Rochers-Rouges, the Petits-Mulets, the Tourette, are the still projecting points of this pyramidal colossus; the remainder is covered with a hood or cap of snow, which does not melt on account of the elevation of the mountain. The temperature of the air, on the summit, is rarely as high as zero, but nearly always very far below it. If the reader asks how it is that the thickness of this hood of snow is always the same,—how it is that the altitude of the mountain does not change according to the seasons, and even according to the years,—we answer that, in reality, the quantity of snow which falls there, the winds which sweep it, the evaporation which diminishes its thickness, the condensation of the clouds which increases it, vary from one year to another; so that the form of the summit is never the same. If he will compare the descriptions of De Saussure, Clissold, Markham Sherwill, Henry de Tilly, and Bravais, recorded successively in 1787, 1822, 1827, 1834, and 1844, he will see that each of these travellers found a difference in configuration, except in the fundamental character, a ridge, like an ass's back, running from north to south. How could it be otherwise? Torrents of snow, brought on the wings of the wind from every point of the compass, descend upon Mont Blanc; they have scarcely fallen before they are swept away, displaced, carried off, until their surface resembles that of a carefully cultivated field. Even in the fairest weather, when the most absolute tranquillity prevails in the plain, a light smoke seems to escape from the summit, drawn out horizontally by a strong wind; if in a southerly direction, it is a good sign. It is, the Savoyards say, "Mont Blanc smoking its pipe." But in the aggregate all these varied causes of ablation and increase balance one another, so that the height of the summit continues uniform. Nature never proceeds on any other principle; nothing is always and absolutely stable; everything changes,—the atom as the ocean. This oscillation round a certain mean is the fixity of life;

immobility is death, and the general forces of Nature, which govern the organic as well as the inorganic world, never rest.

M. Martins had scarcely completed his meteorological and geodesical operations when the sun drew near the lines of the Jura in the direction of Geneva; it was a quarter past six, and the thermometer indicated $-11°.8$ for the temperature of the air, $-17°.6$ for that of the snow on the surface, and $-14°.0$ at eight inches in depth. The travellers found it exceedingly painful to come in contact with the snow, even through their thick boots. However, they endured their sufferings bravely. They would fain have lingered on the peak long enough to kindle some fires which might be visible, according to agreement, to the astronomers of Geneva, Lyons, and Dijon; for these, if simultaneously observed from the three cities, would have enabled their differences of longitude to be accurately determined; but the keen, biting air was so intense that further delay would have been fatal to life. Auguste Simond expressed an intention of remaining behind for this purpose; but his companions very prudently refused to allow him. And since that time the desired result has been obtained without difficulty by means of the electric telegraph. Departure was resolved upon; and the triumphant *ascensionists*— may we use the word?—were beginning to descend, when they were suddenly arrested by the most magnificent spectacle which man has ever contemplated. The shadow of Mont Blanc, forming an immense cone, extended to the whitely-gleaming mountains of Piedmont; it advanced with majestic slowness towards the horizon, and rose high into the air above the Bocca di Nonna. But then the shadows of the other mountains successively blended with it, as the sun sank behind each great peak, and formed, as it were, a regal retinue for the monarch of the Alps. By an effect of the perspective, all converged towards it; and these shadows, of a greenish blue towards their base, were surrounded by a very vivid purple tint which shaded softly into the rose of the heavens. It was a splendid spectacle. A poet might have said that angels with kindling pinions inclined around the throne on which sat the Invisible Presence of the Deity. The shade passed from the sky, and still the travellers stood as if rooted to the spot; motionless, but not mute with astonishment, for their admiration found expression in involuntary cries and exclamations. Only the auroras of Arctic Europe can furnish a spectacle equal in magnificence to the unexpected phenomenon which none before M. Martins and his companions had beheld from the summit of Mont Blanc.

The sun was sinking fast, and the travellers must set out. They fastened themselves all to one rope, and descended hastily towards the Grand Plateau. When passing near the Petits-Mulets, M. Martins found a couple of stones among the snow; and, from the glassy beads upon their surface, knew they were fragments of rock dispersed by the lightning which so often strikes these lofty peaks. After leaving the Petits-Mulets they made no further halt, but descended, "like an avalanche," in a straight line, and without picking out their route; each one was dragged on by his predecessor, and

Mergnier, leading the way, sprang with leaps and bounds down the declivity, sinking at every movement into the snow, which sufficiently moderated the impetus of the swift procession. On reaching the Grand Plateau, they paused a moment to take breath; resumed their rapid march, and finally reached their tent at a quarter to eight. In fifty-five minutes they had descended from the summit, which is fully 2500 feet above the Grand Plateau.

X.

In the Indian Archipelago.

ONE of the great volcanic belts of the world is carried through the superb islands of the Indian Archipelago. It may be traced in a curving line, indicated by numerous active and extinct volcanoes, throughout the entire length of Sumatra and Java, and thence by the islands of Bali, Lombock, Sumbawa, Flores, the Servatty Islands, Banda, Amboyna, Balchian, Makian, Tidore, Ternate, and Gilolo, to Morty Island. After a break of about two hundred miles to the westward, the chain of fire begins again in North Celebes, and strikes through Sian and Sanguir to the Philippine Archipelago. An offshoot of the main belt diverges at Banda, and passes under the sea to the north-eastern coast of New Guinea; whence it may be followed through New Britain, New Ireland, and the Solomon Islands, to the eastern border of the Indian Ocean.

The islands thus occupied are remarkable for the picturesque character of their scenery and the extraordinary fertility of their vegetation. No more singular development of the subterranean fires can be found in any quarter of the globe; for not only does the archipelago owe its natural wealth, but to a certain degree its existence, to their activity. They have piled up ranges of mountains and built up isolated peaks from 7000 to 12,000 feet in height, and have clothed their sides with the fairest fruits and flowers of the Tropical world. Thus Java, though it contains no fewer than forty-five volcanoes, averaging 10,000 feet high, is not the less the very garden of the East, and rich beyond all that the liveliest imagination can suggest. Its mountains are not bare and rugged, like those of Scandinavia,—nor clothed in a cerecloth of perpetual snow, like those of Alpine Europe; but from base to crest exhibit the most luxuriant variety of vegetation. Hence the ascent of a mountain in the Indian Archipelago reveals a constant succession of rich and radiant landscapes, and possesses a peculiar interest for the scientific naturalist.

THE PANGERANGO MOUNTAIN: JAVA.

In 1861, Mr. Wallace, the author of several important works of travel, ascended one of the loftier summits of Java—the Pangerango, an extinct volcanic cone about 10,000 feet above the sea. He started from a town called Tchipanas, situated at its base; with two hunters as companions, and a couple of coolies to carry his baggage. The first mile, he says, was open country; after which they entered the great forest that covers the whole of the mountain from a height of about 5000 feet. Through the dense shades of this forest, up a tolerably

VOLCANO OF BANDA—INDIAN ARCHIPELAGO.

steep ascent, they proceeded for a mile or two; the trees being of great size, and the luxuriant undergrowth consisting of fine herbaceous plants, tree-ferns, and shrubby vegetation. The ferns were as numerous as they were various, and of a beauty that would have enchanted any English fern-grower. It is said that as many as three hundred species may be found on this one mountain.

A little before noon they arrived at the small plateau of Tjeburong, at the foot of the steeper part of the mountain, where, in the neighbourhood of a curious cavern and a picturesque waterfall, a plank-house has been erected for the accommodation of travellers. Continuing their ascent, they came to a rugged, steep, and narrow road, winding zigzag up the cone, which was strewn with irregular masses of rock, and overgrown with a dense but less lofty vegetation. They passed a torrent of water, the temperature of which was little below boiling point; and could not but admire its singular effect as it seethed and eddied over its rocky bed, and sent up clouds of white steam, which lingered among the overhanging profusion of ferns and lycopodia.

At an elevation of 7500 feet the travellers found a hut of open bamboos, at a place called Kandang-Badak, or "Rhinoceros Field;" and here they resolved to rest and refresh themselves. From this point Mr. Wallace made two visits to the summit, occupying the interval in botanical researches. He also made an excursion to the active crater of Gedeh, which is on the same mountain, but at a lower elevation. He describes it as a vast semicircular chasm, bounded by perpendicular walls of black rock, and surrounded by miles of rugged scoria-covered slopes. Its depth is not remarkable. The sides are besprinkled with patches of sulphur and variously-coloured products, and continual streams of smoke and vapour ascend from several vents. The summit-cone of Pangerango is nothing more than an irregular, undulating plain, with a low bordering ridge, and one deep lateral chasm, apparently the remains of an ancient crater. The view from this elevated point is necessarily one of great extent and splendour; including, as it does, a considerable portion of the island, with its rich plains, its deep valleys, and its undulating mountain-ranges.

But what renders the ascent of Pangerango specially interesting, is the gradual transition apparent on its colossal sides from the characteristics of a Tropical to those of a Temperate flora. In climbing the 11,000 feet which constitute its height above the sea, the traveller seems to pass from the prolific nature of Tropical Asia to the more reserved and austere features of Temperate Europe. At first, indeed, he meets with temperate forms, with herbaceous plants; and at 3000 feet encounters the familiar strawberries and violets of the West—though the former are tasteless and the latter pale and small. Weedy compositæ also assist in giving a European character to the wayside growth. From 2000 to 5000 feet the forests and ravines glow with all the profuse magnificences of the Tropical World; the splendour of the general effect being greatly enhanced by the abundance of noble tree-ferns, sometimes fifty feet in height, and always very beautiful and striking.

In places where the ravines have been cleared of timber, they crowd the sides and hollows until nothing but waving fronds is visible; and where the road crosses one of these valleys, the view of their feathery crowns, in varied positions above and below the eye, has a picturesqueness of effect which is never to be forgotten. The splendid foliage, says Wallace, of the broad-leaved musaceæ (the well-known plantains and bananas) and zingiberaceæ, and the elegant and varied forms of plants allied to begonia and melastoma, continually attract the attention in this region. The spaces between the trees and larger plants are filled with hosts of orchids, ferns, and lycopods, which festoon every trunk and branch, and fasten and droop and intertwine their trailing arms in ever-various complexity.

At about 5000 feet the traveller meets with horse-tails (*equisetum*) not unlike those of Europe. At 6000 feet, and from thence to the summit of the mountain, wild raspberries are as plentiful as brambles in an English lane. At 7000 feet cypresses appear, and the forest-trees diminish in size, and are more thickly incrusted with mosses and hoary lichens. These minor forms of vegetation rapidly increase as we ascend, until the rocky masses and blocks of scoria that form the mountain slope are altogether hidden by them.

At 8000 feet we encounter European types in greater plenty. Several species of honeysuckle, St. John's-wort, and Guelder-rose abound; and at about 9000 feet we fall in with the rare and rarely beautiful royal cowslip (*primula imperialis*), which blooms nowhere else in the world, it is said, but on this solitary mountain summit. It has a tall, stout stem, sometimes more than three feet high; the root leaves are eighteen inches long; and instead of a terminal cluster, it throws off several whorls of cowslip-like flowers. The forest-trees, though gnarled and gloomy, and dwarfed to the size of bushes, extend to the very rim of the old crater, but have not made their way into the summit-hollow. Here we find much open ground, with thickets of shrubby artemisias and gnaphaliums, resembling our English southernwood and cudweed, only growing to a height of six or eight feet; while buttercups, violets, whortle-berries, sow-thistles, chickweed, white and yellow cruciferæ, plantain, and annual grasses everywhere abound. In the shelter of shrubs and bushes, wherever these are found, flourish the St. John's-wort and honeysuckle in balmy profusion; and in the damp shade of the thickets thrives the imperial cowslip.

The following genera, belonging to distant and more temperate regions, are found in the Pangerango:—

Two species of violet, three of ranunculus, three of impaticus, eight or ten of rubus, and several kinds of primula, hypericum, swertia, convallaria (lily of the valley), vaccinium (cranberry), rhododendron, gnaphalium (cudweed), polygonum, digitalis (foxglove), lonicera (honeysuckle), plantago (rib-grass), artemisia (wormwood), lobelia, oxalis (wood-sorrel), quercus (oak), and taxus (yew). A few of the smaller plants (plantago major and lanceolata, jonchus oleraceus, and artemisia vulgaris) are identical with European species.

Now, as the flora of the lowlands, for " thousands of miles around," is of an entirely different character, the occurrence of the semi-European vegetation on isolated mountain-peaks in an island south of the equator, is a remarkable fact. No such Alpine flora is found on the Peak of Teneriffe—which is so much nearer Europe, and also of greater height—nor on the mountains of Bourbon and Mauritius. The case of the Javanese peaks calls, therefore, for explanation. Well, an analogous phenomenon exists elsewhere. The loftier peaks of the Alps, and even of the Pyrenees, afford a number of plants exactly identical with those of Lapland, but nowhere found in the intervening plains. On the summit of the White Mountains, in the United States, every plant is identical with species growing in Labrador. In these cases, says Mr. Wallace, all ordinary means of transport fail. Most of the plants have heavy seeds, which could not possibly be carried such immense distances by the wind; and the agency of birds in so effectually stocking these Alpine heights is equally out of the question. The difficulty was so great, that some naturalists were driven to solve it by supposing that all these species had been separately created twice over on these distant peaks; a supposition which all that we know of the order of creation effectually negatives. The ascertained existence at some remote period of a glacial epoch seems, however, to dispose of the question in a satisfactory manner, and to offer an explanation which men of science can accept. In that age of ice, when the Welsh mountains laboured with glaciers, and the mountainous parts of Central Europe and much of America north of the great lakes were covered with ice and snow, and suffered from a climate resembling that of Labrador and Greenland at the present day, an Arctic flora overspread all these regions. When the long, dreary winter-epoch passed away, and the snow-shroud and the glaciers receded up the mountain slopes, and were driven towards the North Pole, the plants peculiar to it receded also—always clinging, as they still cling, to the borders of the perpetual snow-line. And hence it arises that the same species are now found on the summits of the mountains of Temperate Europe and America as in the bleak Polar regions.

But we must carry our explanation a step further. On the higher slopes of the colossal Himalaya, on the mountain-summits of Central India and Abyssinia, occur numerous plants which, though not identical with those of European mountains, belong to the same genera, and are regarded as representing them. The majority of these could not exist in the warm intervening plains. Mr. Darwin accounts for this class of facts in the same way; for, during the extreme severity of the ice-age, temperate forms of plants will have made their way to the confines of the Tropics, and on its departure will have gradually retired up the southern mountains, as well as northward to the hills and plains of Europe. "But in this case," adds Wallace, "the time elapsed, and the great change of conditions, have allowed many of these plants to become so modified that we now consider them to be distinct species. A variety of other facts of a similar nature have led him to believe that the depression of temperature was at one time sufficient to allow a few north-temperate plants to cross the Equator (by the most elevated routes), and to reach the

JAVA AND THE ASIATIC MAINLAND.

Antarctic regions, where they are now found." In this way may we explain the presence of a flora of European type on the volcanoes of Java.

It may be objected to this explanation, that between Java and the Asiatic mainland a great breadth of sea intervenes, which must have effectually prevented the immigration of temperate forms of plants during the long winter of the primeval world. But the answer to this is, that abundant and incontestable proof can be brought forward of the former junction of Java, with the continent. Indeed, Mr. Wallace has almost conclusively demonstrated that the Asiatic mainland at one time included not only the island of Java, but also Sumatra and Borneo, and extended even to the small island of Bali. For evidence of this fact, the reader is referred to Mr. Wallace's charming work on the "Malay Archipelago." It is enough to indicate it here as confirming our explanation of the causes to which is due the European character of the vegetation that so abundantly and vigorously covers the slopes of the mountains of Java.

THE GUNUNG-TALANG MOUNTAIN: SUMATRA.

The great island of Sumatra, which in extent is equal to that of Great Britain, does not possess so large a number of volcanoes, proportionately, as Java, and probably a considerable portion of it is non-volcanic in origin; but some of its peaks are of colossal size and wonderfully romantic character. Among these we may particularize the Gunung-Talang (or Sœlassie), which attains an elevation of 8,480 feet above the sea, and broke out into violent activity in October 1845. At that time it was ascended by several Dutch travellers, one of whom has left on record the particulars of their enterprise.

On their way from Solok to Mocara Pamy, they had caught sight at intervals—when on the higher grounds —of vast columns of smoke rising from the Talang. The view, not unnaturally, begat in them a strong desire to visit the "burning mountain." This desire they resolved to gratify; and having made the necessary preparations, they started, on horseback, at five o'clock in the morning of the 21st of October.

After about a quarter of an hour's travelling, they came upon a deep ravine covered with rolled pebbles, which made the road so dangerous that they were compelled to dismount and lead their horses. Crossing a small bamboo-bridge without parapet, they climbed an acclivity of considerable steepness, and thence enjoyed a prospect so magnificent as amply to recompense them for all their previous exertions. Its principal feature, however, was the Talang, which continued to emit its dense clouds of smoke.

Near Batol-Banjak, where they halted, fragments of trachyte are found in great abundance. In the neighbourhood several thermal springs indicate the wide area of the volcanic action; their waters are pungent and strongly sulphurous.

In the evening they reached Batol-Bedjandjang, situated at the very foot of the volcano. Next morning they resumed their journey in a disagreeable mist and incessant showers of drizzling rain. The thermometer stood at 20° C. The track took them across three abrupt ridges in succession, each about 650 feet in length. From the crest of the highest the view extended over a table-land covered with a rich vegetation of trees and shrubs, at the extremity of which a fresh ascent, of about 1400 feet, awaited them. The soil, composed of a mixture of sulphurous earth and calcareous particles, began to grow perceptibly hot, and jets of white smoke issued from the numerous crevasses that spread across it.

At eleven o'clock they reached the base of the topmost peak,—which rose about 320 feet above them. Though the vicinity of the crater had for some time been evident, from the strong sulphurous odour which infected the air, the activity of the volcano now showed itself much more plainly. In the midst of the blocks of ancient lava which surrounded them vegetation lived a sickly life, and the eye rested with little satisfaction on withered bushes and blackened and burned-up trees. Our travellers pushed forward all the more rapidly that the surrounding landscape offered so little which was attractive, and arrived at a crevasse situated between the two summits, on one of which the crater was visible in all its impressive grandeur.

Truly majestic was the spectacle!

In front yawned the crater, the gloomy basin in which the volcanic forces had toiled for ages; and beyond was the new mouth, still seething and whirling, like a tube surrounded by flames and clouds of smoke. The deadly silence which prevailed was interrupted only at times by the subterranean din of volcanic reports.

To the south-west, about 400 feet from the summit, lay the active crater. Its western border was formed by a vertical wall, through which a portion of the lava escaped. On the south side an inclined crest or ridge disappeared in a depth which the eye could not fathom. To whatever distance the gaze extended, crevasses emitting puffs and cloudlets of smoke were conspicuous.

To obtain a nearer view of this fiery lake, the travellers descended the rapid slope, assisting themselves with their hands as well as with their feet, and taking good care not to quit one rocky projection until they were sure of their footing upon another. Then they were able to survey the violent commotion of the interior of the basin, while almost deafened by a roar like that of the paddle-wheels of a large number of steamships in simultaneous movement.

M. Van der Ven, one of the party, here met with a very narrow escape; for, having advanced close to an opening, the hot lava suddenly yielded beneath his feet: fortunately it rested upon a stratum which had already hardened, and thus he had time to fling himself hastily backwards. They were unable to remain long in the crater, on account of the intense heat; and they proceeded from thence to a small lake of sulphur lying *above* the *aréte* upon which they had been stationed. It was a small circular basin, about 160 feet in diameter. Three of the party descended the length of an almost vertical wall, about twenty-two feet high, to a pool of boiling water. By supporting themselves with one hand at the crevasses, they were able to collect a few spoonfuls with the other; but it emitted so powerful a sulphurous odour that they were glad to beat a retreat in all haste.

Then they recrossed the table-land or summit-plateau to regain the point at which they had commenced their investigations, where they proceeded to secure as comfortable quarters for the night as were available. At about ten o'clock in the evening, they were wrapped up in their mantles and engaged in wooing sleep on their uneasy beds of stone, when the rain began again with great violence. Electric clouds in swift succession swept across the sky, and blazed with incessant gleams of lightning. Thrice was the tent blown down by the furious gale. The water trickled over them in continuous rills, and they trembled with cold. They were immersed in an almost Cimmerian darkness, for the wind had extinguished their lamps; but as the lightning waxed fierce and more frequent they contrived, by its lurid glare, and after many efforts, to pitch their tent securely, and beneath its feeble shelter wait anxiously for the dawn of day.

After contending for some hours with the fury of the unchained elements, they hailed with pleasure a cloudless morning sky, pure, fresh, tranquil, and radiant with sunshine. Recovering their energies, they started on the descent, following the eastern face, where the declivities are less dangerous, as far as the bottom of the extinct crater; and then ascending on the opposite side to the second summit, whence they enjoyed a glorious prospect of hills and vales, lakes, rivers, and islets, all basking in the golden glory of the day.

The descent of the mountain was accomplished without any misadventure.

The mountainous character of Sumatra and Java will best be understood from an enumeration of their principal summits. Sumatra can boast of Indrapura, 12,140 feet; Loesa, 11,150; Dempo, 10,440; Abong-Abong, 10,350; Singallang, 10,150; Merapi, 9,700; and Ganong-Pasaman, 9,500. But the peaks of Java are on even a grander scale: as Slamat, 12,300 feet; Semirer, 11,950; Ardjoono, 11,800; Lawoo, 10,650; Soombing, 10,570; Idjong, 10,170; Sindoro, 10,140; and Geeleh, 9,860. The crater of Taschem contains a lake, nearly a quarter of a mile in length, so strongly impregnated with sulphuric acid that the stream issuing from it poisons the sea for some distance from its mouth, and no fish can survive its influence.

XI.

Chimborazo.

 A GLANCE at the map of South America reveals to us the fact that, on the western side, a grand range of mountains traverses its entire extent, from Tierra del Fuego to the Isthmus of Panama. Nay, this remarkable longitudinal mass is prolonged even into the northern division of the American Continent, extending to the very shores of the Arctic basin. It would seem as if Providence had erected a mighty barrier capable of resisting the wildest fury of the Pacific waters. Beginning at the Panama isthmus, an unbroken line, known as the Andes, which seldom recedes far from the ocean, and frequently descends to the very shore, stretches southward to the Strait of Magelhaens, and after a sudden break reappears in Tierra del Fuego, to terminate in Cape Horn. This line, according to the provinces it traverses, is named the Bolivian, the Peruvian, the Chilian, and the Patagonian Andes. Sometimes the chain consists of a single compact ridge, crested, as it were, by peaks of great loftiness, and of two or even three parallel

ranges, with lofty valleys or table-lands between them; the whole uniting at various points in huge mountain-knots or clusters. There are two such ranges in Ecuador, Bolivia, and Peru; three in New Granada; and only one in Chili. The intervening plains or table-lands, called *puramos* or *punas*, are verdureless wastes, swept by frequent storms. They are available, however, for purposes of transit; as are also the *quebradas*, or passes, which intersect the ranges at irregular intervals. Some of the loftiest volcanoes in the world are included in the Andean system—as Antisana, 19,132 feet; Cotopaxi, 18,875 feet; and Pichincha, 15,976 feet—but, instead of lava, they usually discharge stones, ashes, and torrents of water, mixed with mud and bitumen. Nearly the entire chain, from north to south, rises above the level of the perpetual snow-line.

In Colombia the highest point of the Cordilleras (as they are often called) is found in the central range,—the active volcano of Nevada da Tolima, the summit of which slightly exceeds the elevation of 18,000 feet. In Ecuador we meet with the grand summits of Pichincha, 15,976 feet; Illiniza, 17,380 feet; and Chimborazo, 21,424 feet, in the western range: Cotopaxi, 18,875 feet; Antisana, 19,137 feet; and Cayambe, 19,386 feet, in the inland range. In Peru the principal summits are the Nevada de la Vinda, 16,000 feet; and the truncated cone of Arequipa, 20,320 feet. In Chili, the culminating point is Aconcagua, 23,910 feet. In Patagonia the highest summits are about 8,000 feet in height.

Necessarily, the Andes are comparatively unknown

PANORAMIC VIEW OF THE ANDES

to travellers, and the great majority of its mountains have been unattempted by human enterprise. Some of the most remarkable, however, have yielded to the courage and patience of the explorer; and among others the "giant of the Western star," Chimborazo, which was long considered, though erroneously, the monarch of the Andes.

We propose to describe the ascent of Chimborazo by M. Boussingault and Colonel Hall, as recorded in the former's "Voyages aux Volcans de l'Equateur."

Riobamba, he says, is perhaps the most singular diorama of the universe. Not that there is anything remarkable in the town itself; and it is situated on one of those treeless, grassless table-lands so common in the Andes, which have all, at their lofty elevation, a characteristic wintry aspect, impressing the spectator with a certain feeling of melancholy. This is due, perhaps, to the circumstance that, in order to reach it, we pass at first through the most picturesque scenes; and it is always with regret that we quit the climate of the Tropics for the frosts and keen winds of the North.

From this point, however, the traveller beholds a vast sweep of mountain-heights,—the Capac-Urcu, the Tunguragua, the Cubilla, the Carguairazo, and finally, in the north, the snow-crowned Chimborazo; besides the celebrated peaks of the Paramos, which, though they possess not the glory of the eternal snows, are full of interest to the geologist.

This magnificent amphitheatre, which everywhere

limits and contracts the horizon of Riobamba, is a continual subject of varied observations. It is curious to observe the aspect of its glaciers at different hours of the day, to see their apparent elevation modified from one moment to the other by the effect of atmospheric refraction. With what interest, too, do we see, in a space so circumscribed, all the great phenomena of meteorology produced! Here it is one of those clouds, of vast breadth, aptly designated by Saussure a "parasite cloud," which clings midway to a lofty trachytic cone; clings so closely that not even a strong wind has any effect upon it. Soon the thunder bursts from the heart of this mass of vapour; hail and rain deluge the base of the mountain, while its snowy summit, soaring far above the storm, shines in the golden light of day. Farther on, it is a pinnacle of ice resplendent with glory; it is so sharply outlined against the intense azure of the firmament that all its contours, all its irregularities can be distinguished: the purity of the atmosphere is remarkable, and though the snowy summit is wreathed with a cloud which seems to emanate from its bosom, it is but as a ring of smoke; already it is nothing more than a silvery vapour; and now it has disappeared. Again it reproduces itself, once more to melt into "thin air." This intermittent cloud-formation is a very frequent phenomenon on the summits of snow-shrouded mountains; it is chiefly observed in fair and tranquil weather, and always some hours after the culmination of the sun. In such conditions, the glaciers may be compared to condensers launched towards the upper regions of the atmosphere, to dry the air by cooling it, and thus to conduct to the surface of the earth the water which it contains in the state of vapour.

These table-lands, with their belts of glaciers, sometimes present a singularly gloomy aspect; especially when a warm wind fills them with humid air from the lower regions. The mountains become invisible, and the horizon is masked by a ring of clouds which apparently touch the earth. The day is cold and damp, the mass of vapour being almost impenetrable to the solar light. A prolonged twilight prevails, the only one known between the Tropics; for under the equatorial zone night abruptly follows day, and it seems as if the sun were extinguished when it sets.

Let us now turn our attention to Chimborazo. For the purpose of studying it geologically, it might be sufficient to approach its base; but the enthusiasts of science have been led to cross the threshold of perpetual snow, and accomplish its ascent, in the hope of making some additions to the stores of meteorological knowledge.

From Riobamba Chimborazo presents two declivities or slopes of very different inclination. The one, which faces the Arenal, is very abrupt, and covered with numerous pinnacles of trachyte which force their way through the encrusting ice. The other, which descends towards the site called Chillapullu, not far from Mocha, is, on the contrary, of a very gentle gradient, but of considerable extent. After a careful examination of the environs of the mountain, M. Boussingault and Colonel Hall resolved to attack it on this side. On the

14th of December 1831, they took up their quarters in the "métairie" of Chimborazo, where they found some dry straw to sleep on, and some sheep-skins to protect them from the cold. This "métairie" is situated at an elevation of 12,000 feet; the nights there are fresh, and it is not an agreeable place of sojourn owing to the scarcity of fuel. It lies within that botanical zone of the graminaceæ which must be crossed before the traveller can reach the perpetual snow-line; and it is there that all woody vegetation terminates.

On the 15th, at seven o'clock, the two explorers started on their enterprise, accompanied by an Indian guide. They followed up the winding course of a brook, enclosed between two walls of trachyte, which derived its waters from the glacier; and then, quitting this crevasse, skirted the base of Chimborazo in the direction of Mocha. The ascent was gradual; but the mules picked their way with difficulty through the fragments of rock accumulated at the foot of the mountain. The slope became very rapid; the soil was loose and shifting, and at almost every step the mules halted, paying no attention to the spur. Their breathing was difficult and accelerated; they panted laboriously. The travellers had gained a height equal to that of Mont Blanc, for the barometer indicated an elevation of 15,650 feet.

After covering their faces with masks of light taffetas, as a protection against atmospheric inconveniences, they began to climb an *aréte* which abuts high up the glacier. It was noon. They mounted slowly, and as they entered upon the snow suffered more and more from difficulty of respiration; however, by pausing for a moment at every eighth or tenth step, they were able to recover themselves. Continuing the ascent, they experienced much fatigue from the want of consistency of the snowy soil, into which at every step they sank up to their waists. In spite of all their efforts, they found it impossible to advance; and, in fact, a short distance beyond, the crumbling snow was upwards of four feet deep. They betook themselves to rest on a block of trachyte, which resembled an island in the midst of a sea of snow. The elevation, according to their instruments, was 16,735 feet; so that after great fatigue they had ascended only 925 feet above the point where they had begun their march.

At six o'clock they were on their way back to the "métairie." The weather had been magnificent; never had Chimborazo appeared so majestic; but after their fruitless journey they could not contemplate it without a feeling of vexation. They resolved to attempt the ascent on the more precipitous side—that is, on the side facing the Arenal. They knew that Humboldt, in his ascent of the mountain, had taken this route. At Riobamba the point to which he attained had been distinctly shown to them, though they had found it impossible to obtain any exact particulars of the route he had followed. None of his Indian guides were alive.

At seven o'clock, on the following day, they started on the Arenal route. The sky was remarkable for its purity. To the east was visible the famous volcano of Sangay, situated in the province of Macas,—which, nearly a century before, M. la Condamine had seen in a state of permanent incandescence. By degrees, as they pressed forward, the level rose perceptibly. In general, the trachytic table-lands which support the isolated peaks that form so remarkable a feature of the Andes, rise gradually towards the base of these same peaks. The numerous deep crevasses which furrow these table-lands seem all to radiate from a common centre, and at the same time to contract as they recede from that centre. They may aptly be compared to the cracks noticeable in a broken pane of glass.

When they dismounted from their mules, they had reached an elevation of 16,000 feet. The ground had become impracticable for these animals,—which sought, moreover, with their usual extraordinary instinct, to make known to their riders the fatigue they suffered: their ears, generally so erect and attentive, were entirely prone, and during their frequent halts for breath they incessantly gazed towards the plain. Few cavaliers, it may be assumed, have ridden their steeds to such an elevation; and before one can mount, on mule-back, over a shifting soil, to a point beyond the perpetual snow-line, one must have had several years' equestrian experience in the Andes.

After examining the character of the surrounding localities, they discovered that, to gain an *arête* which rose towards the summit of Chimborazo, they must first ascend an exceedingly steep precipice immediately in front of them. To a large extent it was formed of blocks of all sizes disposed slope-wise; here and there these trachytic fragments were covered by more or less extensive sheets of ice; and at many points it could plainly be seen that these rocky fragments rested on the hardened snow, consequently they were the result of landslips which had recently taken place in the upper part of the mountain. Such landslips are frequent; and among the glaciers of the Cordilleras, what the traveller has most reason to fear is the avalanches, in which stones have a much larger share than snow.

At eleven o'clock they completed the passage of a tolerably extensive sheet of ice, in which they had been compelled to cut steps with their axes to steady their feet. It had not been accomplished without danger,—a stumble would have cost them their lives. Again they plunged into the midst of fragments of trachyte; but this they regarded as a kind of *terra firma*, and progressed with considerable rapidity. They marched in single file—Boussingault first, then Colonel Hall, and the negro last; he followed exactly in Boussingault's footsteps, so as not to compromise the safety of the instruments intrusted to him. Absolute silence was preserved during the march, experience having shown that nothing is so exhausting as a conversation maintained at so great an elevation; and when the travellers halted, if they exchanged a few words, it was always in a low voice. To this precaution Boussingault attributed, in a great degree, the health he had always enjoyed during his numerous ascents of the American volcanoes. "This salutary precaution," he says, "I imposed despotically on all my companions; and on the Antisana Peak, an Indian who neglected it, and shouted with all the strength of his lungs to Colonel Hall, who had wandered from the route during a thick mist, was seized with vertigo, and experienced a slight hemorrhage."

In due time they arrived at the ridge or *arête* by which they hoped to gain the summit; but it proved in reality to be something very different from what it had appeared at a distance. There was not much snow upon it, but its escarpments were difficult to climb. They found themselves compelled to make almost incredible exertions; and in these aerial regions gymnastics are painful! At length they reached the foot of a vertical wall of trachyte several hundred feet in height. For a moment the adventurers felt discouraged, when the barometer told them that they were at only 18,400 feet of elevation. Considerable as this will seem to "home-keeping youth" and dwellers in the plains, it was a trifle to them; for it was not even the height they had attained upon Cotopaxi, and Humboldt had ascended much higher upon Chimborazo. Mountain-climbers, when baffled, are always strongly disposed to seat themselves, and Boussingault and his companions yielded to the inclination. It was the first time they had rested, sitting. They had suffered much from excessive thirst, and their first care was to suck some icicles, so as to relieve it.

Though it was past noon, the cold was very keen, and the thermometer had sunk to 0° 4. A thick mist surrounded them. When it cleared away, they took account of their situation. Looking towards the Pena-Colorada, or Red Rock, they had on their right a frightful abyss; on their left, towards the Arenal, they distinguished an advanced rock resembling a belvedere or prospect-tower. It was important to reach this, in order to discover whether it were possible to double the

Red Rock, and, at the same time, whether they could ascend higher. It was no easy task to scale this rocky belvedere; but Boussingault, with the help of his two companions, succeeded. He then saw that, if they contrived to master a steep snow-slope which abutted on a face of the Red Rock opposite to the side by which they had approached it, they might attain a very considerable elevation. To obtain a sufficiently clear idea of the topography of Chimborazo, let the reader figure to himself an immense mass of rock, supported on every side by flying buttresses. The *arêtes* are the flying buttresses which, from the plain, seem to abut on the enormous central block in order to steady it.

Before undertaking this dangerous passage, Boussingault sent his negro to test the consistency of the snow. It proved to be of satisfactory hardness. Hall and the negro succeeded in doubling the base of the position occupied by Boussingault, and the latter joined them as soon as they were planted firmly enough to receive him. Just as they were on the point of resuming their march, a stone from the upper part of the mountain fell close beside Colonel Hall. He stumbled, and came to the ground. At first his companion thought he was wounded, but was reassured on seeing him rise and examine with his lens the fragment of rock so uncourteously submitted to his investigation; the unlucky trachyte was identical with that on which they were marching.

Very cautiously they moved forward. On the right, they were able to support themselves against the rock; on the left, the declivity was frightful, and before pushing ahead they familiarized themselves thoroughly with the precipice; a precaution which should never be neglected in mountain-climbing whenever a dangerous place has to be passed. Saussure gave this warning long ago, but it cannot be too often repeated; and M. Boussingault asserts that in all his adventurous explorations of the Andean summits he never lost sight of this prudent precept.

They now began to feel more powerfully the effect of the atmospheric rarefaction. At every two or three steps they were compelled to halt, and often even to lie down for some seconds. The moment they were seated, all painful sensations vanished; their suffering lasted only while they were in movement. The snow soon threw in their way an additional and a very formidable obstacle. Of soft snow, the depth did not exceed three or four inches; underneath was a compact and very slippery ice, in which the travellers were obliged to cut steps. The negro went first, in order to dig out these standing-places; the work exhausted him in a moment. In endeavouring to pass ahead to relieve him, Boussingault slipped; but fortunately he was seized by Hall and the negro. For a second all three were in extreme peril. This incident produced a moment's hesitation; but taking fresh courage, they resolved to push forward. The snow became more favourable; they made a last vigorous effort, and at three-quarters past one stood upon the long-desired *arête*. There they felt convinced that more was impossible. They were at the foot of a prism of trachyte, of which the upper base, crowned with a cupola of snow, formed the summit of Chimborazo.

The *arête* to which their indomitable courage had carried them, was only a few feet wide. All around them gloomy precipices frowned, and deep chasms yawned. The deep colouring of the rock contrasted strongly with the dazzling whiteness of the snow. Long stalagmites of ice appeared suspended above their heads, as if a magnificent cascade had suddenly frozen. The weather was admirable; only a few light clouds perceptible in the west. The air was perfectly calm, and their gaze embraced a prospect of immense extent. The situation was as superb as it was novel, and the adventurers enjoyed a keen sensation of triumph.

The point to which they had attained—namely, 19,500 feet above the sea-level—was considerably higher than had hitherto been reached by any explorer.

After a brief interval of repose, they threw off all fatigue; and, indeed, they do not seem to have experienced the "bad quarter of an hour" which most mountaineers are doomed to undergo. Three-quarters of an hour after their arrival, Boussingault's pulse, as well as Colonel Hall's, beat only one hundred and six pulsations in a minute. They were thirsty and slightly feverish, but not to a painful extent. Colonel Hall was particularly lively, and never ceased to utter the smartest sayings, though busily engaged in drawing what he called "the hell of ice" which surrounded them. The travellers noticed that the intensity of sound seemed remarkably attenuated; Boussingault affirms that the voice of his companion was so modified, that in any other circumstances he would have failed to recognize it. He was much astonished also by the feeble noise produced by the hammer with which he struck some smart blows on the rock. It is well known that the rarefaction of the air generally affects in a very marked manner persons who ascend the loftier heights. On the summit of Mont Blanc, Saussure experienced much physical uneasiness and pain at the heart; and his guides, though inhabitants of Chamounix, all suffered in the same way. Acosta informs us that the first Spaniards who ascended the great American mountains were attacked by nausea and internal pain. Bouguer suffered several times from hemorrhage among the Cordilleras of Quito; so did Zumstein on Monte Rosa; and, finally, Humboldt and Bonpland, when they ascended Chimborazo on the 23rd of June 1802, experienced a desire to vomit, and bled at the lips and gums. As for Boussingault and Colonel Hall, though they were conscious of much difficulty of breathing, and of extreme lassitude while in motion, they felt quite at ease as soon as they rested. The cause of this insensibility to the effects of the highly-rarefied air is difficult to determine; but M. Boussingault himself attributes it to their prolonged sojourn in the elevated towns of the Andes. "When one has seen the movement," he says, "which goes on in towns like Bogota, Micuipampa, Potosi, at an elevation of 8200 to 13,000 feet; when one has been a witness of the strength and prodigious agility of the toreadors in a bull-fight at Quito, at an elevation of 9700 feet; when, finally, one has seen young and delicate women abandoning themselves to the dance all night in localities almost as elevated as Mont Blanc—there, where the celebrated Saussure found scarcely strength enough to consult his instruments, and where his vigorous mountaineers fell into a swoon while digging a hole in the snow; if I add, too, that a celebrated battle—that of Pichincha—was fought at an altitude little below that of Mont Blanc, one will understand, I think, that man may accustom himself to breathe the rarefied air of the highest mountains."

While the explorers were making their observations upon the summit of Chimborazo, the weather had maintained its serene and equable character; the sun was even powerful enough to cause them some slight inconvenience. About three o'clock, however, they perceived some clouds forming below, in the plain. The thunder soon began to peal below their station. The noise was not intense, but it was prolonged; they thought at first that it was a *bramido*, or subterranean roaring. Dense clouds quickly surrounded the mountain base; slowly they rolled their way upward: the adventurers felt they had no time to lose; for unless they cleared the dangerous passes before the storm reached them, the peril would be great. A heavy snow-fall, or a frost rendering the path slippery, would have been sufficient to render impracticable their return; and they had no provision for a sojourn upon the glacier.

The descent was difficult. After from 1000 to 1300 feet had been accomplished, they entered the upper part of the belt of clouds; lower down they were caught in a storm of hail, which greatly cooled the air; and at the moment of their falling in with the Indian in charge of the mules, the clouds hurled upon them a volley of hailstones large enough to wound them severely on the hands and face.

As they continued their descent, they noticed that sleet mingled with the hail. Night surprised them on the way; and it was eight o'clock before they re-entered the "métairie."

The observations collected by Boussingault during this expedition, all tended to confirm his theory as to the nature of the trachytic mountains which form the crest of the Cordilleras. Upon Chimborazo he remarked all the characteristics which he had already noticed on the volcanoes of the Equator. Chimborazo itself is an extinct crater. Like Cotopaxi, Antisana, Tunguragua, and the mountains generally which cover the table-lands of the Andean system, its mass is composed of trachytic débris, accumulated without order. These fragments, often of enormous size, have been upheaved in the solid state; their angles are always sharp; there is no indication that they were fused, or even soft. In none of the Andean volcanoes did Boussingault observe any flow of lava; and in this he has been confirmed by later travellers: from their craters have issued only muddy torrents, showers of ashes, and incandescent blocks of more or less solid trachyte, often hurled to considerable distances.

XII.

In Hawaii.

IN the North Pacific Ocean, at an almost equal distance from California, Mexico, China, and Japan, between the parallels of 18° 50′ and 22° 20′ north latitude, and the meridians of 154° 53′ and 160° 15′ west longitude, lie the fair and flourishing group of the Sandwich Islands, discovered by Captain Cook in 1778. They enjoy the advantages of a fertile soil and an equable climate; and their beauty of scenery and luxuriance of vegetation entitle them to be described as oases of the ocean—

"Summer isles of Eden, lying in dark purple spheres of sea."

Their formation is entirely volcanic; and the principal island, Hawaii, or Owhyhee, possesses the largest perpetually active and the largest extinct crater in the world. All of them are mountainous, with bold, romantic outlines; and on Hawaii the two culminating summits are nearly 14,000 feet in height. Their natives are of a quiet and orderly race, and have freely adopted the manners and customs, as well as the system of government, of civilization. They profess the Christian religion; and have constituted their islands an independent kingdom, with legislative houses and courts of justice. Apparently this insular state is destined, from its position, to become in the future a centre of great commercial importance.

But in these pages our object is mountains, and nothing but mountains; and we are attracted to the Hawaiian Archipelago by the great volcanic peaks which crown its principal island. These have been the subject of description by several writers—by Admiral Wilkes, the Rev. William Ellis, Mr. Brigham, and Mr. Manley Hopkins—but for our present purpose we shall adopt the narrative of Miss Isabella L. Bird, who visited Hawaii in 1873, ascended its colossal crater-mountain, and has recorded her experiences in graphic and picturesque language.*

The two peaks of Hawaii are named Mauna Kea (which rises to the height of 13,950 feet) and Mauna Loa (which has an elevation of 13,760 feet). The latter presents a singularly impressive aspect from the sea, with its abrupt precipices and dome-like summit. On its eastern slope, at an altitude of 4000 feet, is situated the terrific crater of Kilauea,—a "sea of fire,"—one of the most extraordinary volcanic phenomena on the face of the globe. A pilgrimage to this crater was undertaken by Miss Bird, and we cannot do better than repeat it under her guidance.

The starting-place is the village of Hilo. After about

* "Six Months in the Sandwich Islands." London, 1875.

AN EXPANSE OF LAVA.

four miles of tolerable road, the track, formed of rough, hard lava, and reduced to a width of twenty-four inches, plunges into the depths of a Tropical forest. It is difficult to imagine a scene of more luxuriant beauty: palms, breadfruit trees, eugenias, candle-nuts of immense size, bananas, bamboos, papayas, and tree-ferns are bound together by lianas of every description, with stems varying in size from the thickness of a man's arm to the slenderness of whipcord; binding all in an impassable network, and waving with festoons and delicate tendrils in the breeze. It is a striking change to emerge from this rich greenery upon a grove of cocoa-nut trees, suffused with the glow of day; and another change is experienced when the traveller quits the grove and enters upon an immense expanse of lava, the remains of a torrent which once flowed from Kilauea towards Hilo, and now lies hardened into hummocks, coils, rippled waves, smooth still pools, and great dark hollows. Here, as Miss Bird remarks, we may vividly realize the universally igneous origin of Hawaii. From the hard black rocks which border the sea, to the loftiest mountain dome or peak, every stone, every atom of dust, every foot of fruitful or barren soil bears the Plutonic mark. In truth, the island has been built up, course upon course, ridge upon ridge, mountain upon mountain, to a height nearly equal with that of Mont Blanc, by the same volcanic forces which are still in operation, and may hereafter augment at intervals the elevation of the blue dome of Mauna Loa. Hawaii is actually and at the present time being wrought up from the ocean; and this great sea of lava, or *pahoehoe*, is no vindictive eruption, spreading ruin and death over a fertile region, but an architectural and formative process.

There is no water, except a few deposits of rain-water in holes, but the moist air and incessant showers have aided nature to mantle this frightful expanse with an abundant vegetation,—principally ferns of an exquisite green, the most conspicuous being the sadleria, the gleichenia Hawaiiensis, a running wire-like fern, and the exquisite microlepia tenuifolia, dwarf guava, with its white flowers resembling orange flowers in odour, and ohelos (vaccinium reticulatum), with their red and white berries, and a profusion of small-leaved ohias (metrosideros polymorpha), with their deep crimson tasselled flowers, and their young shoots of bright crimson, relieved the monotony of green. These crimson tassels, deftly strung on thread or fibres, are much used by the natives for their *leis*, or garlands. The *ti* tree (cordyline terminalis), which abounds also on the lava, is most valuable. They cook their food wrapped up in its leaves. The porous root, when baked, has the taste and texture of molasses candy, and when distilled yields a spirit; and the leaves form wrappings for fish, hard *poi*, and other edibles. Occasionally a clump of tufted cocoa-palms, or of the beautiful candle-nut, rose among the smaller growths. To the left a fringe of palms marked the place where the ocean and the lava met; while, on the right, the traveller is seldom out of sight of the dense timber belt, with its fringe of tree-ferns and bananas, which girdles Mauna Loa.

The ascent is gradual—that is, about 4000 feet in

thirty miles. Only strong and sure-footed horses are useful on the journey, for it is a constant scramble over rocks, up or down natural steps, or along difficult ledges. But the track is generally discernible, owing to the vegetation having been worn off the lava.

Of a volcano in general we think as a colossal cone; but Kilauea is something wholly different. Though situated at a height of nearly 4000 feet on the flank of Mauna Loa, it resembles a vast abyss sunken on a rolling plain. An abyss of nine miles in circumference, and from 800 to 1100 feet in depth, according to the condition of the molten sea below in different years. Sometimes the seething lava-tide is at its flow, sometimes at its ebb. All around its margin, and upon its dreary sides, are indications of violent volcanic force: steam-cracks, deposits of sulphur-crystals, blowing cones, and jets of sulphurous vapour. Frequently the abyss is rent by earthquakes, and at intervals it is the theatre of eruptions of extraordinary but dreadful magnificence. The activity of Kilauea, however, is not confined to these occasional outbursts; its wonderful phenomena are always being manifested in a lake or lakes in the southern part of the crater. Well might the imagination of the Hawaiian represent it as the abode of their all-powerful goddess Pelé. Earth has scarcely any scene more dreadful or more majestic; it is, indeed, a *Haleman-man*, a House of Everlasting Fire. Had Dante seen it, what new horrors he would have introduced into his "Inferno"! The very heaven above shines with a lurid glare, as if, like the abyss, it were involved in perpetual conflagration.

The first descent down the terminal wall of the crater is very steep; but it is covered, and so is the slope which extends to the second stage, with a bright carpet of ohias, ohelos, sadlerias, polypodiums, silver grass, and bulbous plants with berry-clusters of vivid blue. Then the explorer comes to a stretch of rough blocks and ridges of broken lava, apparently forming part of a break which surrounds the entire crater, and marks, in all probability, a tremendous subsidence of its flow. All below is a region of desolation and darkness, filled with weird sights and sounds; broken up into rugged cliffs and terraces, into lakes and rivers, into whirlpools and chasms of lava,—sometimes black and shining, sometimes of an ashen gray, sometimes white with alum, or yellow with sulphur.

The lowest level of the crater, which measures about a mile across, and has from the brink the appearance of a sea at rest, is really an expanse of hardened waves and convolutions of ashy-coloured lava, traversed by huge cracks of black lava of recent formation, and by fissures emitting hot and sulphurous vapours. "Strange to say, in one of these," on the occasion of Miss Bird's visit, "deep down in that black and awful region, three slender metamorphosed ferns were growing, three exquisite forms, the fragile heralds of the great forest of vegetation, which probably, in coming years, will clothe this pit with beauty. Truly they seemed to speak of the love of God." In some of the crevices may be seen the curious filamentous lava, like spun glass of a greenish or yellowish-brown colour, which is called "Pelé's hair."

CRATER OF KILAUEA, ISLAND OF HAWAII.

After threading his way for some distance across this lava-desert, with its hummocks and depressions, exactly resembling a storm-tossed sea which has been suddenly petrified, the traveller reaches the brink of Hale-man-man, the crater within the crater, the lake or pit of fire that boils with ceaseless fury. It is the most unutterable of wonderful things; and Miss Bird declares that the words of common speech are quite useless to describe it. In fact, it is *in*describable, as it is unimaginable; a sight which at once takes possession of every faculty of sense and soul; a sight which realizes in the most dreadful manner the Scriptural images of that "fire which is not quenched," "the place of hell," "the lake which burneth with fire and brimstone," "the everlasting burnings." Then, as if billows of fire broke upon a fiery coast, the air is rent with groanings, and rumblings, and detonations, with seething, hissing, splashing noises, with a roar like that of breakers on remote reefs and rocks. And the lava rises in jets and waves, in bubbling fountains, in burning cones; never the same in appearance for two minutes together; but always terrible, always sublime, always striking the spectator's soul with an ever-deepening impression of awe!

For what he sees, perhaps, is some such spectacle as this:—*

An irregularly-shaped lake, possibly 500 feet at its narrowest part, and nearly half a mile at its broadest, almost divided into two by a low bank of lava, which

---

* In the following description we have adopted Miss Bird's language with some slight alteration.

stretches nearly across its narrowest diameter. The sides of the lake nearest to us are absolutely perpendicular, but nowhere more than forty feet high; but on the opposite side they are bold and craggy, and probably attain an elevation of 150 feet. The prominent object is *fire in motion;* but the surface of the double lake is continually skimming over for a second or two with a cooled crust of a lustrous gray-white, like frosted silver, broken by jagged cracks of a bright rose-colour. Nearly always the movement is made from the sides to the centre, but the central motion in itself always appears independent, and takes a southerly direction. Before each outburst of agitation much hissing is audible, with a throbbing internal roaring, as of imprisoned gases. Now it seems furious, demoniacal, as if no power on earth can bind it; then playful and sportive; then for a second languid, but only while it is accumulating fresh force. At first no fewer than eleven fountains of fire were playing joyously around the lakes; and sometimes the six of the nearer lake ran together in the centre, to go wallowing down in one vortex, from which they reappeared bulging upwards, till they formed a huge cone thirty feet high. Then this cone too, in its turn, plunged downwards in a seething whirlpool; only to reappear in exactly the same number of fountains in different parts of the lake, leaping, tumbling, raging, soaring on high! Sometimes the whole lake, abandoning its usual centripetal motion, as if impelled southwards, assumed the form of mighty waves, and beating heavily against the partial barrier with a roar like that of the Pacific surf, lashed it, and rent it, and boiled over it in clots of liv-

A WAVE OF FIRE, CRATER OF KILAUEA.

ing fire. It was all confusion, commotion, force, terror, glory, majesty, mystery, and even beauty. Then the colour! "Eye hath not seen it!" Molten metal has not that crimson glow, nor blood that vivid light.

The crust perpetually broke up into ridges and furrows, and great pieces were sucked downwards, to be thrown up again on the billowy crests. The eleven lurid fountains played the greater part of the time,— leaping round the lake with "a strength of joyousness" which was perfectly beautiful, on which the spectator, after his emotions of awe and dread, learned to look with pleasure. For three hours the lava-bank which partially separated the lakes rose considerably, owing to the cooling of the spray which overflowed it, and within it was formed a considerable cavern, with a roof of fiery stalactites. Meantime, the surges of the further lake broke in a southerly direction, and tumbled like Atlantic breakers against the bold and craggy cliffs which form its southern boundary, throwing up a fiery foam, and filling the air with unutterable noises.

Almost close below the spectator was an intermittent jet of lava, which kept cooling round what was possibly a blow-hole forming a cone with an open top; the cone being about six feet high on its highest side, and about as many in diameter. Up this cone or chimney the lava sprang every second or two, and cooling as it fell over the edge, rapidly increased its size and elevation. Its fiery interior, and the singular sound with which the lava was regurgitated, had an awful effect. No smoke rose from the lake, but the wind carried a light blue lava in the opposite direction.

Then the lava was possessed with a new impulse. The fire was thrown to a great height; the fountains and jets all wallowed together; new ones appeared and floated merrily round the margin, until suddenly converging towards the centre they united in one glowing mass, which upheaved itself pyramidally, and disappeared with a mighty crash. Suddenly, innumerable billows of fire flung themselves into the air, and the lake divided into twain, recoiling on either side; and then all its fires blended together, and rose as if upheaved by some subterrene force, and the lake surged over the temporary rim which it had formed, flowing majestically downwards, while the central surface dashed and swayed in wild commotion, as if disturbed by some mysterious but irresistible force.

Such is the crater of Kilauea.

Kilauea seems to act as a kind of gigantic safety-valve to the volcano of Mauna Loa. At least, each time that an eruption has taken place from the summit-crater, this lateral crater has been abnormally quiescent. These eruptions have been of a terribly formidable character. As, for instance, in 1855 (the fourth eruption *recorded*), when for several months the lava-flood rolled steadily towards Hilo,—spreading through the dense forests, and creeping shorewards until it seemed as if for that portion of the island was reserved the awful fate which swept Herculaneum and Pompeii from the face of the living world. For thirteen months the inundation continued its progress, until arrested by some natural obstacles which piled the waves up in hillocks, only eight miles from Hilo. It had travelled forty miles, as the crow flies; or sixty, including sinuosities. Its breadth varied from one to three miles, and its depth from two hundred to five hundred feet, according to the configuration of the mountain-slopes over which it took its way. In all it covered nearly 300 square miles of land, and its cubic contents were estimated at 38,000 millions of feet!

In 1859 occurred another eruption. On this occasion the lava-flood ran fifty miles in eight days; and then, slackening its course, steadily progressed towards the sea, into which it extended a new promontory.

But far more disastrous were the circumstances attending the eruption of 1868.

It began on the 27th of March, with a shock of earthquake; and the shocks were repeated daily, with increasing violence, until "the island quivered like the lid of a boiling pot" in the intervals, or trembled like a ship struck by a heavy wave. Then the summit-crater, Moknarveorveo, sent up columns of smoke and steam and lurid fiery light; and the southern slope of its dome was cloven in four deep chasms, and from each chasm issued a river of molten matter, the four rivers flowing down the mountain-sides in divergent lines. Suddenly these paused in their impetuous onset, and the blue mountain-dome rose into the still air without any sign of fire, steam or smoke.

The lull, however, was of brief duration. The earthquake shocks returned, and became nearly continuous; the throbbing, jerking, and quivering motions grew more positive, intense, and sharp; they were vertical, rotary, lateral, and undulatory. Late in the afternoon of a beautiful day (April 2nd), the catastrophe came. The crust of the earth swelled and sank, like a sea in a storm. Hills were overthrown and rocks cloven in twain; houses were shattered to the ground; trees swayed like reeds; and a great terror fell upon men and animals. The earth opened in numerous clefts and fissures, and horses and their riders were laid prostrate. To all it seemed as if "the rocky ribs of the mountains, and the granite walls and pillars of the earth, were breaking up." At Kilauea the shocks were as frequent as the tickings of a watch. In Kau, to the south of Hilo, three hundred were counted on this day of dread; and an eye-witness has recorded that the earth swayed to and fro, north and south, then east and west, and round and round, while the trees crashed as if torn by a strong rushing wind. People sat on the ground, steadying themselves with interlocked hands and feet to avoid being rolled over. They saw an avalanche of "red earth," which they supposed to be lava, break from the mountain-side, and rush downwards with fearful velocity; in three minutes it travelled as many miles, and buried a hamlet with thirty-one inhabitants and five hundred head of cattle beneath its ruins. The shore subsided; and, simultaneously, a wave, estimated at from forty to sixty feet in height, hurled its mass upon the coast and receded five times, destroying whole villages, and even strong stone houses, and carrying away six-and-forty natives.

Five days later, the ground south of Hilo was sud-

CASCADE OF LAVA, HAWAII.

denly broken open, and a lava-flood, which had travelled subterraneously for twenty miles, poured forth with tremendous fury. Four great fountains threw up glowing lava, and rocks weighing several tons, to a height of from 500 to 1000 feet. "From these great fountains to the sea," says Mr. Whitney, "flowed a rapid stream of red lava, rolling, rushing, and tumbling, like a swollen river,—bearing along in its current large rocks that made the lava foam as it dashed down the precipice and through the valley into the sea, surging and roaring throughout its length like a cataract, with a power and fury perfectly indescribable. It was nothing else than a river of fire from 200 to 800 feet wide and 20 deep, with a speed varying from ten to twenty-five miles an hour." On its way to the sea it again divided into four streams, between which men and beasts were hopelessly shut up. One stream hurried to the shore in four hours, but the others occupied two days in travelling ten miles. The aggregate width was a mile and a half. "Where it entered the sea, it extended the coast-line half a mile; but this worthless accession to Hawaiian acreage was dearly purchased by the loss, for ages at least, of 4000 acres of valuable pasture-land and a much larger quantity of magnificent forest. The whole south-east shore of Hawaii sank from four to six feet, which involved the destruction of several hamlets and the beautiful fringe of cocoa-nut trees. About one hundred lives were lost on this occasion.

MAUI, another of the Hawaiian group, has a great extinct volcano, known to the natives as Haleakala, the "house of the sun." It was ascended in 1873 by Miss Bird.

She started, with several companions, and a train of mules and horses, loaded with mountain-gear, at two in the morning. The road, at first very good, soon degenerated into a wood road, then into a bridle track, and finally into a mere trail; and at dawn the excursionists found themselves more than half-way up the mountain, with rocks, scoriæ, tussocks, ohelos, and a few common compositæ all around them. The vegetation grew coarser and scantier the higher they ascended, but nowhere entirely ceased. Even at the summit, which is 10,200 feet above the sea, bloomed a few tufts of grass and some dwarf ferns. The cold was severe, and the rarefied air rendered walking difficult.

The sunrise flushed the cloud-belt below with delicate rosy tints, and now and then the vaporous masses parted, and revealed enchanting gleams of verdurous meadows and deep-blue sea. At seven, after a rough ascent, the travellers reached the summit, where the view was barred by a rugged wall of rock. Entering through a gap, they found themselves in the presence of the largest crater on the face of the globe. Owing to its peculiar formation, its entire extent, though the surrounding precipices stretch over a circuit of nineteen miles, can be seen at once, and the effect is singularly impressive. Two thousand feet deep lies its huge irregular floor, which is strewn with numerous cones, in clusters or standing alone, as high as Arthur's Seat. On the north and east are the Koolau and Kaupo Gaps, through which, in the remote ages, tremendous lava-torrents have found their way to the sea. The spectator might be forgiven for imagining that once upon a time the volcanic forces broke into sudden tumult, shattered the mountain-summit, exhausted all their fury, and then subsided into an everlasting calm.

The crater is composed of a hard gray clinkstone, traversed by innumerable fissures. Its internal cones are regular in shape, with fiercely red sides, and their central cavities lined with layers of black ash. They are all built up of cinders of light specific gravity, and the ash is largely tinged with the hydrated oxide of iron. Small quantities of sulphur are scattered about, but there are no hot springs, no jets of steam or sulphurous vapour. The volcano is absolutely lifeless.

Our travellers divided the time between glimpses into this abyss of desolation, and watching the ever-varying cloud-scenery which lends so great a charm to the view from Haleakala. Before them spread the gaunt, desolate, hideous pit, with its lurid red cones and its congealed rivers and surges of black lava and gray ash, crossing or mingling all over the area,—with splatches of yellow or rusty colour and coils of satiny rock,—with dark, gloomy walls, everywhere riven and splintered, and clouds sailing in through the deep valley-gaps, and filling the crater with their white swirling masses. "Before noon clouds surrounded the whole mountain—not in the vague, flocculent, meaningless masses one usually sees, but in Arctic oceans, where lofty icebergs, floes, and pack, lay piled on each other, glistening with the frost of a Polar winter; then Alps on Alps, and peaks of well-remembered ranges gleaming above glaciers, and the semblance of forests in deep ravines loaded with new-fallen snow. Snow-drifts, avalanches, oceans held in bondage of eternal ice,—and all this massed together, shifting, breaking, glistening, filling up the broad channel which divides Maui from Hawaii; and far away above the lonely masses, rose, in turquoise blue, like distant islands, the lofty Hawaiian domes of Mauna Kea and Mauna Loa, with snow on Mauna Kea yet more dazzling than the clouds. There never was a stranger contrast, than between the hideous desolation of the crater below and those blue and jewelled summits rising above the shifting clouds. After some time the scene changed, and through glacial rifts appeared as in a dream the Eeka mountains which enfold the low valley, broad fields of cane 8000 feet below, the flushed palm-fringed coast, and the deep-blue sea sleeping in perpetual calm. But, according to the well-known fraud which isolated altitudes perpetrate upon the eye, it appeared as if we were looking *up* at our landscape, not down; and no effort of the eye or imagination would put things at their proper levels."

The travellers began to descend soon after noon, and reached the village of Makawao at nightfall, fatigued physically, but delighted with the recollections of their enterprise.

Let us now return to Hawaii, and undertake the ascent of Mauna Loa.

We start, as usual, in single file, the guide leading the way, and follow a difficult path through long grass and ferns and dead and living koa trees,—all, dead and living, encrusted with a long gray hairy lichen, which gives them the appearance of being coated with frost.

After two hours' ascent we reach the boundary of the wooded region, and halt while our mules are fed, and our native attendants collect fuel for the fire we shall certainly need upon the summit. On resuming our journey, we cross wide up-reaching tracts of *pahoehoe*, or smooth lava,—a dreary wilderness extending seven thousand feet towards the crest. A dreary wilderness of lava, broken up into such a variety of shapes that it fatigues the imagination to dwell upon them. Here, indeed, we recognize something of the awful character of the volcanic power. Mauna Loa occupies the whole of the southern districts of Hawaii; it is nearly three miles high, and its base is one hundred and eighty miles in circumference. Yet the colossal bulk of this huge mountain, exceeding 8000 feet in height, is one hopeless waste of unproductive lava.

It is no easy work to toil up its barren, broken, contorted, and deep-furrowed acclivities. Pinnacles have to be doubled, crevasses crossed, impracticable lava-streams avoided. We are called upon to wind round the bases of fissured hummocks, to leap from crag to crag, to scale precipitous steeps, and to tread warily over crusts that ring with an ominously hollow sound. No animal but a mule could carry us safely through such a labyrinth of difficulties;—stepping over deep clefts which lead downwards, it may be, to the sea of fire,—traversing hilly lakes shattered by frequent earthquakes,—painfully labouring up the sides of mounds of scoriæ frothed with pumice-stone,—and again, for miles, stumbling over rolling surfaces of billowy lava! And all this under a Tropic sun and a cloudless sky.

Towards the afternoon, however, the clouds begin to gather, and accumulate below us in wonderful snow-like masses,—pure and brilliant to us who look down upon them from a sunlit height, though dark and gloomy enough to the eyes of the dwellers in the plains,—and these masses soon interpose between us and the "nether world" an impenetrable screen, which confines us to the solitariness of the mountain-top.

The cold now becomes intense, though the rarefied air so quickens the circulation of the blood that our pulses beat one hundred a minute. We wrap ourselves in our thickest coverlets, and press forward and upward,—forward and upward,—climbing dizzy ledges and skirting yawning crevasses,—until we surmount the topmost terrace, and stand upon the "ghastly volcanic table-land, creviced, riven, and ashy, and twenty-four miles in circumference," which forms the summit of Mauna Loa. Dismounting from our mules, we cross this table-land until we come to the edge of the great crater of Moknarveorveo, which is 11,000 feet in length by 8000 feet in width, or about six miles in circumference. Moreover, it is about 800 feet in depth. A fitting theatre for the action of forces so vast and terrible as those of the Hawaiian volcano!

In a deep gorge at one end of the crater rises a jet or fountain of pure yellow fire—a jet composed of several smaller jets, which unite together and leap upwards to a height of 200, 300, and even 600 feet. And all around spreads a mighty murmur, like that of far-off ocean-breakers, now rising and now swelling, and filling the soul with a sense of unutterable awe. This, indeed, is one of those voices of Nature which compel the attention even of the most indifferent, and seem to speak of the mutability of worldly things and the eternity of the Creator.

The area of the crater appears from our standing-point like "a dark gray and tolerably level lake,"—the dark gray relieved here and there by stains of white and yellow, and blotches of black, and the level interrupted by numerous irregular fissures. No steam or smoke proceeds from any part of the surface, which wears the peculiar look of deadness and gloom so eloquent of the past action of fire. About thirty feet above the level projects a ledge or ancient beach, marking the former elevation of the lava; and here are various signs of present volcanic activity, such as smoke-jets and steaming sulphur-banks.

When the sun has set, and night come on with its sudden darkness, as it does in the Tropics, the hitherto dead and dreary crater seems to leap into life. Gleams of fire, burning steadily in rows like blast-furnaces, chequer the wide expanse; others, isolated at vast intervals, shine like stars; rows of tiny jets indicate the margin of the lowest level of the crater; it is fire above and below, fire everywhere! Fire calm and stationary; fire flickering in irregular gusts; fire streaming in wavy lines; and thus betraying that beneath the dark crust of lava lurks an incandescent sea, descending, it may be, to the very centre of the earth! "Broad in the glare, giving light enough to read by at a distance of three-quarters of a mile, making the moon look as blue as an ordinary English sky, its golden gleam changed to a vivid rose colour, lighting up the whole of the vast precipices of that part of the crater with a rosy red, bringing out every detail here, throwing cliffs and heights into huge black masses there, rising, falling, never intermitting, leaping in lofty jets with glorious shapes like wheat-sheaves, coruscating, reddening, the most glorious thing beneath the moon is the fire-fountain of Moknarveorveo."

The crater looks by night a wholly different thing from what it does in the day. By day its crust was black and even sooty, with a jet of molten gold playing upwards from it; by night it was incandescent everywhere, with "black blotches of cooled scum," which were continually absorbed and continually reappearing. In the centre the lake glowed with a white heat, and waves of white lava revolved in a swirling vortex; and from this centre rose the fountain, solid at its base, which is estimated at 150 feet in diameter, but tapering and thinning as it mounted, and falling from its great elevation in a shower of fiery spray. "When one jet was about half high, another rose so as to keep up the action without intermission; and in the lower part of this fountain two subsidiary curved jets of great volume continually crossed each other. So, 'alone in its glory,' perennial, self-born, springing up in sparkling light, the fire-fountain played on as the hours went by."

That the entire interior of the huge dome-like summit-peak of Mauna Loa is fluid, would seem to be probable; for the eruptions from its crater are not the result of an overflow, but of the yielding of the mountain-sides to an irresistible pressure. Thus, in 1855, the mountain-side split open, and the lava poured forth for thirteen months in a slow-moving stream, which extended sixty miles in length, and covered an area of three hundred square miles.

The appearances of the crater alter every hour. "Blowing cones" are formed with a report like that of cannon; the lava-river broadens and advances; fresh banks of lava are thrown up; and stars of fire sparkle over the blackened crust. The great fire-fountain plunges upwards to a greater height, and intercrossing jets play across its lurid base. The colours deepen into an intense crimson, or soften away into rose-red, and ruby flashes shoot across the wonderful scene. It is very beautiful, but the beauty is of an unearthly character, and awes rather than pleases, terrifies rather than charms.

We close this chapter with an adaptation of Miss Bird's account of her ascent of Hualalai ("offspring of the rising sun"), another of the Hawaiian volcanoes, about 10,000 feet high.

She made the ascent twice: the first time guided by her host and hostess; the second time, somewhat adventurously, by herself alone. Forests of *koa*, sandal-wood, and *ohia*, with an undergrowth of raspberries and ferns, clothe its base; the fragrant *mailé*, and the graceful sarsaparilla vine, with its clustered coral-coloured buds, nearly smother many of the trees; and in several places the heavy *ié* forms the semblance of triumphal arches over the track. This forest terminates abruptly on the great volcanic wilderness, with its starved growth of unsightly scrub. But Hualalai, notwithstanding its height, is covered with bracken, coarse burnt grass, and similar vegetation to its very summit, which is crowned by a small, solitary, blossoming *ohia*.

For two hours before reaching the top, the way lies over streams and beds of lava, considerably disintegrated. Pit craters extend over the whole mountain, all of them more or less clothed with a coarse unhandsome vegetation. The edges are often very rugged and picturesque. The depth varies from 300 to 700 feet, and the diameter from 700 to 1200 feet. In some the walls are of a smooth gray stone, in others they are composed of tufa. In not a few places they are so crowded together that the ridge dividing them is only wide enough for two people to walk abreast upon it. The mountain was rent by an earthquake in 1868, and a great fissure stretches for some distance across it. From every point of view on this side it is very striking, being a "complete wilderness of craters,"—and upwards of one hundred and fifty lateral cones have been counted.

The object of Miss Bird's second ascent was to visit one of the most magnificent of the summit-craters. It is bordered by a narrow and very curious ridge of rock, which is crowned by a mound, some 60 feet in height, composed of fragments of black, orange, blue, red, and golden lava, with a cavity or blow-hole in the centre, estimated by Brigham as having a diameter of 1800 feet and a depth of 25. The interior is dark brown, much grooved horizontally, and as smooth and regular as if turned. No steam-cracks or signs of heat are anywhere visible. Superb caves or "lava-bubbles," formed by the sudden cooling and contraction of the lava, abound at a height of 6000 feet. These are draperied with ferns, and the drip from their roofs is the water-supply of this porous region.

Owing to the vegetation which partially conceals its ruggedness, Hualalai looks as if it had slept for ages; but it has been quiescent only since 1801, when it broke out into violent eruption, flooding several villages, destroying many plantations and fish-ponds, filling up a deep bay twenty miles in extent, and forming the present coast. The panic-stricken inhabitants threw living hogs into the destructive lava-torrent, and even costlier offerings, with a view to propitiate their offended gods; but all proved useless, until King Kamehameha, attended by a large retinue of priests and chiefs, cut off a portion of his hair, which was considered sacred, and flung it into the flood. Then it ceased to flow. Probably the king or his counsellors had discovered some signs of its approaching abatement before he essayed this proof of his royal power.

And here we close our description of the Hawaiian volcanoes.

XIII.

Mount Ararat.

ARARAT, strictly speaking, is the name given to a mountainous district of Asia Minor, in the province of Armenia, which has acquired a peculiar interest from its connection with the Scriptural records of the Deluge. It was unknown to the ancient geographers, as it is to the modern Armenians; but evidence exists to prove that it was an old and indigenous name for a portion of Armenia,—and it seems to have been applied to the elevated table-land which overlooks the plain of the Araxes on the north, and of Mesopotamia on the south. At a very early date this table-land was put forward as the spot where the ark rested after the subsidence of the Noachian Flood. Thus, Berosus the Chaldean, contemporary with Alexander the Great, places that event on the mountains of Kurdistan, which form the southern frontier of Armenia. His opinion was adopted by the Syriac and Chaldee versions of the Old Testament, and afterwards by the Koran. Tradition's finger still points to the Jebel Judi as the scene of the event, and legends record that fragments of the ark still lie upon its lonely summit. And, indeed, it was only natural that the Ararat range should be selected by an inhabitant of the Mesopotamian plain, to whom it must have represented the world's furthest limit, or at least its loftiest summits. With this neighbourhood, at all events, are connected all the Noachian associations and traditions; and European travellers have confirmed the opinion of the natives so far as to confine the name Ararat to the loftiest and most striking mountain in the district,— the great peak which the Armenians call *Massis;* the Turks, *Agri-Dagh,* or the "Steep Mountain;" and the Persians, *Kah-i-Nuh,* or "Noah's Mountain." Ararat, then, as it is now called, starts immediately from the plain of the Araxes, and terminates in two conical summits, the Great and the Less Ararat, about seven miles distant from each other; the former attaining an elevation of 17,260 feet above the sea-level, while the latter is about 4000 feet lower. The crest of the former, for about 3000 feet of perpendicular height, is shrouded in eternal snow. Its middle region abounds in immense masses of cinders, lava, and porphyry, indicating the volcanic origin of the mountain; and a chasm on its northern side has been regarded as a crater. On the 2nd of July 1840 it was the scene of an outbreak, in which the village of Arguri and the monastery of St. James were destroyed. A violent earthquake brought down an avalanche of earth and stones from the upper heights, which buried beneath its ruins both the convent and the village. As the shock was followed by clouds of reddish smoke and a pungent sulphurous odour, it is assumed that the volcanic forces of Ararat are not extinct.

It was long believed that the summit of Ararat was inaccessible, and the Armenians still adhere to the belief; though its ascent was accomplished in 1829 by Parrot,* and several later travellers have successfully followed in his footsteps. The region immediately below the snow-line they describe as bare and desolate, unvisited by beast or bird, and haunted by a silence and a solitude which are completely overpowering. Arguri, the only village known to have been erected on its slopes, was the spot where, according to an ancient tradition, Noah planted his vineyard; and at Nachdjevan, in the plain of the Araxes, the patriarch is reputed to have been buried.

Mount Ararat forms the culminating point of Western Asia, and the loftiest peak of the Ala-dagh chain, an eastern prolongation of the Anti-Taurus. It is situated in lat. 39° 42′ N., and long. 44° 35′ E.

One of the legends connected with it relates that, in the early ages of Christianity, a poor monk conceived the idea of offering his prayers on the sacred summit, and thrice attempted the ascent, but was thrice brought back by angels to his starting-point,—where he was ordered to build the chapel destroyed along with the village of Arguri in 1840.

We shall now borrow a few extracts from the narratives of travellers who have been more successful than the monk. M. Bellinger, in his "Voyage aux Indes," says:—

---

* Tournefort, the botanist, had made the attempt in 1700, but failed. Some English travellers accomplished it in 1857.

MOUNT ARARAT.

"Early in the morning of the 23rd of April we set out from Ouchayan; we descended the escarpment of the ravine watered by the Asterck, which we crossed upon a bridge remarkable for its architectural gracefulness. Afterwards we reascended by a very abrupt path, carried over volcanic rocks, which appeared to me to have furnished the materials of the bridge. It is impossible to give any idea of the difficulties our horses surmounted in climbing this steep; twenty times mine was on the point of stumbling and dragging me into the river. At length we reached the summit without accident, and found ourselves in a plain covered with volcanic wreck, and clumps of artemisia and euphorbia. From this plain we perceived very distinctly the snowy summits of Ararat; which, owing to its great elevation, seemed close upon us, though it was more than twelve leagues distant. This colossus of Armenia exhibits itself under the form of two pyramids, the lesser of which terminates in a sharp cone, while the other, with its truncated crest, has the appearance of an extinct crater."

Geographers differed in opinion as to the height of this celebrated mountain until 1829, when the question was solved by Professor Parrot, of Dorpat. As soon as the district of Ararat had been conquered by the Russian armies, M. Parrot formed the project of a pilgrimage, at his own cost, to the famous mountain which is consecrated in Holy Writ as the second cradle of the human race. He set out in the middle of March 1829. Let us now leave him to speak for himself, in the letters which he addressed to his father:—

"MONASTERY OF ST. GREGORY, ON THE LOWER SLOPES OF ARARAT,
"*September 22, 1829.*

"We set out from Tiflis on the first of September, and arrived—it was snowing all the way—at the monastery of Etchmiadzin on the eighth. We started again on the tenth, crossed the Araxes, passed the night in the open air, and reached the monastery on the evening of the eleventh.

"In our first tentative ascent of Ararat, on the east side of the mountain, we attained an elevation of 12,996 feet above the sea; but when we had gained this altitude, we saw very clearly that to reach the summit on this side would be impossible, owing to the precipitousness of the icy slope we should have to traverse. I followed, therefore, some days later, the advice of a peasant,—to attempt the north-west side,—accompanied by Messrs. Behagel and Shleman, scholars of the university, the brave Deacon Abojan, two infantry soldiers, a Cossack, and five of the people of the village. On the first day, we mounted to the perpetual snow-line, where we spent the night around a bivouac-fire. At daybreak we set out for the summit, hoping to reach it at noon; but at that hour we had only succeeded in ascending as high as 14,400 feet. As it appeared to me that we had still upwards of 1800 feet to climb, at a pace which continually slackened,—and more, seeing that masses of cloud and fog were advancing towards the mountain, and at nightfall would cover it with snow, I found myself compelled to redescend."

"MONASTERY OF ST. GREGORY,
"*September 28th.*

"I hasten to announce that I have succeeded in accomplishing the ascent of Ararat. It was the third attempt which I undertook on the 25th of this month, when I was accompanied by the robust and intrepid Abojan, by five peasants, and two Russian soldiers. We arrived at the summit on the 27th, at three o'clock in the afternoon. The difficulties were numerous, and probably I owe the entire success to the ardour of the two soldiers and one of the peasants, the others having been unable to follow us. From our first entry on the frozen snow up to the summit, we were compelled to dig out with the hatchet a series of steps or notches in which to place our feet. These were even more necessary in the descent than in the ascent; for the *coup d'œil*, plunging from so great an elevation upon those immense precipitous surfaces of shining ice, intersected by deep and obscure precipices, has really an imposing character even for him who is inured to such enterprises. This time, as on our second attempt, the weather proved as favourable as could be wished. We had spent the night in the midst of the frosts, in an atmosphere so tranquil and serene that I scarcely felt the cold, which is extremely keen at these great heights. The moon herself took care to guide our uncertain steps on the cone of ice, when, after sunset, I found myself far beyond the region of perpetual snow. The barometer then gave 16,200 feet as our altitude above the sea-level."

Though M. Parrot did not discover on the summit any crater of the ordinary form, and though it is difficult to believe that it is represented by the enormous crevasse which cleaves the mountain on its northwest side, there can be no doubt, as we have said, of its volcanic origin. Ararat and the plain present a succession of lava-tracts, from the snow-line to a circumference of twelve miles round the base. This fact, and its situation equi-distant from the Black Sea and the Caspian, entitle us to regard it as a Mediterranean volcano, one of the most ancient and considerable in Asia.

We conclude with an account of the proceedings of the scientific expedition conducted by M. Khodyko, in August 1850, and recorded by M. de St. Martin in the "Nouvelles Annales des Voyages."

"On the 29th of July, we pitched our camp on the

Great Ararat, at a distance of seven versts from the source of Saretai-Boidak, and in proximity to the snow-belt, the lower boundary of which stretched very far down the mountain that year. After receiving a final supply of fuel and provisions, Colonel Khodyko decided on commencing the march on the 1st of August.

"The weather proving auspicious, we proceeded without delay to pack up the instruments. The baggage of the individuals who were to take part in the ascent were placed on horseback, and our tents were struck at six in the morning. At the outset, the beasts of burden advanced without any difficulty upon the snow which covered the ground; but soon the extraordinary precipitousness of the acclivities made them stumble and yield under their load in such a manner that we were compelled to abandon them. The stores were then placed upon four sledges, which had been previously prepared in case of accident. The soldiers of the detachment were harnessed to them, and began to haul them up with all their might, animating one another by lively sayings and shouts of cheerful encouragement.

"Colonel Khodyko made light of every difficulty, and kept close beside the sledges, while the idler members of the expedition skirted the rocks on the left side of the ravine, the course of which we carefully followed. At the head of the column marched an Armenian, named Simon, who, in 1845, had acted as guide to M. Abich. He bore a cross, which we proposed to plant on the summit of Ararat.

"Though frequently delayed by the slowness with which the transportation of the baggage was necessarily effected, the detachment succeeded in reaching, about two o'clock in the afternoon, the first gap on this side of the rocky mountain-ridge. At three o'clock we crossed the ravine, keeping to the right, where we were rejoined by M. Khodyko. We pushed forward for some distance, and then halted under the enormous rock of Taset-Kelessi, which constitutes in a certain degree the lower stage or terrace of the summit. Here, the abruptness of the incline, and the insufficient amount of shelter from the snow, rendered the establishment of a camp exceedingly difficult. Nevertheless, thanks to the zealous exertions of the soldiers, the area was swept clear, and our small company disposed themselves to rest. We waited the dawn with the more impatience that clouds were accumulated around the summit and sharp ridges of the Taset-Kelessi, and that the pealing of the thunder, joined to the glare of the lightning, incessantly disturbed the silence of night.

"At six o'clock on the morning of the 2nd of August, our company resumed their march; but obstacles multiplied at every step. We gained the rocky crest which stretches along the ravine on the left, and gradually rose to the upper regions. The sky, which was tolerably clear in the morning, gradually darkened with accumulating clouds; and towards noon a west wind arose, bringing with it whirling clouds of hail and frozen snow. This storm compelled Colonel Khodyko to empty the sledges of all their contents, with the exception of the instruments. The Cossacks employed in the work of transportation, stimulated by the example of their chief, did not the less gaily resume their laborious task, with all the audacity, carelessness, and energy characteristic of the Russian soldier.

"About one o'clock they reached the north-eastern extremity of the chain of rocks, which at some distance beyond loses itself in a formation composed of stony débris, crossed in all directions by beds of snow and ice. This tract extends to the base of the last escarpment of the summit-peak, near which we found, erect, and firmly planted in the ground, the cross planted in 1845 by one of M. Abich's servants. Here we halted for a while, hoping the storm would subside. But in vain. At half-past two the wind increased in violence, and, what was worse, a dense fog enveloped the summit of the mountain. We resolved, therefore, to push forward, so as to secure some degree of covert among the rocks of the escarpment from the rapidly gathering hurricane. We toiled up the height about half-way, and then were convinced against our will of the impossibility of making any further progress on that day. Our attendants were harassed and half-frozen; the snow lashed their faces and blinded them; while incessant gusts of wind obstructed the passage of the heavy sledges with the instruments. To find a refuge seemed difficult. Abrupt rocks were accumulated so close together, that we could nowhere find a corner spacious enough for our accommodation. M. Khodyko at length decided, at five o'clock, to dismiss half his men; ordering them to return to our camp at Taset-Kelessi, where, as a matter of precaution, we had left a tent. Then the rest of us, six in number, took possession of a small plateau, open to every wind. We made some preparations for the night. Huddling ourselves together in the smallest possible space, we had for our coverings a carpet and a skin which had been used to protect the instruments from the rain. And this uncomfortable position was ours until morning.

"Meantime, the wind continued to augment in fury. Rending at times the thick mantle of clouds which shrouded the mountain on every side, it opened up to us, by the pale gleam of the moon, either a nook of the valley of the Araxes, or the outlines of the Lesser Ararat, the summit of which sank already beneath our feet, or the sombre steeps which surrounded our inhospitable asylum, situated at an elevation considerably exceeding that of Mont Blanc. About ten o'clock in the evening, to complete our misery, the tempest came; and by the vividness of the lightnings and the force of the thunder we soon felt assured that we were caught in the very bosom of the electric clouds. At each explosion, the lightning did not flash through the air in a zigzag path, as is usual, but instantaneously filled the void with a dazzling lustre, shaded with reflections of green, red, and white. The thunder-peals followed almost immediately on the passage of the lightning; their awful detonations were long and distinctly repeated by the innumerable echoes of the mountain-gorges. Towards midnight the storm subsided, but the snow continued to fall in flakes. Those of us who had not changed our places were covered three to four inches deep. The day at length began to break, but not with any promise of favourable weather. The summits, it is true, were released from their vaporous shrouds; but, in revenge, the flanks of the Lesser Ararat, and all the lower region accessible to the eye, disappeared beneath a screen of clouds which, seen from above, resembled an undulating icy sea. As the sun gradually rose above the horizon, it emerged from the midst of these vapours; light at first like wreaths of smoke, but afterwards condensing into thick and snowy mists. Towards three o'clock the sky slightly cleared, but the wind did not diminish in impetuosity. Our situation became so intolerable that we determined on continuing the ascent, in the hope of discovering, beyond the rocks, a smooth breadth of ground which we knew to be contiguous to the summit.

"At four o'clock we quitted our resting-place, but we did not reach the plateau in question until we had crossed a third chain of rocks. It proved to incline at an angle of 50°, and was strewn with small-sized pyrites, which emitted a strong odour of sulphur. To the right stretches the ravine which touches on the Taset-Kelessi and abuts on the summit-peak; on the left extends another, terminating at the Makinsk glacier, and not less rude or precipitous than the former. On gaining the centre of the table-land, we were forced to halt, though only nine hundred paces from the summit,—fatigue and the wind preventing our further progress. We succeeded, after almost incredible efforts, in pitching a couple of tents, at a part where the ground was less precipitous than elsewhere, though its slope was still equal to 30°, and even 40°. And this position we maintained for three days and two nights,—from the 3rd to the 5th of August,—during which period the wind, snow, hail, and sleet continued almost uninterruptedly.

"Sunset, on the 5th of August, marked the conclusion of the storm. On the morning of the 6th, the wind had completely sunk; all the ravines of Ararat, the Great and Less, were clear and open; and on the horizon remained only a slender wreath or girdle of clouds, crowning the distant peaks of the Karabagh and the gigantic terraces of the Savalan, whose outline was distantly defined to the east.

"M. Khodyko resolved to employ the morning in exploring the summits, as well as in seeking an advantageous site for the establishment of his instruments and his camp. At three-quarters past eight he set out with his Cossacks, and a quarter of an hour later planted his feet on the topmost platform of the mountain. Three summits dominate it. On two of these we discerned pyramidal eminences, or cairns, built up of fragments of stone, and crowned by beacon-posts; they had been erected by some soldiers who, a month before, had voluntarily undertaken the ascent of the Ararat. We rapidly climbed the nearest summit, and afterwards crossed the second, which Abich had visited in 1845. But great was our surprise when, having gained the topmost stone, we saw before us a third summit, considerably higher than the others, and separated from them by a deep depression. The sides of this depression were almost perpendicular, and it was with difficulty we accomplished the passage. However, all obstacles gave way before our perseverance, and at ten o'clock in the morning—it was the Feast of the Transfiguration—we stood in triumph on the culminating point of the Greater Ararat.

"Here, first of all, we proceeded to erect the cross. In the absence of the guide Simon, it had been intrusted to a Cossack, named Dokhnoff. On arriving at the indicated spot, he fell on his knees, prostrated himself before the symbol of human redemption, and immediately set to work to plant it in the ground. This done, the assistants gathered around the Christian memorial, which they had thus erected on the summit of the Biblical mountain; and the ceremony terminated with a fervent prayer, at which was present a Persian and a Mohammedan, Nooarsaz-Ali, who had arrived that day from the lower encampment. Colonel Khodyko then made arrangements for our departure, fearing that the wind, which still blew violently, might render dangerous a prolonged sojourn on the mountain. The descent from the heights of Ararat exposed us to considerable hazard, particularly on account of the rapid and slippery declivities near its summit: the slightest false step might have hurled us into the snow-wreaths of the Taset-Kelessi ravine; but, with the help of our iron-shod alpenstocks, we escaped every danger, and about noon regained our camp in safety."

When M. Abich ascended Ararat, July 29, 1845, he and his six companions remained an hour on the summit, without suffering any inconvenience from wind or cold. Prior to undertaking the ascent, he had pitched his tent for some time on the upper slope of the mountain, in the valley or depression between the two peaks already spoken of, at an elevation of about 6000 feet above the sea. He declares that from this point the summit may be reached with considerable facility. As the period most suitable for such an enterprise, he names the latter weeks of July or the opening days of August, when the summer attains its maximum heat, and the sky is clear and unclouded, the atmosphere calm and undisturbed. After the middle of August fine weather is not to be expected; atmospheric disturbances increase in fury and frequency; and the traveller incurs great peril from violent thunderstorms, accompanied by tornadoes of hail and snow.

We have referred to the eruption of July 2, 1840—which took place at the head of the great ravine, and destroyed the monastery of St. James and the village of Arguri. Its principal features are thus described by Wagner, in his *Reise nach dem Ararat*:—" Half an hour before sunset, on the 2nd of July, when the air was perfectly clear, the inhabitants of Armenia were alarmed by a thunderous din, that rolled loudest and most fearfully in the neighbourhood of the Great Ararat. During an undulating motion of the earth, lasting about two seconds, which extended from the mountain in an easterly and south-easterly direction, and accomplished great havoc in the districts of Sharur and Nakhichevan, a rent was formed at the head of the great chasm, about three miles above Arguri, from which gas and vapour rose, ejecting with immense force stones and earth over the mountain-slope and down into the plain. Very speedily the vapour rose higher than the summit of the mountain; it seems to have been wholly of aqueous composition, for in the same night a heavy rain fell in the vicinity,

—an unusual occurrence in this country during summer. At first the vapour was tinged with various colours, red and blue prevailing. Whether flames burst forth could not be ascertained; the smoke or vapour-columns, however, had a reddish tint, which, had the outbreak taken place during night, would probably have been found to be due to flame. Soon the blue and red of the vapour passed into black, and the air became filled with a strong and pungent smell of sulphur. While the mountain continued to heave, and the earth to shake, along with the incessant thunder, and noises as of a subterranean cracking and growling, might be heard the whiz as of bombs, caused by the force with which stones and large masses of rock, some upwards of fifty tons weight, were hurled through the air; and the hurtling of these tremendous missiles as they met in their wild flight, could be distinguished from the thunderous sounds rolling in the interior of the mountain. These large stones generally lay where they fell; for, in consequence of the gentle inclination of the ground at the base of Ararat, to roll far was impossible.

"The eruption lasted an hour. When the vapour had cleared away, and the shower of earth and stones had ceased, the rich village of Arguri, and the monastery and chapel of St. James, were no longer visible; all, along with their inmates, had been buried under the ejected mass. The earthquake which accompanied the eruption destroyed, it is said, six thousand houses in the neighbouring districts of Nakhichevan, Sharur, and Ardulad.

"Four days later a second catastrophe occurred, and

spread still further the area of destruction at the mountain's base. After the rent in the chasm, from which the stones and vapour had issued, closed, there remained in the same place a deep basin filled with water by the melting of the snow, the rain, and a streamlet from above, so as to form a small lake. The mass of stone and clay, which served as a dam, and encircled the lake like the rim of a crater, was burst by the weight of water, and poured down the declivity of the mountain with irresistible fury a deluge of thick mud, which spread into the plain, and partially filled up the bed and diverted the course of the small river Karasa. So much of the gardens of Arguri as had escaped the eruption were now destroyed, and the mud-torrent carried trees, rocks, and the bodies of the inhabitants of the village, down into the plain, and into the bed of the Karasa. This flood was thrice repeated, and each time accompanied by subterraneous noises."

Ararat derives its name, it is said, from Arai, a king who lived 1750 years B.C. He was killed in a great battle on an Armenian plain, which was thence designated Arai-arat, the "fall of Arai." Before him reigned Amassis, the sixth in descent from Japhet, and after him the country was named Amasia; hence comes Massis, by which appellation to this day the Armenians know the great and famous mountain. It is not to be supposed that Noah's Ark rested on the summit of Ararat. Such a theory is contradicted by the difficulties of the descent, and by the low temperature of the atmosphere, which would have proved fatal to many of the animals. And besides, in Genesis we read only that it rested "on the mountains of Ararat." But as the olive flourishes nowhere in the neighbourhood, it seems very doubtful that this can be the mountain intended by the author of the Mosaic record. Many authorities prefer to identify it with the Gordyæan mountains, which run to the south of Armenia, and divide the valley of the Tigris from Iran.

The fauna of Ararat is of a very uninteresting character. Birds are numerous to a point about half-way up the great chasm; and among them the most remarkable is the rose starling, which has acquired celebrity as a locust killer. The only mammal is the common hare. Vegetation is not very abundant, owing to the want of water; but the sides of Little Ararat are tolerably well covered with birches. The Alpine flora met with is the same as that of the Caucasus, and include various species of pyrethrums, centaureas, campanulas, and asters.*

* The ascent of Mount Ararat was accomplished in the year 1877 by Mr. James Bryce.

XIV.

Mount Sinai.

"God from the mount of Sinai (whose gray top
Shall tremble, he descending) will himself,
In thunder, lightning, and loud trumpets' sound,
Ordain them laws."—MILTON.

"With such a horrid clang
As on Mount Sinai rang,
While the red fire and smouldering clouds outbrake."—MILTON.

STRICTLY speaking, Sinai is the general name given to the cluster of mountains which occupies and forms the southern extremity of the Arabian peninsula; that peninsula, rugged, rocky, and desolate, which extends between the two ramifications of the Red Sea, separated from Egypt on the west by the Bay of Suez, and from another portion of Arabia on the east by the Bay of Akabah.

The general configuration of this mass of granite, greenstone, and porphyry, which bears no trace of having undergone volcanic action since its original elevation, is that of a wedge-shaped plateau, traversed by intersecting ravines or *wadys*, from which spring the bold cliffs and soaring peaks, gradual at first, but terminating in a very steep ascent. A recent authority

(Dean Stanley, in his "Sinai and Palestine") distinguishes three chief and comparatively distinct groups:—

1. The north-west cluster above Wady Feirân; the culminating point of which is the fivefold peak of Serbal, 6342 feet above the sea.

2. The eastern, which is also the central; of which the apex, 8063 feet high, is the Jebel Katherin. This includes the Jebel Mûsa, variously estimated at 6796, 7033, and 7097 feet.

3. The south-eastern group, closely connected with the central, which contains the highest Sinaitic summit, Um Shaumer.

The three great peaks of Jebel Katherin, Jebel Mûsa, and Um Shaumer, lie in a line about nine miles long drawn from Mûsa, which is the most northerly; and a perpendicular to this line, traced on the map westwards for about twenty miles, traverses almost the entire length of the five-peaked chain of Serbal. From the boldness of their outlines and the depth of their valleys, the Sinaitic mountains present a succession of landscapes remarkable for sublimity.

Which of the great peaks of the Sinaitic peninsula is to be regarded as the Mount Sinai of the Mosaic record, the Mount of the Law, where "the red fire and smouldering clouds outbrake"?

The question is one which has been a fertile source of discussion among geographers.

Lepsius and Burckhardt identify Sinai with Serbal, which lies thirty miles to the westward of Jebel Mûsa, and close to the Wady Feirân and El Hessnæ. The latter is considered by Lepsius to be the ancient

Rephidim, one of the halting-places of the Israelites in their march through the wilderness. But this view brings the Israelites to Sinai on the same day that they fought and defeated the Amalekites, which is hardly probable. On the other hand, the most ancient traditions are in favour of Serbal, which is the grandest of the Sinaitic mountains.

Objections apply to the hypothesis of Ritter, who represents Jebel Mûsa as Sinai, and in the Wady es Sebayeh, on the south-east side, finds the scene of the encampment of the Israelites.

The theory now very generally accepted is that of Dr. Robinson; who suggests that the modern Horeb of the monks—that is, the north-west and lower face of the Jebel Mûsa, crowned with the glorious cliffs of Râs Safsâfeh, and overlooking the plain Er-Râhah—is the scene of the giving of the law, and the "Mount Sinai" which Moses ascended. The great support of Dr. Robinson's suggestion is the conjunction of mountain with plain which this site affords. Dean Stanley observed at the foot of the precipices some alluvial mounds, which answer exactly to "the bounds of the people;" and the broad sweep of comparatively level ground, stretching away into ample lateral valleys, would furnish sufficient space for the evolutions of the Israelite host, when they "removed and stood afar off." From every point of it the wondering and awe-stricken people could easily see the tremendous spectacle of "the mountain burning with fire to the midst of heaven."

At the foot of the mountain, and overlooking the Wady Mûsa, stands the famous monastery of St.

Catherine, the patron-saint of mountains,—a quadrangular pile of building, enclosed by walls, varying in height from thirty to fifty feet, and so strengthened by bastions as to assume the grim appearance of a mediæval fortress. In addition to cloisters and apartments for the monks, we find in the interior a principal church; twenty-three smaller churches or chapels, each dedicated to a different saint; and a library, in which some valuable manuscripts were formerly preserved.

A visit to this convent, and to the mountain above it, is described in the *Tour du Monde*, by Messrs. Bida and Hachette. We borrow some interesting passages from their narrative:—

It was at noon, on the 28th of February, they reached the consecrated spot. After a brief interval of repose, they bent their steps towards the convent, the external aspect of which, they remark, is by no means religious in character. The traveller sees himself confronted by massive crenelated walls, forming an irregular square of 245 feet in length by 204 in breadth, and constructed of blocks of granite about twenty inches in height, and a little more in length. Its small bastions are a warning to the Bedaween that, in case of need, their attacks could be repelled by artillery.

The great gate of the convent is kept shut; and is opened only when the superior, one of the four independent archbishops of the Greek Church, comes from Cairo, at long intervals, to honour the monks with a visit.

Founded, it is said, in the year 527, by the Emperor Justinian and his wife Theodosia, on the site of a tower

MONASTERY OF ST. CATHERINE, MOUNT SINAI.

raised by the Empress Helena, this monastery was protected in the following century by Mohammed himself,—who, as is well known, borrowed largely from Christianity in building up his new creed. In 1403, a treaty concluded between the Knights of St. John of Jerusalem and the Sultan of Egypt refers to the taxes levied on the pilgrims of the Holy Land, among whom were included the visitors to the convent of Mount Sinai. About this time, the buildings were repaired and enlarged. There were then many other monasteries upon Mount Sinai, "beloved of God, and worthy of all honour," as the Emperor Marcian writes in an imperial rescript. The French general Kleber, on his way to Egypt, in the early years of the French revolution, rebuilt some portions of the convent-walls.

We were impatient to penetrate into the interior. From a postern in the wall hung a rope, to which we fastened our letter of recommendation. It was received by a monk. After waiting half an hour we obtained admission; not, as formerly, being hauled up to the postern in a loop of the rope or in a basket, but by a small side-door, low, and loaded with iron—truly formidable is its apparatus of bolts and bars. Yet all these precautions are useful only so far as they impose upon the Bedaween. A dozen European soldiers would carry the monastic fortress by storm in a quarter of an hour.

The superior came to meet us, and placed at our disposal everything which we might find agreeable; the *useful*, we had stowed away in our tent. He conducted us into every part of the convent. We found the interior a confused mass of irregular buildings, arranged without order on the different levels of an uneven and broken site. Through a labyrinth of narrow passages, corridors, and courts, we visited the cells, communicating with outer galleries of timber,—the apartments, plainly furnished, reserved for the accommodation of strangers,—the cellars, the workshops, the small factories of things necessary for the existence of the "religious" and the support of the convent,—the great church dedicated to St. Catherine, the twenty-three chapels, and, what most astonished us, an ancient mosque situated in the centre of the enclosure. The superior informed us that it had been erected for the use of the Arabs employed in the convent. Probably, too, it was a concession enforced by Moslem authority; and it is a kind of palladium against the tribes of the Sinaitic peninsula. Externally, the church is more than modest; in the interior, it is profusely decorated. It is divided into three aisles, separated by granite columns, which support a roof of timber, painted, and sown with golden stars. The sanctuary is enclosed by a screen, carved and gilded; the altar, in mosaic work of shell and mother-of-pearl, is loaded with the specimens of jewellery offered by wealthy devotees; the episcopal throne is of wood, carved and gilded; the pavement of marble, serpentine, and granite.

The superior pointed out to us some Byzantine paintings; the medals of the founders, Theodosius and Helena; in the apse, a mosaic representing Moses— young, handsome, beardless—on his knees before the burning bush; and, in another scene, receiving from the hands of God the tables of the Law. The site of the bush, we are told, was on the left hand of the high altar; it has been enclosed in a chapel, into which we were not allowed to enter until we had removed our shoes—not, unquestionably, as is often asserted, in imitation of a Mohammedan custom, but in remembrance of Jehovah's words to Moses, when He spake to him from the midst of the flaming bush: "Put off thy shoes from off thy feet, for the place whereon thou standest is holy ground."

This church is dedicated to St. Catherine, whose tomb, ornamented and surrounded by lamps and tapers always lighted, attracts a great number of pilgrims.

In the library, we were allowed to glance at rather than to see the Greek and Arabic manuscripts, about fifteen hundred in number. We obtained leave to examine more closely the "gospels" of the Emperor Theodosius, and a psalter which belonged (it is said) to St. Catherine.

We afterwards walked through the gardens, which glowed with flowers; their verdure, in the midst of the sterile rocks around us, had a charming effect, recalling to us the vineyards of France in the sunny days of May and June. The trees are all white or rose-tinted. The almond trees, the figs, the olives, the vines, the peaches, and especially the pear trees, produce—so the monks assured us—excellent fruit.

March 2nd.—Ascent of Sinai, or Jebel Mûsa ("Mount of Moses"), at eight o'clock. Our excursion lasted five hours. We set out through the gardens to the south of the convent, and plunged into a maze of pathways, with steps dug out of the rock. We passed between the Mountain of the Jews and Mount Horeb; and, in succession, reached a fountain, a chapel dedicated to the Virgin, and finally a small plateau, where we paused to rest under a cypress tree, near a spring of pure and crystal water. Ascending still higher, our guides pointed out to us the ruins of a chapel formerly erected in a hollow or depression, identified with the cave in which Elijah took refuge when pursued by Jezebel.

On the summit of Sinai may be seen the ruins of a chapel and a mosque, both consecrated to Moses.

It marks the site, according to tradition, from which Mohammed was transported to heaven. His camel has left on the rock the imprint of one of his hoofs.

Whatever the creed or the philosophical conviction of the traveller, he alone is to blame if he remains frigid and unmoved on this narrow table-land, this mountain-summit, hallowed by such noble memories, while his gaze wanders from peak to peak, in the midst of the solemn silence, in which the thought of man is free to rise from earth to heaven.

A very full and interesting account of the Monastery of St. Catherine and the Sinaitic peaks is given by Dean Stanley. He speaks of the emotion with which the pilgrim finds in the heart of the desert so stately a convent, with its massive walls, its gorgeous bannered church, its galleries of chapels, cells, and guest-chambers, its library of precious manuscripts, the sound of its rude cymbals calling to prayer, and changed by the echoes into music as it rolls through the desert valley, the double standard of the Lamb and Cross floating high upon its topmost towers. The fact that the monks are not Arabs but Greeks—that there in the midst of the wilderness, the "very focus of the pure Semitic race," he hears the accents of the Greek tongue, meets the natives of Thessalonica and Samos, sees in the convent-garden the produce of the isles of Greece—not tamarisk, and palm, and acacia; but olive and almond, poplar and cypress—is also not less strange than impressive. Another circumstance which he cannot forget is, that the monastery is not, as it were, of native growth; was founded by no patriarch, no pilgrim prince, no ascetic king, but by a Byzantine emperor, the most worldly of his race. The renown of Justinian, as of one who loved to rear great architectural monuments, had spread even to the recesses of Sinai; and the hermits, "when they heard that he delighted to build churches and found convents, made a journey to him, and complained how the wandering sons of Ishmael were wont to attack them suddenly, eat up their provisions, desolate the place, enter the cells, and carry off everything; how they also broke into the church and devoured even the holy wafers." Justinian was by no means unwilling to raise for them such an asylum as they desired, because it enabled him to convert it into a point of defence against the Arabian tribes. The choice of the site was dictated by the existence of an old tower, ascribed to the Empress Helena. It stood close to the localities associated by tradition with the Well of Jethro and the Burning Bush, in what is truly "hallowed ground."

As centuries have passed away, even the convent in the mountain-solitudes of Sinai has not escaped their influence. The numerous cells with which the heights were formerly thronged have long been vacant. The episcopal city of Paran—probably owing to the growth of Justinian's foundation—has perished almost without a history. The Nunnery of St. Episteure has disappeared; we see only the ruins of the Convent of the good physicians Cosmo and Damian, the Hermitage of St. Onufrius, the Convent of the Forty Martyrs; and if the Convent of St. Catherine has been preserved, its preservation is due more to the massiveness of its walls than any other single cause. Yet, as Dean Stanley says, it is a thought of singular, almost of melancholy interest, that amidst all these revolutions the Sinaitic convent is still the one seat of European and of Christian civilization and worship, not only in the peninsula of Sinai, but in the whole country of Arabia. Even now it retains, or until recently it *did* retain, its hold on the superstitious feelings, if not on the affections, of the Bedaween. Burckhardt, and after him Dr. Robinson, relate the deep conviction cherished by these wild children of the desert that the rains of heaven, on which the produce of the peninsula depends, are withheld or poured down at the bidding of the monks.

We append, with some slight alterations, Dean Stanley's account of his ascent of Jebel Mûsa, Râs Safsâfeh, and St. Catherine.

In the ascent of Jebel Mûsa there were two points which especially struck him: first, the little plain just before the last ascent; the long flight of rude steps, leading from the base to the summit, winds through crags of granite until it brings you in sight of a grand archway standing between two of these huge cliffs. You pass this, and yet another, and then find yourself in that world-renowned spot.* The tall cypress which stands in the centre of the little basin is seen towering above the rocks before you catch sight of the whole. A ruined church on the hill-slope is built over the so-called Cave of Elijah; and a well and tank on the other side of the basin are also ascribed to the prophet. It is a solemn and beautiful scene, entirely secluded, and entirely characteristic, with the exception of the cypress, which marks the hand of strangers.

Next, the summit itself, whatever else may be its claims, bears evident indications of being, or having been, regarded as the spot most universally sacred on

---

* "Between the Egyptian and the Arabian deserts, formed by two gulfs of the Erythræan Sea, is a peninsula of granite mountains. It seems as if an ocean of lava, when its waves were literally running mountains high, had been suddenly commanded to stand still. These successive summits, with their peaks and pinnacles, enclose a series of valleys, in general stern and savage, yet some of which are not devoid of pastoral beauty. There may be found brooks of silver brightness, and occasionally groves of palms and gardens of dates, while the neighbouring heights command sublime landscapes, the opposing mountains of Asia and of Afric, and the blue bosom of two seas. On one of these elevations, more than five thousand feet above the ocean, is a convent; again, nearly three thousand feet above this convent is a towering peak, and this is Mount Sinai.

"On the top of Mount Sinai are two ruins—a Christian church, and a Mohammedan mosque. In this, the sublimest scene of Arabian glory, Israel and Ishmael alike raised their altars to the great God of Abraham. Why are they in ruins? Is it that human structures are not to be endured amid the awful temples of nature and revelation; and that the column and the cupola crumble into nothingness in sight of the hallowed Horeb and on the soil of the eternal Sinai?

"Ascending the mountain, about half-way between the convent and the utmost height of the towering peak, is a small plain surrounded by rocks. In its centre are a cypress tree and a fountain. This is the traditional scene of the greatest event of time."—*Tancred*, bk. iv., c. 7.

earth; for there, side by side, and from reverence for the same event, on which both religions are founded, stand the ruins of a small Christian church—once divided amongst all the Christian sects—and of a small Mohammedan mosque. From whatever point this famous peak is seen, these two fragments of worship, almost always visible upon it, more distinctly than anything else proclaim what it is.

Dean Stanley next proceeded to gain the summit of the other end of the range, called the Râs Safsâfeh (or "Willow-Head"), which overlooks the great plain of the Er-Râhah. The whole party descended, and after winding through the various basins and cliffs which compose the range, reached the crest of the rocky precipice. The effect of the scene was instantaneous. They gazed with admiring awe on the great amphitheatre of granite peaks around them, and on the deep, wide, yellow plain below, sweeping to the very base of the cliffs. A yet higher mass of granite, immediately above this elevated point, should be ascended, for the greater completeness of view which it affords. The plain below is then seen stretching, not only between the ranges of Ilaha and Furci'â, but also into the lateral valleys which, on the north-east, unite it with the wide Wady of the Sheikh. Behind extends the granite mass of the range of Jebel Mûsa, cloven into deep gullies and basins, and ending in the traditional peak, crowned by the memorials of its double sanctity.

Next day the Dean and his companions ascended the highest peak,—not of the whole peninsula, but of the Sinai range. Its historical or legendary interest is con-

THE RAS SAFSAFEH AND PLAIN OF ER-RAHAH (MOUNT SINAI.)

nected solely with the story from which it derives its name: that a retinue of angels bore the body of St. Catherine from Alexandria, over the Red Sea and the desert, and placed it on this mountain-crest. The rock here assumes the likeness of a human body, with its arms swathed like that of a mummy, and headless—the counterpart, say the monks, of the corpse of the decapitated Egyptian saint.

The view from the summit is glorious, embracing not only the labyrinth of bare granite peaks visible from Jebel Mûsa, but a panorama of the whole peninsula,—including the five-peaked ridge of Serbal, the masses of Um Shaumur, and the gulf of the Red Sea, with the high mountains of Egypt and Arabia on the remote horizon.

XV.

The Himalaya.

THE Himálaya*—that is, Hima-alaya, the "Abode of Snow"—is a range of mountains extending from the Equator to the 45th parallel of north latitude, and over 73 degrees of longitude. But, in fact, as a glance at any good map of the world will inform the reader, this great central range, which the Arab geographers termed "The Stony Girdle of the Earth," may really be traced from the mountains of Formosa, in the China Sea, to the Pyrenees, where they sink into the Mediterranean. The Himálaya proper, however, are not more than 1500 miles in length. Their western prolongation is called the Hindú Kúsh. Or we may take another division; and, starting from the Pamir Steppe, or "Roof of the World," as a centre, may regard the western range as a boundary wall to the high table-land of Western Asia, separating the waters of the Arabian Gulf from those of the Caspian, the Black Sea, and the Aral. That portion consists of the Hindú Kúsh, the Paropamisan Mountains, the

* Pronounced as if written Himah-láyá.

Elburz, the Zagros of Kurdistan, Ararat and the Armenian Mountains, the Taurus and Anti-Taurus, which are continued through Europe, as already hinted, in the mountains of Greece and European Turkey, the Alps, the Cevennes, and the Pyrenees. Turning to the southeast, we find a range stretching from the Pamir to the China Sea, with branches running down into the Malay Peninsula and Annam. The eastern prolongation consists of the Kuen-lung, which reaches the Pacific; and the Pe-ling, which separates the Yang-tsze from the Yellow River. And, lastly, a north-east range strikes from the Pamir to Behring Strait, including the Tengu Tagh, and several ranges in Siberia and Kamtchatka.

We shall here, however, confine ourselves to the Himálaya proper,—the palace or Pantheon of the Hindú gods,—which may be said to be enclosed by the Indus, the Brahmapútra, and the great northern plain of India. Of this magnificent mountain-mass, which raises its principal peaks to an elevation of nearly 30,000 feet, very ample descriptions have been furnished by recent travellers, and especially by Mr. Andrew Wilson and Mr. Frederick Drew.

In Hindú mythology, says Mr. Wilson, these mountains are personified as the husband of Manaka. He was also the father of Dúrga, the great goddess of destruction, who became incarnate as Parvati, or the "daughter of the mountain," in order to beguile Siva and withdraw him from a penance which he had undertaken to perform in the Himálaya. Siva himself is also known as Himálaya, and under this title is celebrated in Kálidása's beautiful poem of the *Kumara Sambhana*, or "Birth of the War-God." It is, then, with the god of destruction, and his no less terrible spouse, that the Himálaya are more specially associated, rather than with the brighter form of Vishnu, the Preserver; but, says Mr. Wilson, the whole Hindú Pantheon are also regarded as dwelling among the inaccessible snowy peaks of these inaccessible mountains. And, assuredly, neither Cretan Ida nor Thessalian Olympus can boast of so divine a company. The Aryan imagination seems to have been inspired by the tremendous character of the scenes among which it flourished; and, with much that is mean and debasing, there is so much of the grand and exalted, that, looking up to the snow-crowned heights of the Kailas, we may justly affirm that—

> "Every legend fair
> Which the supreme Caucasian mind
> Carved out of Nature for itself, is there."

On the Indian side the Himálaya are steep and abrupt; on the north, as a rule, they incline gradually towards the great central table-lands of Asia. Yet it is on the Indian side that the snow-line—that is, the lower boundary of the region of perpetual snow—reaches the lowest level. This is owing to the dryness of the atmosphere on the northern side, while on the southern a considerable quantity of moisture is accumulated by the Indian monsoon. From Bhotan to Kashmir, the snow-line on the southern slope descends to 16,200 feet; on the higher Himálaya we may place it at 18,600. The rule must not be made arbitrary, however; and where snow can lodge, it is not common to find exposed

PASS IN THE HIMALAYA.

tracts above 16,000 feet at any period of the year; and even in August a snowstorm will often cover everything down to 10,000 feet, or even lower.

Glaciers of immense size are abundant in the Himálaya, and descend far below the snow-line. The lower portions of them are thickly covered with débris of rock, and in some places among the débris flourishes living grass. Mr. Wilson describes a remarkable glacier-scene in the neighbourhood of the Chandra River, which cuts its way through high mural precipices, the clefts of which are filled with the frozen torrents. Here nothing is to be seen but snow, rocks, and glaciers; and "the great ice-serpents crept over into this dread valley as if they were living monsters." In the local dialect *Shigri* means "a glacier;" but the word is applied to the upper Chandra valley,—which, therefore, may fairly and really be described as the "Valley of Glaciers."

Greensward there is none; woodland shade there is none:

"Bare is it, without house or tract, and destitute
Of obvious shelter as a shipless sea."

That, however, is by no means the worst of it; and in the course of the afternoon, on the occasion of Mr. Wilson's traversing it, a fierce storm of wind, rain, and snow increased the savagery of the scene. It seemed as if some of the clouds of the monsoon had been driven across the ranges of lofty mountains which shut out the valley from the Indian plain; and soon the storm-clouds began to roll grandly among the snowy peaks which towered on every side. So far the spectacle was

bridges there are none; and it was impossible not to pity the poor women who, on so cold a morning, were forced to wade shivering through the streams, with the rapid water rising almost up to their waists. Still onward moved the travellers, with twenty-thousand-feet snowy peaks and overhanging glaciers on every side, and great beds of snow fringing the margins of the mural precipices. After a few miles the Chandra ceased its southerly flow, and diverged to the westward; but the scenery retained its character of terror and sublimity. Out of the huge beds of snow above, wherever a gap in the mountain-walls presents itself,

> "The glaciers creep
> Like snakes that watch their prey; from their far fountains
> Slow rolling on; there many a precipice,
> Frost and the sun, in scorn of mortal power,
> Have piled—dome, pyramid, and pinnacle—
> A city of death, distinct with many a tower
> And wall impregnable of beaming ice.
> Yet not a city but a flood of ruin
> Is there, that from the boundaries of the sky
> Rolls its perpetual stream."

Before long the travellers made closer acquaintance with some of these colossal glaciers. They came to one which, as it stretched right down into the river, defied all attempts to flank it. "At first," says Mr. Wilson, "it looked as if we were painfully crossing the huge ridges of a fallen mountain; but this soon proved to be an immense glacier, very thickly covered over with slabs of clay-slate, and with large blocks of granite and gneiss, but with the solid ice underneath exposed here and there, and especially in the surfaces of the large

bridges there are none; and it was impossible not to pity the poor women who, on so cold a morning, were forced to wade shivering through the streams, with the rapid water rising almost up to their waists. Still onward moved the travellers, with twenty-thousand-feet snowy peaks and overhanging glaciers on every side, and great beds of snow fringing the margins of the mural precipices. After a few miles the Chandra ceased its southerly flow, and diverged to the westward; but the scenery retained its character of terror and sublimity. Out of the huge beds of snow above, wherever a gap in the mountain-walls presents itself,

> "The glaciers creep
> Like snakes that watch their prey; from their far fountains
> Slow rolling on; there many a precipice,
> Frost and the sun, in scorn of mortal power,
> Have piled—dome, pyramid, and pinnacle—
> A city of death, distinct with many a tower
> And wall impregnable of beaming ice.
> Yet not a city but a flood of ruin
> Is there, that from the boundaries of the sky
> Rolls its perpetual stream."

Before long the travellers made closer acquaintance with some of these colossal glaciers. They came to one which, as it stretched right down into the river, defied all attempts to flank it. "At first," says Mr. Wilson, "it looked as if we were painfully crossing the huge ridges of a fallen mountain; but this soon proved to be an immense glacier, very thickly covered over with slabs of clay-slate, and with large blocks of granite and gneiss, but with the solid ice underneath exposed here and there, and especially in the surfaces of the large crevasses which went down to unknown depths. Some of these edges must have been two or three hundred feet in height."

Some of Mr. Wilson's attendants accounted for the rocks which covered this glacier as being due to the fall of a mountain-peak that had formerly existed in the immediate neighbourhood. They acknowledged, moreover, that the apparently immutable ice-river *must* move, because every summer they had to strike out a new path across it, and to erect fresh marks to indicate the way. So numerous are the crumbling peaks and precipices about the great fountains of this glacier, that its rock-strewn surface is easily explained without the intervention of a landslip. Its formation is plainly due to the junction of several large glaciers in a great valley above. When they had filled this up, they overflowed its rim in one huge ice-stream descending to the river. So thick and compact was the débris on its surface, that it afforded sustenance to delightful clusters of flowers and grasses. Coleridge, in his "Hymn to Mont Blanc," tells of

" The living flowers that skirt the eternal frost;"

but here the blossoms bloom sweetly on the eternal frost itself.

Mr. Wilson also describes his journey through the Great Schinkal Pass; which opens from the province of Lahaul into that of Zanskar, and attains an elevation of 18,000 feet.

"The first day and a half," he says, "were the worst part of this journey. Its features changed greatly after we reached the point where the Kado Tokpho divides into two branches, forded the stream to the right, and made a very steep ascent of about 1500 feet. Above that we passed into an elevated picturesque valley, with a good deal of grass and a few birch bushes, which leads all the way up to the glacier that covers the summit of the pass. The usual camping-ground in this valley is called Ramjakpúk, and that place is well protected from the wind; but there are bushes to serve as fuel where we pitched our tents a mile or two below, at a height of about 15,000 feet. Towards evening there was rain and a piercing cold wind, with the thermometer at 36° F., and many were the surmises as to whether we might not be overtaken by a storm of snow on the higher portion of the pass next day."

They found the thermometer in the morning at 32°; the hoar-frost sparkled on the grass, and a crust of ice spread over every stream. For some distance they pursued an easy path; afterwards came a long ascent, and then they entered upon the colossal glacier which forms the crest of this awful Pass. The ground bordering on the glacier was broken up by immense ridges of granite and slabs of slate. Some of these rested on the ice-river itself, and others had been thrown up by it on the rocky mountain-side. Soon, however, the travellers got clear of these obstacles, and were fairly on the glacier; which was intersected by innumerable narrow crevasses, many of them concealed by white honeycombed ice,— diversified by blocks of stone erect upon small platforms or tables of ice,—and by a few rills, and even large brooks, the results of the morning's sunshine. It was not properly an ice-stream, this huge glacier, but an ice-lake, for it was nearly circular; and all around it was fed by glaciers and snow-slopes, while it overlapped into the valleys beneath in several directions.

When the travellers reached the centre of the glacial lake, at the summit of the Pass, they saw at once whence it derived its perennial supplies. Steep slopes of snow or *névé*, overhung by immense beds of snow, frowned on every side. It was more like a "Place de la Concorde" than the basin of the Aletsch glacier in Switzerland; and the encircling masses of *névé* were far more abrupt, precipitous, and impressive than in any similar Alpine scene. On the right the long deep inclines of snow—sheeted declivities—shone with a striking grandeur. A precipice of unbroken snow rose up steeply, for more than a thousand feet, to vast overhanging walls of "stratified *névé*," which occasionally yielded in immense masses with a tremendous din. Wherever the eye rested, it rested upon ridges and fields, domes, walls, and cliffs of snow. Nowhere else would it be possible, not even in the Arctic wastes, to gain a more vivid idea of the might of the eternal Winter, or of the mingled power, savageness, and beauty of high Alpine life.

Mr. Wilson introduces here an episode of travelling, which proves that Himalayan explorations, however carefully conducted, are not without danger. He had given strict orders that all the bigarrés, or porters, should keep close in his rear; but on reaching the summit of the Pass he found that three of them were missing, and that these three carried his tent-poles, his bedding, and the portmanteau containing his money. He might have dispensed with the tent-poles, though the want of them would have caused much inconvenience in a treeless region, where they could not have been replaced. The lack of bedding could have been supplied only by purchasing sheep-skins, furs, or vermin-haunted blankets; but this would have been impossible, owing to the loss of the rupees.

No wonder that our traveller's indignation was excessive, for he and his followers were placed in a position of some peril. Though the morning had glowed with sunshine, bad weather had been threatening for several days; even now the sky was dark and lowering; clouds were gathering all around; and to have been overtaken by a snowstorm on the grim glacier would have been death to all. It was not difficult to cross it while the sky was clear, and the snow-walls indicated the track; but what must have been their fate in a blinding snow-drift, on a glacier fully 18,000 feet high, with no central moraine, and overlapping in several directions? Moreover, the snow would quickly have concealed the rotten honeycombed ice which partially bridged over numerous crevasses. Resolved not to retrace his route, Mr. Wilson ordered his servants and the bigarrés to continue the passage of the glacier, and to encamp at the first suitable spot on the Zanskar side; while he himself, with one attendant, rode back in quest of the missing coolies and their loads. In this resolution lay an obvious hazard, for Mr. Wilson might have been cut off from his people and baggage; but it was the only thing to be done in the circumstances, unless he had been willing to turn back.

"So I waited," says Mr. Wilson, "until my party disappeared on the brow of the glacier, and then rode back in a savage and reckless humour over ice which I had previously crossed in a very cautious manner. I could easily retrace our track until we got to the great stony ridges, and then the mare I had taken with me was useful. On getting off there, and descending the valley a short way, I found my three light-laden gentlemen quietly reposing, and immediately forced them to resume their burdens and go on before me. Even then they showed some unwillingness to proceed; and I had to act the part of the Wild Horseman of the Glacier—driving them before me, and progging whoever happened to be hindermost with the iron spike of my heavy alpenstock, which considerably accelerated their movements. There was the most urgent reason for this, because, had we been half an hour later in getting over the summit of the Pass, the probability is that we should have been lost. It began to snow before we got off the glacier; and when we descended a few hundred feet it was snowing so heavily on the ice-lake we had just left that we could not have seen there two yards before our faces, and it would have been quite impossible to know in which direction to turn, the tracks of our party being obliterated, and the crevasses, which ran in every direction, affording no guidance. Even on the narrow glaciers of the Alps, a number of people have been lost by being caught in snowstorms; so it can be imagined what chance there would have been for us on a great lake of ice above

18,000 feet high. Without the tracks and a sight of the surrounding snow-walls to guide us, we could only have wandered about hopelessly in the blinding storm; and if we did not fall into a crevasse, through rotten ice concealed by the new-fallen snow, we might have wandered on to one of the outlets where the ice flowed over in steep hanging glaciers which it would have been impossible to descend."

We have referred to the various levels of the limit of perpetual snow. These differ greatly, as we have seen, according to the exposure of the mountain-face, the dryness of the atmosphere, and other local conditions. Thus, for that portion of the Himálaya which lies between the Sutlej and the north-west frontier of Nepál, General Strachey records the following figures:—

<blockquote>
On the south..15,500 feet.
On the north..18,500 feet.
On the southern face of Kailas, which lies further within Tibet..........................19,500 feet.
</blockquote>

Hence it appears that the westernmost Himálaya, though in a higher latitude, exhibit a higher level for the snow-line than the easterly ranges. Glaciers, in this district, occur at an elevation of about 17,000 feet; though where the air is free from moisture they are not found even at an altitude of 18,000 feet.

Let us glance at the mountain-peaks and glaciers of the great Himálayan chain which borders Kashmir on the north-east, and sends down lofty branches to enclose and protect its Eden-valley.

Beginning with the mass of the Nariga Parbat, we

find that many points of its ridges and spurs are 20,000 feet high; while its apex, the one which bears the name, is no less than 26,629 feet, or 11,000 feet higher than Mont Blanc. This colossal summit rises from a lofty ridge that for ten miles is upwards of 22,000 feet in height; the faces of this ridge, on the east and south, form an enormous cliff or precipice, of from 6000 to 10,000 feet, on the greater part of which hangs a perpetual shroud of snow, white and deathly; from the most elevated point great buttresses radiate; and the clefts and fissures are filled with large glaciers. Such is the majestic height of the great ridge and its gigantic peak, that they are visible from long distances over the neighbouring ranges of 16,000 feet altitude, which become quite dwarfed to the eyes.

The southern portion of the ridge serves as the watershed between the Indus and Jhelum basins, and is about 20,000 feet high. On both sides it is furrowed with glaciers. From thence, the chain for about 120 miles takes a general south-easterly direction.

For the first fifty or sixty miles it is not of such a height as to bear perpetual snow or give birth to glaciers. The average elevation may be taken at 14,000 feet. Its line is broken by several gaps, through two of which run the much-traversed roads that connect the Kishanganga and Aster rivers; these passes are respectively 13,200 and 13,500 feet high, and are available for laden horses.

After a length of sixty miles the range increases in height; some of the peaks tower to 17,000 and 17,400 feet, and collect sufficient snow to form small glaciers.

Further on, still pursuing a south-east course, we come to a gap in the mountain-barrier, which is the lowest passage—between the Indus on the one side, and the Chīnāb and Jhelum basins on the other—along the whole length of 300 miles from the eastern sources of the Chīnāb to the head of the Khāgān tributary of the Jhelum. This is the celebrated Drās Pass; the Zojī Lā of the Tibetans.

According to Mr. Drew, the height of this mountain-passage is 11,300 feet. An important characteristic of it is its steep ascent from the Kashmir side, while it falls but slightly to the elevated table-land of Ladākh. The traveller from Kashmir rises steeply, in the last mile or so, a height of about 2000 feet to the level of the Pass; he then finds himself in a narrow valley, the floor of which sinks with so gradual an incline that in twenty miles we do not descend more than 1000 feet. The Pass itself—that is, the high-level valley at the top of the breathless ascent, up which men and beasts toil pantingly and with laborious effort—is a level grassy hollow slightly exceeding a quarter of a mile in width. Rugged and rocky are the mountains which border it; the peaks immediately visible are 2000 or 3000 feet above the valley, but the ridges of which they form the ends reach in the distance to 5000 and 6000 feet above it, or 16,000 and 17,000 feet above the sea. By this noble gateway, this "enchanted portal" in the vast mountain-barrier, the traveller rises into the high-level country of Ladākh, where the valleys even are at no lower level than 10,000 feet,—or more than twice the height of Ben Nevis. Indeed, nowhere in the Upper

Indus basin south of the latitude-parallel of this Pass shall we find any ground, even in the valleys, so low as 10,000 feet.

Continuing along the main chain, we find that the summits rise higher and higher; peaks of 18,000 feet, and some that approach even 20,000 feet, occur, and the *general* level is not much below them. Long spurs, too, or branch ridges that jut out, are very lofty. Ten miles east-south-east from the Pass a distinct ridge branches off; and this, making a bold curve, forms the eastern and southern boundary of Kashmir. Then, after some further travel—about twenty-six miles from the east Pass—the traveller arrives at an opening which, though not so low as the other, yet, considering the loftiness of the mountains it traverses, must be regarded as a considerable depression. It is named the Bhot Kol Pass, and bristles with ice and snow.

From the Drās Pass hither the peaks have been of a height to form glaciers, and there is a glacier in every hollow of the ridge. These ice-rivers are found also in the recesses of many of the branch ridges. Usually they are of no great dimensions; generally two or three miles in length. They do not extend very low; but one—the Mechuhir Glacier—has its foot at 10,850 feet above the sea. Looking from a point near the Bhot Kol Pass to the north-east, the traveller can see at a glance a number of these small glaciers embedded in the hollows of the mountains, the narrow rock-ridges of which curve round and enclose them.

From the last-named Pass eastwards the range continues at a great elevation, and frequently attains to

20,000 feet nearly. Lastly, at a distance of twelve to fourteen miles from the Pass, rise two colossal summits, each of them a few hundred feet over 23,000. They are called Nun and Kun—or together, Nun Kun; and as they tower fully 3000 feet above their neighbours, are conspicuous from afar. According to the point from which they are viewed, their aspect varies greatly.

We have dwelt in detail upon this part of the Himálayan range, in the belief that such particulars will assist the reader in forming a distinct idea of the enormous magnitude of that vast mountain-barrier. But we must now proceed to a few more generalizing sketches.

At Arandu, in the Būsha valley (province of Baltistān), occurs a remarkable glacier, of which Mr. Drew has furnished an interesting description.

The village of Arandu lies close at its foot, and all the valley above is filled with the great mass of ice. The elevation of the village and of the foot of the glacier is between 10,000 and 11,000 feet. This is one of those colossal glaciers which sweep down from the highest mountains, and occupy a great length of the valley.

The valley which it fills up with its burden is a mile and a half wide; the height of the ice at its irregular termination is about 200 feet; but probably increases higher up. Crossing not far above the end, says Mr. Drew, we find a very irregular mass of ice, with ridges and hollows of no even run, so covered with stones that in going over the whole mile and a half, which is the width of the glacier, the traveller hardly once puts his feet on ice. On the higher part are thick mounds of stones; on the slopes are fewer; again in the hollows are accumulations of them: all this is because the ice has been so much melted as it nears its terminal moraine that the stones of the lateral and central moraines have slipped and become mixed together. "Thus it is," says our authority, "for some miles up; but when we go further up still, then the moraine matter appears in lines, and strips of clean ice come into view between them. If, when one has passed along, say fifteen or twenty miles of the glacier, one rises on the hill-side to gain a view over it, one sees the great ice-stream lying with its enormous length in the valley, with a very low slope of surface; at this part the incline is not more than $1\frac{1}{2}°$ or $2°$, though below the slope had been rather more; in the centre is a wide strip of snow-white ice, moulded by melting into such forms as to give the appearance of waves of a rapid stream; on either side are lines of moraines; steep rocky banks make the boundary of all; above these are mountains with an immense spread of perpetual snow, from which spring glaciers, some ending off abruptly high above the main valley, others continuing on and coming down, with a steep slope, to join and coalesce with the large glacier. As we go up, large glaciers come in which themselves have a moderately low slope; to these again join some of the steeper ones, leading from the mass of perpetual snow above. The highest spot I reached was in the centre of the glacier twenty or twenty-five miles up from its foot; up to this place the width had been very regular. I should say from a mile and a quarter to a mile and a half; but here a greater expanse of ice was visible; the ice was white-surfaced, looking like a frozen and snow-covered lake, and here it was far clearer of débris than it was below—still moraine-lines lay along the centre. This wider part (which is about 13,500 feet above the sea) is where several glaciers, meeting, combine to form the great stream which thence, as before said, flows on with a gentle incline. From the foot of the glacier at Arandu to the summit of the feeding glaciers the distance must be over thirty miles."

As might be expected, the snows and springs of the Himálaya give birth to numerous rivers, some of which are remarkable for their volume of water and extent of course.

Thus, in the Western Himálaya rises the rivers of the Panjáb (or "five waters"), the Chilum, the Chinab, the Ravee, the Bejah, and the Sutlej.

Then, from the south-west base of Kailas flow the mighty streams of the Indus and the Brahmapútra.

At the foot of Jumnutie, a triple-peaked mountain, 25,749 feet high, rises the Jumna; and in the shadow of the lofty Panchaparvata (or "five mountains") well up the streams which unite to form the sacred Ganges. Of these sources the holiest and most famous is the Gangavatari or Gangútri, about 13,000 feet above the sea, in lat. 31° N.

The Gogra or Saraja has its source in the mountains to the south-east of Nanda Devi. These are the loftiest summits of the Himálaya,—the Dhawalagiri, the Kunchain-junga, and Mount Everest,—all of which exceed 28,000 feet in elevation.

The Kósi or Kooso has its rise in several springs between the Gosainthair and the Kunchain-junga, and traverses the kingdom of Nepál.

The Eastern Himálaya, from Sikkim to the Brahmapútra, contributes all its waters to that noble river. Its peaks form the boundary of Bhotan, into which country it projects in numerous spurs and branches.

Some of the finest Himálayan scenery is to be found in the neighbourhood of the head waters of the Ganges. The "sacred river" is formed by the junction of two considerable streams, the Bhagirathi and the Alaknunda; which junction takes place at Deoprag, about ten miles below Serīnagur, in lat. 30° 10′ N., and long. 78° 35′ E., at about 1000 feet above the sea-level. The Bhagirathi, which is usually regarded as the true source of the Ganges, and occupies a conspicuous position in the Hindú mythology, wells up in the shadow of a wild deep glen, above Gangútri; the cold crystal waters issuing from a low-arched cave at the bottom of a tremendous glacier—called the "Cow's Mouth."

A pilgrimage to the sources of the Ganges was made by Mr. Hodgson, and as his narrative furnishes many interesting glimpses of the grand scenery of the Himálaya, we shall transfer it to these pages.

After doubling the spur of Mount Gangútri, Mr. Hodgson and his companions came in sight of the

MOUNT EVEREST.

noble Miauri peak. In the distance rose, one above another, the masses of the Rudr-Himálaya, surmounted by the lofty summit of the Dudgé, the snows of which shone with dazzling lustre in the cloudless noon. At a great depth beneath them rolled the foaming river in its narrow and rocky channel. Above Gangútri, they observed a great peak of singular form. A cascade precipitated itself into the middle of a vast expanse of snow, which stretched almost from the mountain-crest to the river-bed. The travellers mounted above a torrent which roared from the brink of a rock of granite. Of granite, too, were the rocks among which the rapid river made its way. On its bank, to the right, could be seen Gangútri, a small temple dedicated to the gods Ganga Maï and Bhagirathi.

Pursuing their upward course, the travellers were delighted with the succession of glorious landscapes that opened upon them—landscapes in which were blended the savage and sublime. The rocks are of a remarkably clear bright granite, and sprinkled with black shining spots like felspar. Near Gangútri the river widens. The temple is built of stone, and contains images of Ganga, Bhagirathi, and other gods. It is situated on a platform of rock, on the right bank of the river, and about twenty feet above its level. In the vicinity is a wooden building, intended for the accommodation of strangers. Farther on, if you follow the course of the river, you come to some "cedar-covered plains;" but, in general, nowhere can you see aught else than fragments of rocks which have fallen from the neighbouring mountains.

Fatigued with a long day's march, our travellers had betaken themselves to rest, when, between ten and eleven o'clock P.M., they were aroused by earthquake-shocks. They rushed from their tent, and became eye-witnesses of the effect of the earth's convulsive movement, during which they keenly felt all the horror of their situation. Their tent was pitched between enormous masses of rock, some of which exceeded one hundred feet in diameter, and had probably been heaped up by former earthquakes. The scene which surrounded them, illuminated by the sad gleam of a sickly moon, was truly frightful. At the second shock, the rocks rolled in all directions from the crest of the peak into the river-bed. The terrific din caused by their descent is beyond all description, and Mr. Hodgson writes that "it would never be effaced from his memory." When the noise of falling stones had ceased in their immediate neighbourhood, the travellers could hear afar the report of similar catastrophes. They regarded with alarm the rocks above their heads, in the fear that the next shock would detach some fragments, under which they would be crushed to death. But, happily, no more shocks occurred that night.

On the 27th, however, and on the day following, some light movements were experienced. In spite of their desire to quit as soon as possible so dangerous a neighbourhood, Mr. Hodgson and his companions resolved, having ventured so far, to trace the course of the river as far as they could. Consequently, they set out on the 29th of May, with the view of reaching its source. The two Brahmins of Gangútri could give

KUNCHAIN-JUNGA.

them no information as to the distance, never having travelled beyond the precincts of their temple.

After dragging themselves laboriously among the débris of rocks and newly-fallen avalanches, they entered upon a field of snow which covered the river, and was about thirty feet in depth. Beyond, where its bed again became visible, it was loaded with enormous masses of granite that had been precipitated into it. On each side rose an uninterrupted range of lofty rocks, like a wall. They plunged after a while into the very midst of the wreck and ruin of a recent avalanche of snow. A similar avalanche, five hundred feet thick, had fallen across the river's channel, and was completely frozen. Near at hand were visible the remains of a great landslip. Hemmed in by rocks, the river was broken up into a series of cataracts; and the path of the travellers became toilsome and difficult in the extreme. Towards the head of the stream rose several lofty peaks, shaped like towers. Soon afterwards they arrived at a point where the waters of the river, literally churned into foam, are precipitated, cataract-wise, into a snow-field. This they left behind them, and ascended to a torrent which issues from a cavern situated on the left. Here, in an opposite direction, the Ganges winds around a great snowy peak; to the left rises a rampart of precipitous rocks. Judging now that the river-source lay at a greater distance than they had supposed, the travellers sent to Gangútri for a small tent.

As they continued their slow ascent, they continuously skirted a wall of rock, while, on the right, towered peaks of snow with their summits fully 6000 feet above their heads. They recrossed the river near some landslips, leaping from rock to rock. The snow-line was not more than two hundred feet above them; a proof of the great elevation to which they had attained.

The cedars had now disappeared; but the river-banks and the slopes of the valley were occasionally relieved by clumps of birches and dwarf pines. The place being in many respects safe and convenient, the travellers determined on halting for rest and refreshment. The volume of water having greatly diminished, they hoped on the following day to reach the source. The march was very laborious and painful, owing to the rocky débris which fall daily at this season when the snow is melting. And it is necessary for the traveller to seek a place of shelter towards noonday, if he does not wish to expose himself to the danger of being crushed. Our explorers suffered much from the cold, for all night the thermometer was below freezing-point; but with wood from the neighbouring thickets they kindled a great fire. The earth was spongy, and strewn with stones. Frequently the silence of the night was interrupted by the fall of avalanches.

At sunrise, on the 30th of May, they resumed their march across a field of snow. A broad torrent, the banks of which were fringed with icicles, rushed tumultuously towards the Ganges. They mounted a frozen avalanche, which completely concealed the river, though its channel had become much wider. Among the rocks they saw large fragments of ice suspended. By a rough and rocky road, crossing a small stream, they pursued their way, with masses of granite on the right, and on the left snow-crowned peaks soaring to a height of 7000 and 8000 feet above their own level. Here the Ganges attained a breadth of 2200 feet or more. They then found themselves beyond the boundary of the wooded region, and left behind them the last stunted pines. It is true they continued to meet here and there with a few bushes, but they had ceased to be trees, and were nothing better than large bushes. Before them rose the most glorious object on which the eye of man ever rested,—the majestic snow-shrouded mountain, with its triple-peaked summit. As these three peaks had hitherto been unknown and unnamed, Mr. Hodgson availed himself of the usual privilege of discoverers, and christened them St. George, St. Patrick, and St. Andrew,—the patron saints of the United Kingdom. Advancing still further, they discovered, between St. George and St. Patrick, a fourth and less lofty peak, to which, in honour of Wales, they gave the name of St. David. The four peaks were afterwards included in the general designation of the "Four Saints." In this vicinity the river receives several tiny falls, and one which is about twelve feet high. The incline of its bed is considerable, and it is strewn with blocks of granite, white, yellow, and red. Our explorers began to toil and pant, breathless and exhausted, for the track was difficult in the extreme, and by a steep ascent conducted them to masses of shattered rocks.

The summits of the mountain, rent and torn, were fully 4000 feet in height: huge boulders threatened an immediate fall; and many, indeed, came tumbling, ever and anon, down the deeply-furrowed sides. Mr. Hodgson, in all his wanderings, had never seen so dangerous a ruin; which spread over an area of half a mile. The travellers hastened to escape from the perilous pass, where the fractures of the rocks were so fresh that it seemed probable they had been occasioned by the recent earthquake.

They halted at a point where they felt themselves safe from landslips or falling rocks, and from which they could leisurely contemplate the magnificent appearance of the mountain. The "Four Saints" are situated on the uppermost plane of the Valley of Snow, to the right of which rises another gigantic peak, shining brilliantly with ice and snow,—the formidable Moira. The valley of snow, in the depth of which the river lies concealed, appeared to the travellers of great extent, and they waited impatiently for the daylight that they might examine its features.

They were now about one hundred and fifty feet beyond the river-bed. During the day the sun had much power, because the mountains reflected its rays; but as soon as it sunk behind them the air turned very cold, and a keen frost prevailed during the night.

Wherever the explorers discovered table-lands, or platforms, in the neighbourhood of great snow-crowned mountains, they observed that their position was horizontal. The colour of the rocks of the "Four Saints" seemed to be a bright yellow, mingled with brown and black. The St. George peak, according to Mr. Hodgson's measurement, rose 22,240 feet above the sea; and that of St. Patrick, 22,385 feet.

From Gangútri, the travellers had been accompanied only by a small train of attendants; but here they sent back all whom they could possibly spare, in order to make their supply of barley last some days, if they succeeded in passing the snowy masses that towered before them. After completing their computations and measurements, they felt at liberty to examine the wonderful scene that spread around them.

The dazzling splendour of the snow was enhanced by its contrast with the deep dark blue of the firmament, which is to be attributed to the rarefaction of the air; throughout the night the stars sparkled with a brilliancy which is never seen in a denser atmosphere. They rose above the snowy summits, and their lustre shone with the swiftness of flashes of lightning. The stillness was awful, and interrupted only by the din of the fall of an occasional avalanche. In the pale moonlight everything seemed drear, wild, frightful; a Pagan might have thought the place a haunt of evil spirits.

To give an idea of the imposing aspect of one of these snow-crowned mountains, we may mention that its summit, at a distance of three miles, appeared to the travellers under a very wide angle which raised its elevation upwards of eight thousand feet above their standing-point; and that the same peak when viewed from the remotest districts of Hindustan, and necessarily at a very slight angle, never fails to excite the spectator's admiration. The reader can judge how this feeling is deepened when this gigantic mass, in its shroud of snow, stands revealed from summit to base in all its immensity.

On the 31st of May, following the course of the river, though at some distance above its banks, the travellers came upon an astonishing spectacle. At the foot of a huge bed of snow, the Ganges issued from a small cave or grotto. On both sides the river was fenced in by rocks. But in front, and beyond, and above the cave, rose a glacier, three hundred and eighty feet high, the formation of several centuries, and completely perpendicular. Even its isolated fragments were several feet thick. On the edge of this wonderful wall of frozen snow, and immediately above the opening from which the river issued, hung great pieces of gray ice, formed by the drops of water which fall when the snow melts; for, towards noon, the sun's rays have much force. The Brahmin of Gangútri, who accompanied Mr. Hodgson, had never heard of this remarkable spot, and was ignorant that any person had penetrated to it. However, this ignorance would seem to be of modern growth; at least, nowhere else is the name of the "Cow's Mouth" so applicable as to this wonderful spring, and this name supposes that curious Hindus in times long past had found their way to its shades. Such a shower of blocks of snow rained about the heads of our explorers, that they had scarcely time to complete their observations. With a peal from their hunting-horns they saluted the fountain of the Ganges, and then ascended on the left the bed of snow which lies beyond it.

This vast snow-field extends over a breadth of two miles and a half, and fills the entire space between the right and left part of the summit. Before our travellers stretched a view of about two thousand feet. There it is limited on the left by the base of the "Four Saints," and on the right by the valley which lies at the back of Moira. The base of the latter appears to be planted at a higher elevation even than that of the "Four Saints," and the snow-field mounts up to a point where it appears to terminate in the shape of a ridge.*

* J. A. Hodgson. In "Asiatic Researches."

XVI.

Hekla.

ICELAND, the "Ultima Thule" of the ancients, is the largest island in the North Atlantic. It lies at a distance of 130 miles east of Greenland, and 500 miles north-west of Scotland; and extends from N. lat. 63° 22′ to 60° 44′, or 202 geographical miles, and from W. long. 13° 38′ to 11° 25′, or about 168 geographical miles. Its circumference is variously given at 752 to 830 miles, and its superficial area at 37,000 and 40,000 square miles. It is about five times the size of Sicily, about one-sixth larger than Ireland, and one-fifth the size of Portugal. Owing to the character of its soil and climate, its population is very scanty; assuming it to number 70,000 souls, it rates only at 1.75 per whole area.

Early writers have been accustomed to speak of Iceland as a realm of fire and frost,—a region of almost perennial winter, where Nature presents herself in her most savage and inhospitable aspects. Thus, Chasby asserts that the whole of Iceland may be described as a burnt-out lava-field, from eruptions previous to the peopling of the country. Henderson speaks of it as a most rugged and dreary country, where all life dies, death lives, and nature breeds all monstrous and prodigious things. Even Professor Forbes paints it in the gloomiest colours. Undoubtedly, the island has been the scene of volcanic phenomena on a startling scale. Undoubtedly, it has suffered severely from wintry storms, and rains, and avalanches; and the greater portion of its table-land consists of black rock and glittering ice. There is no prodigality of colour, though vivid contrasts are not wanting. The sunny freshness and fairness of southern lands is nowhere visible. The green shadows of the woods are absolutely wanting in valley, and plain, and on sloping hill. But let it not be thought that Iceland can show the traveller no landscapes worthy of his admiration, or that it is one unbroken waste of snow and lava. "During the delightfully mild and pleasant weather of July and August, seen through a medium of matchless purity, there is much to admire in the rich meads and leas stretching to meet the light blue waves; in the fretted and angular outlines of the caverned hills, the abodes of giant and dwarf; in the towering walls of huge horizontal steps which define the fjörds; and in the immense vistas of silvery cupolas, 'cravatted' cones, and snow-capped mulls, which blend and melt with ravishing reflections of ethereal pink, blue, azure, and lilac, into the gray and neutral tints of the horizon. There is grandeur, too, when the storm-fiend rides abroad: amid the howl of gales, the rush of torrents, the roar of waterfalls; when the sea appears of cast-iron; when the sky is charged with rolling clouds torn to shreds as they meet in aërial conflict; when the pale-faced streams shudder under the blast; when grim mists stalk over the lowlands; and when the tall peaks and 'three-horns,' parted by gloomy chasms, stand like ghostly hills in the shadowy realm. And often there is the most picturesque of contrasts: summer basking below, and winter raging above; peace brooding upon the vale, and elemental war doing fierce battle upon the eternal snows and ice of the upper world."

Iceland is of volcanic formation, and nowhere else do we meet with lava-streams of such immense size. The principal portion of its area is occupied by volcanoes, extinct or active, or by the secretions and accumulated growth of volcanic material. Its outline is curiously irregular, and broken by jökulls, or immense mountainous masses of glacier-like ice, formed by the enormous pressure of the superincumbent snow; by fells, or mountain-peaks; by snow-heights; and true glaciers. In the north-eastern quarter are fifteen considerable summits, of which the highest is Herdubreid, 5,447 feet. In the south-eastern, twenty, of which the loftiest is Oræfajökull, 6,426 feet. In the north-west we meet with twenty-three, including Hvammsfell, 3,897 feet; and in the south-west, sixteen, including Eyjafjallajökull, 5,593 feet, and Hekla, 5,108 feet. The perpetual snow-line varies, according to position, from 2,000 to 3,500 feet above the sea-level; the mean may be stated at 2,830 feet. Glaciers are not numerous, and seem to be confined to the southern and south-eastern shores.

The volcanoes have been arranged by Captain Burton

into eight great systems:—1. The Oranga-Glámu; 2. the Leirhnúkr, Krafla, and Heidurfjall, near the My-vatn Lake; 3. the Snæfellsjökull; 4. the Hofsjökull; 5. the Hekla system; 6. the Vatnajökull, which reaches its apex in the colossal Oræfa; 7. the Katla, or Kötlu-gjá; and, 8. the Reykjanes system.

During the present century several formidable proofs of the activity of the volcanic force have been given. As, first, in December 1820 to June 1822, and January to June 1823, by the Austjökull. In 1823, by the Kötlu-gjá, when the eruption of sand and ashes extended over a hundred square miles. In February 1827, by the Skeidarjökull. In 1831, a submarine eruption occurred off Cape Reykjanes. The twenty-sixth eruption of Hekla took place on September 2, 1845, when its ashes fell in the Orkneys. Kötlu-gjá showed some activity in May 1860; and an outburst of ashes from Trölladyvegzier is recorded as having taken place in 1862.

An eruption of the Skaptárjökull, in the north-west corner of the Vatnajökull group, occurred in 1873. The following account of its phenomena appeared in the *Times*:—

"REYKJAVIK, *March 23, 1873.*

"On Thursday, the 9th of January, about three o'clock A.M., we observed from Reykjavik a grand fire in east-north-east direction, and all agreed that it was 'some neighbouring farm burning,' with hay-stacks. The fire shot up like lightning, displaying beautiful evolutions in combination with the electricity above. Indeed, it was exactly like a fine display of rockets and wheels; and so bright was it, that during the dark morning hours we all thought it must be very close to Reykjavik. But when daylight dawned, and we could discern the mountains, we observed a thick and heavy column of vapour or steam far in the background, beyond all mountains visible; so it was clear that it was far off, and, according to the direction, it seemed most likely to be in Skaptárjökull, the west part of Vatnajökull—the great waste of glaciers in the east and south of the island. Morning and night this grand display was visible during the 9th, 10th, 11th, and 12th, and during the day the column of steam and smoke stood high in the sky.

"When similar news came from east, north, and west, all came to the same conclusion, that it must be in Skaptárjökull; and according to the different points of observation, the position of the crater ought to be between 64° 7′ and 64° 18′ N. lat., and 30° 45′ and 30° 55′ W. long., from the meridian of Copenhagen.

"In the east, near Bernfjörd, some shocks were felt, and fire was seen from many farms. Ashes, too, had fallen over the north-east coast, so that pasture-fields were covered so far that the farmers had to take their sheep into the huts and feed them. The Reykjavik newspaper says:—'In the south no earthquakes were felt, or noises heard in the earth, far or near, as far as Markarfljot (near Eyjafjakajökull). Nowhere has been observed any fall of ashes or dust, but all over a bad smell was felt, and also here in Reykjavik in the forenoon of the 10th. The people of Landeyjar (opposite Westmann Islands) assert the same to have been the case there on the first day of the eruption; but here, at Reykjavik, it was not observed that day, but we felt the air very close, particularly on the 9th, from three to five o'clock in the afternoon, with some smell of sulphur and powder, very like the smell from a lately discharged gun-barrel.'

"No change was observed in the sun, moon, &c. The sky was clear all these days. The direction of the wind was from north-west, west-south-west, and the weather fine. At Landeyjurn the wind had been east-north-east on the 10th, with a strong breeze, and the columns of steam got very high, and mist hid all the eastern horizon, but no fall of ashes took place.

"This eruption lasted only four or five days, and is not likely to have done any damage to inhabited parts or pasture grounds.

"The weather has been very changeable during the whole winter, but very little snow has fallen in the southern part of the country. The cod-fishing has been very favourable when the boats have been able to go out. During the stormy weather some fishermen were lost. On the 1st of March we had a very heavy fall of snow, but since then the weather has been mild but rather stormy."*

The most celebrated of the Icelandic volcanoes, however, is Hekla; either because its eruptions have been the most frequent and destructive, or because their consequences have been the best known. Its ascent has been often accomplished; but its explorers, in their

* The Vatnajökull was ascended by Mr. W. Watts in 1876.

narratives, seem to have drawn freely upon their imagination for details. And so it has come to pass that Hekla ranks, or has hitherto ranked, among the "Wonders of the World;" and readers have been accustomed to picture it to themselves as a colossal cone, or "pillar of heaven," upon the formidable summit of which "white, black, and sanguine red lay in streaks and patches, with volumes of sooty smoke and lurid flames, and a pitchy sky." The Hekla of reality, however, is described by Captain Burton * as a commonplace heap, half the height of Hermon,† and a mere pigmy compared with Alps or Andes, rising isolated from the plains; not more than three miles and a half in circumference. How all the illusions of our childhood are passing away,—vanishing into the thinnest mist! Mont Blanc has ceased to be formidable; the Sahara is no longer "a sea of sand;" and Hekla proves to be a very tame and ordinary protuberance! Seen from the north-west, says Burton, it shows now four, then five, distinct points: the north-western lip of the northern crater, which hides the true apex; the south-western lip of the same; the north-eastern lip of the southern crater, which appears the culminating point; and the two eastern edges of the southern bowls. A pair of white patches are all that the traveller sees of the so-called "eternal snows." On the right of the picture is the steep, but utterly unimportant, Thréhyrningr, crowned with its beach-mark; to the left, the Skardsfjall, variegated green and black;

---

* R. F. Burton, "Ultima Thule; or, a Summer in Iceland," ii. 162.

† Hekla is the fifth in rank of the mountains of Iceland. The four highest are Oræfajökull, 6426 feet; Snæfell, 5964 feet; Eyjafjallajökull, 5593 feet; and Herdubried, 5447 feet. Hekla is about 5000 or 5100 feet.

MOUNT HEKLA

and in the centre, the Bjólfell, a western buttress of the main building, which becomes, from various points of view, "a saddle-back, a dorsum, and an elephant's head, trunk, and shoulders."

We propose to adopt Captain Burton's graphic account of his visit to Hekla; and as the gallant explorer wields an accomplished pen, we shall transfer his language to our pages with little alteration.

We came, he says, upon the valley of the Western Rángá at a rough point, a gash in the hard yellow turf-clad clay, dotted with rough lava blocks, and with masses of conglomerate, hollowed, turned, and polished by water: the shape was a succession of S's, and the left side was the more tormented. Above the ford a cascade had been formed by the lava of 1845, which caused the waters to boil; and below the ford, where the stream divided, leaped a second. We then entered an Iceland "forest," at least four feet high,—composed of red willow, woolly-leaved willow, and birch. About mid-afternoon we reached Næfrholt (birch-back hill), the "fashionable" place for the ascent, and we at once inquired for the guide. Upon the *carpe diem* principle, he had gone to Reykjavik with the view of drinking his late gains; but we had time to engage another,—and even alpenstocks with rings and spikes are to be found at the farmhouse.

In the evening we scaled the stiff slope of earth and palagonite which lies behind, or east of Næfrholt: this crupper of Bjólfell, the Elephant Mountain, gives perhaps harder work than any part of Hekla on the normal line of ascent. From the summit we looked down upon a dwarf basin, with a lakelet of fresh water, which had a slightly (carbonic) acid taste, and which must have contained lime, as we found two kinds of shells, both uncommonly thin and fragile. Three species of weeds floated off the clean sandstrips. Walking northwards to a deserted byre, we found the drain gushing underground from sand and rock, forming a distinct rivervalley, and eventually feeding the Western Rángá.

Before nightfall we received a message that three English girls and their party proposed to join us. This, says Captain Burton jocosely, was a "scare;" but happily the Miss Hopes proved plucky as they were young and pretty, and we rejoiced in offering this pleasant affront of the feminine foot to that grim old *solitaire*, Father Hekla.

We may here introduce a few historical details in reference to this "Vesuvius of the North." The first recorded eruption occurred in 1004, and since that time about twenty-two have been noticed, according to the Icelandic historians, Olafsen and Paulsen. One of extraordinary violence broke out in 1766. Then, after an interval of seventy-nine years, the volcanic forces again manifested their activity. On the 1st of September 1845, the inhabitants of the neighbouring districts were alarmed by a severe earthquake, followed by awful subterranean noises. Next day, about noon, two new vents suddenly opened in the sides of the volcano; and from these poured forth two torrents of incandescent lava, which spread over the barren heaths and scanty pastures, scorching and destroying all they touched. It was almost impossible to discern the outlines of the mountain, owing to the ash-showers and clouds of vapour which were almost continuously ejected. The water in the river-channels grew so hot that all the fish were killed, and it was impossible to cross them, even on horseback.

A fortnight elapsed, and the commotion was renewed. Loud reports and dense discharges accompanied it, which resounded over the whole island, and lasted for two-and-twenty hours. Again two new craters opened,—one on the southern, and the other on the eastern side of the cone,—and the lava rolling from them descended a distance of upwards of twenty-two miles. They united in one thick seething stream, which, at a point three thousand yards from its origin, measured a mile in breadth, and forty to fifty feet in depth. The damage caused by it was necessarily very extensive.

On the 12th of October, a fresh stream issued from the southern crater, and accumulated at the mountain-foot a mass of scoriæ, slag, and fused materials, from forty to sixty feet in height. At the same time, from each of the other new vents a vast column of dust, ashes, and vapour mounted upwards.

During the remainder of the year, and in the early months of 1846, the volcanic forces maintained their extraordinary activity. The eruption finally terminated in October, with an explosion of increased fury; volumes of ashes and scoriæ being hurled to an immense height, while, illuminated by the reflections of the molten lava within, they glowed in the distance like huge pillars of flame.

Some idea may be formed of the pressure exerted by the subterranean fires and gases, from the fact that a block of pumice weighing nearly half a ton was hurled a distance of five miles. The burdens of ice and snow with which the mountain-sides were charged, melted in the great heat, and, descending in vast floods, swelled the rivers and inundated the lower grounds. So many terrible and ominous circumstances attended the prolonged eruption, that the spectator might well have been forgiven for imagining the "foundations of the earth" to be broken up.

Like Etna, Vesuvius, and especially Stromboli (says Captain Burton), Hekla became mythical in medieval Europe, and gained an extensive fame as one of the gates of "Hel-viti." It was said that "Witches' Sabbaths" were held upon its summit. The spirits of the wicked, driven by demons, might be seen trooping into the infernal crater; and the minds of men do not easily dismiss such traditions as these. So the Danes still say, "Begone to Heckenfjæld!" the North Germans, "Go to Hackelberg!" and the Scotch consign you to "John Hacklebirnie's house." Even Goldsmith, in his "Animated Nature," refers to the local creed: "The inhabitants of Iceland believe the bellowings of Hekla are nothing else but the cries of the damned, and that its eruptions are contrived to increase their tortures." Uno Von Triol, who in 1770, together with Sir Joseph Banks and Dr. Solander, "gained the pleasure of being the first who ever reached the summit of this celebrated volcano," attributes its virginity to the popular superstitions.

He writes about its wonders with much moderation; and rightly explains its great renown by its position on the great water-way from Greenland to North America. His English companions, however, do not imitate his soberness of tone. As Burton says, it may be granted that an unknown ascent "required great circumspection;" and that in a high wind excursionists should lie down. But the facts of the case do not explain the "dread of being blown into [or down?] the most dreadful precipices, for these do not exist." Moreover, to "accomplish this undertaking," they travelled over three hundred to three hundred and sixty miles of continuous lava-tracts; which is more than the maximum length of the island, from north-east to south-west.

And now let us resume the narrative of Captain Burton's ascent.

The next morning (the Captain *loquitur*), July 13th, broke fair and calm, and the Miss Hopes were punctual to a minute; an excellent thing in travelling womanhood.

We rode up half-way, somewhat surprised to find so few parasitic craters; the only signs of independent eruption on the western flank were the Kandhóbar (red hills), as the people call their lava hornitos and spiracles, which are little bigger than the bottle-house cones of Leith.

At an impassable divide we left our poor nags to pass the dreary time, without water or forage, and we followed the improvised guide, who caused not a little amusement. His general port was that of a bear that has lost its ragged staff, for his alpenstock had been given to one of the ladies, and he was plantigrade rather than cremnobatic; he had stripped to his underalls, which were very short, whilst his stockings were very long, and the heraldic gloves converted his hands into paws.

The two little snow fonds ("steep glassy slopes of hard snow") were the easiest of walking. We had nerved ourselves to

"Break neck or limbs, be maimed or boiled alive;"

but we looked in vain for the "concealed abysses," for the "crevasses to be crossed," and for places where "a slip would be to roll to destruction." We did not sight the "lava wall, a capital protection against giddiness." The snow was anything but slippery; the surface was scattered with dust, and it bristled with a forest of dwarf earth-pillars, in which the ice was preserved by a coating of blown volcanic sand. In about an hour and a half we gained the crater which opened at nine A.M. on September 2nd, 1845, and poured out lava till the end of November. An inexperienced man might pass it without observation. The sole remnant is the upper lip prolonged to the right; the dimensions may have been one hundred and twenty by one hundred and fifty yards, and the cleft shows a projecting ice-ledge ready to fall. The feature is well marked by the new lava-field of which it is the source: the bristly "stone-river" is already mouldering to surface-dust. A short distance beyond this bowl the ground smokes, discharging snow-steam made visible by the cold air. Hence, doubtless, the veracious travellers of old experienced, at one and the same time, a high degree of cold and heat.

In fifteen minutes more we reached the first or southern crater, the Ol-bogi (elbow or rim) of which is one of the horns conspicuous from below. It is a regular formation, about one hundred yards at the bottom each way, with the right (or east) side red and cindery, and the left yellow and sulphury; mosses and a few flowerets grow on the lips; in the bottom rise jets of steam, and a rock-rib bisects it diagonally from north-east to south-west.

From the First Crater we walked over the left or western dorsum, across which it would be perfectly feasible to drive a coach, and we congratulated one another upon the achievement. Former travellers, "balancing themselves like rope-dancers, succeeded in passing along the ridge of slags, which was so narrow that there was scarcely room for their feet," the breadth being "not more than two feet, with a precipice on each side several hundred feet of depth." It might be supposed that the features of the scene had been altered by the effects of an eruption; but no eruption took place between 1766 and 1845. Moreover, the lip would have diminished, not increased. And one of the most modern visitors repeats the "very narrow ridge," with the classical but incorrect adjuncts of "Scylla here, Charybdis there." Scylla—which is, let us say, the crater slope—is disposed at an angle of 30°, and Mr. Chapman coolly walked down this "vast" little hollow. Captain Burton adds: I descended Charybdis (the outer counterscarp) far enough to make sure that it is equally easy.

Passing the "carriage-road"—for so we named it—we crossed a *névé* without any necessity for digging foot-holes. It lies where sulphur is notably absent. The hot patches which account for the freedom from snow, even so high above the congelation-line, are scattered about the summit; in other parts, the reading of the thermometer, when placed in a hole eighteen inches deep, made earth colder than air. After a short climb we reached the apex; the ruddy-walled north-eastern lip of the Red Crater (No. 2); its lower or western rim forms two of the five summits seen from the prairie, and hides the highest point. We thus ascertained that Hekla is a linear volcano of two mouths,—or three, including that of '45,—and that it wants a true apical crater. But how is it possible to reconcile the accounts of travellers? Pliny Miles found one cone and three craters; Madame Ida Pfeiffer, like Metcalfe, three cones and no crater.

When the summit was reached the guides raised a song of triumph, whilst we drank to the health of our charming companions, and, despite the cold wind which eventually drove us down, carefully studied the extensive view. The glorious day was out of character with a scene *niente che montagne*, as the unhappy Venetian described the Morea; the picture would have been more complete with sleet and rain and blinding snow, but happily they were conspicuous by their absence. "Iceland, beyond a steep snow-bed, unpleasantly crevassed, lay a grim photograph all bleak and white; Lángjökull looking down upon us with a grand and freezing stare; the Hrafortiunu Valley marked by a dwarf cone, and beyond, where streams head, the gloomy regions stretching to the Springisandur, dreary wastes of utter sterility, howling deserts of dark ashes, wholly lacking water and vegetable life, and wanting the gleam and the glow which light up the Arabian wild. Skaptár and Oræfa were hidden from sight. Seawards, ranging from west to south, the view, by contrast, was a picture of amenity and civilization. Beyond castellated Hljódfell and conical Skjaldbried appeared the familiar forms of Esja, and the long lava projection of the Gold Breast country, melting into the western main. Nearer stretched the fair lowlands, once a broad deep bay, now traversed by the network of Olfusá, Thjórsá, and Markarfljót; while the sixfold bunch of the Westmann Islands, mere stone lumps upon a blue ground, seemingly floating far below the raised horizon, lay crowned by summer sea. Eastward we distinctly traced the Fiskivötn, or fish-lakes. Run the eye along the southern shore, and again the scene shifts. Below the red hornitos of the slope rises the classical Three-horned, not lofty, but remarkable for its trident top; Tindfjall (tooth-fell), with its two horns or pyramids of ice, casting blue shadows upon the untrodden snow; and the whole mighty mass known as the Eastern Jökull; Eyjafjall (island-fell), so called from the black button of rock which crowns the long white dorsum; Kátlá (Kötlu-gjá), Mukrjökull, and Godalands, all connected by ridges, and apparently neither lofty nor impracticable. I venture to predict that they will succumb to the first well-organized attack."

www.ingramcontent.com/pod-product-compliance
Lightning Source LLC
Chambersburg PA
CBHW022115290426
44112CB00008B/677